Controversies Over The Imitation of Cicero in the Renaissance

With translations of letters between
Pietro Bembo and Gianfrancesco Pico

On Imitation

and

A Translation of Desiderius Erasmus,

The Ciceronian (Ciceronianus)

by
Izora Scott

Hermagoras Press
1991

Published by Hermagoras Press,
P.O. Box 1555, Davis, California 95617.
Manufactured in the United States
by Braun-Brumfield, Ann Arbor, Michigan.

Typesetting & Camera-ready Production
of covers, spine and frontispages
by Graphic Gold, Davis, California.

Originally published as *Controversies Over The Imitation of Cicero as a Model for Style and Some Phases of Their Influence on the Schools of the Renaissance.* Teachers College, Columbia University, Contributions to Education, No. 35. New York: Teachers College, Columbia University, 1910.

ISBN 0-9611800-8-0

FOREWORD

This classic, frequently-cited study of "Ciceronianism" has long been unavailable except in a few research libraries. Originally published in 1910, it has been out of print for decades.

Izora Scott's work is particularly valuable because she presents not only her own clear analysis of the issues involved, but also translations of key texts by major Renaissance humanists who were involved in the controversy. These include a set of letters (1512-1513) between the Italians Pietro Bembo (1470-1547) and Gianfrancesco Pico della Mirandola (1469-1533), and, more importantly, "The Ciceronian" (Ciceronianus) (1428) of the Dutch humanist Desiderius Erasmus (1466?-1536).

The issues were complex. At one end of the spectrum were the "ultra Ciceronians," mainly Italian, who believed that no Latin word or syntactical structure should be used that was not in Cicero's works; at the other end of the spectrum were those who felt that a number of authors (Cicero included) were worthy of emulation. It was not however a mere quibbling about literary style, since the debate came to involve charges of paganism versus Christianity, and, indeed, challenged the basic concept of humanism developed first in Italy and then in France during the fifteenth and sixteenth centuries.

Erasmus' Ciceronianus *is a dialogue between three figures: an ultra Ciceronian, Nosoponus (Mr. Workmad), Bulephorus (Mr. Counsellor), and Hypologus (Back-up). Bulephorus, who also calls himself Dr. Word, eventually suceeds in curing Nosoponus of his disease of Ciceronianism. In the course of the dialogue Erasmus has the characters discuss a wide range of issues connected with the imitation of Cicero; Nosoponus is also asked to judge a large number of writers, ancient and contemporary, as to their true Ciceronianism—a development that enraged scores of the writers named, and produced enmities which dogged Erasmus for the rest of his life. The* Ciceronianus, *then, can serve as an index to the whole Ciceronianism controversy.*

Biographies of the Renaissance writers named in the Ciceronianus *may be found in* Contemporaries of Erasmus: A Biographical Register of the Renaissance and Reformation. Ed. Peter G. Bietenholz and Thomas B.

Deutscher. Three volumes. University of Toronto Press, 1985-87.

There is as yet no single definitive history of the Ciceronianism controversy. *Charles Lenient published a Latin dissertation, De* Ciceroniano bello *(Paris: Joubert, 1855), in which he declared that the long squabbles over what he calls "the religion of words" (p. 73) had produced little of value fr either Latin or the vernaculars. The next major work was Remigio Sabbadini,* Storia del Ciceronianismo e di altre questioni letterarie *(Turin: Ermanno Loescher, 1886); while Sabbadini discusses 68 humanists he is primarily interested in the Italian phase; he divides the controversy into three periods beginning with Angelo Poliziano (1454-1494) and ending with J. C. Scaliger (d. 1558). The Ciceronianism controversy permeates the detailed discussion of French literary culture by Marc Fumaroli,* L'Age de l'Eloquence: Rhétorique et "res literaria" *de la Renaissance au seuil de l'époque classique. Hautes études médiévales et modernes, 43. (Geneva: Droz, 1980); he describes what he calls two separate renaissances of Cicero. Another valuable work is Kees Meerhoff,* Rhétorique et poétique au XVI[7] siécle en France: Du Bellay, Ramus et autres. *(Leiden: E. J. Brill, 1986); though he devotes the major part of the book to Ramus (pp. 175-330), Meerhoff like Fumaroli is deeply concerned with the relation of Ciceronianism and the development of the French vernacular; he terms the controversy "d'une importance primordial" (p. 45). The best modern summary in English is probably Martin L. McLaughlin,, "Imitation in Literary Theory and Practice in Italy, 1400-1530" (Oxford D. Phil thesis, 1983), esp. pp. 246-362; McLaughlin concludes that the controversy was essentially over by the time of Pietro Bembo (1470-1547), and that later writers did little but repeat the same ideas. (McLaughlin's work is to be published shortly in England.)*

This present edition, then, is offered as an aid to our understanding of an important episode in the intellectual life of early modern times.

James J. Murphy
July, 1991

PREFACE

Though the term Ciceronianism could be applied to Cicero's influence and teaching in the field of politics, philosophy, or rhetoric, it is limited in the present study to the technical department of rhetoric and represents the trend of literary opinion in regard to accepting Cicero as a model for imitation in composition. The history of Ciceronianism, thus interpreted, has been written with more or less emphasis upon the controversial aspect of the subject in various languages. Jean Lévesque de Burigny wrote a short sketch *Sur la querelle qui s'eleva dans le XVIe siècle au sujet de l'estime qui était due à Cicéron* in 1756; C. Lenient published a thesis *De Ciceroniano bello apud recentiores* at Paris in 1855; Professor Sabbadini in 1855 described the movement in his *Storia del Ciceronianismo;* and Professor Sandys has most recently (1905) told the story in a short lecture at Harvard, entitled "The History of Ciceronianism."

In view of these publications the only justification for the present study may be found in the statement of a somewhat different aim: to furnish to the English reader some of the controversial matter in direct translation or full analysis, and to connect the doctrine more particularly with the schools of the Renaissance. The major field of the study will lie after the middle of the fifteenth century and will deal with controversial writings on imitation, though the earlier period of the historical development, previous to 1450, will receive brief notice where it will be the purpose to show how the influence of Cicero manifested itself through various phases until it hardened and narrowed into that "pedantry and purism" of the sixteenth century which assumed the name of Ciceronianism as a doctrine of style advocated by a cult of servile imitators. The work, consequently, will fall into three divisions: (a) an introductory chapter on the influence of Cicero from his own time to that of Poggio and Valla (c. 1450) when men of letters began a series of controversial writings on the merits of Cicero as a model of style; (b) a series of chapters treating of these controversies; (c) a study of the connection between the entire movement and the history of education. Translations of the controversial letters of Pico and Bembo along with the translation of Erasmus's *Ciceronianus* will be placed in a separate division of the volume, Part II, pp. 1-130.

There will be found some variation in the spelling of proper names, but in general I have adopted the plan of translating the Latin form into the language of the country of which the man was a native, varying from this only in cases where the Latin name has become fixed by familiar usage, as in the case of Erasmus. To secure uniformity in this throughout the volume I have added a note of corrections to the translation of the *Ciceronianus* which appears in this volume in the text of the edition of 1908.

Most grateful acknowledgment is rendered to those friends who have inspired and assisted me in my work: to Professor Paul Monroe for suggesting the theme, directing and criticising the scope and method of treatment; to Professor Nelson G. McCrea for most kindly assisting and advising in the translation of the *Ciceronianus*. Acknowledgment is also due to the officials of the British Museum and the Bodleian Library for courtesies and valuable assistance in rendering accessible much of the material used.   I. S.

New York, May, 1910.

CONTENTS

PART I

PART II

Part I
History of the Controversies

CHAPTER I

THE INFLUENCE OF CICERO BEFORE 1450

As an introduction to the main theme it is considered desirable to make a brief survey of the influence of Cicero previous to the period chosen for special investigation in order to present the general trend of the development of Ciceronianism and thus to preserve the historical continuity throughout.

When Cicero entered public life there were two distinct schools of stylists at Rome: one professing studied simplicity and brevity after the Attic orators; the other studied ornamentation after the Asiatic. The genius of Cicero lent itself to neither but freely and independently fashioned a third called the Rhodian school which was destined to supplant them both. His theory of rhetorical excellence is embodied in *de Oratore* and *Brutus,* where he sets forth the requirements of an ideal orator. The usual kinds of oratory are considered and accepted,—forensic, deliberative, panegyric,—as well as Aristotle's divisions of the art of rhetoric,—invention, arrangement, style, memory, and delivery.[1] The orator must have, as a basis for eloquence, wide general culture.[2] He may then apply himself to the imitation of the best models, exercising great care to copy their virtues and not their faults.[3] His aim is to teach, to delight, to move,[4] and the means of accomplishing this aim is by a kind of speaking which Cicero variously characterizes as *pure, Latine, plane, dilucide, ornate, apte, decore dicere*[5] and *Latine, plane, ornate, et apte dicere*[6] and *copiose et ornate dicere.*[7] By this we understand that the language must be appropriate not only to the subject but to the audience, that it must be pure and standard Latin, that clearness must be studied, and that there must be artistic development and rhythmical struc-

---

[1] De Oratore, i, 141–143.
[2] Ibid, iii, 127–132.
[3] Ibid, ii, 90–93.
[4] Brutus, xlix.
[5] De Oratore, i, 144.
[6] Ibid, iii, 38.
[7] Ibid, ii, 153.

3

ture. Cicero himself explains *ornate dicere* as follows: *Qui in-luminate et rebus et verbis dicunt et in ipsa oratione quasi quen-dam numerum versumque conficiunt, id est, quod dico ornate.*[8] Cicero's style exemplifying so well his *copiose et ornate dicere* did not win favor without opposition. Brutus and Calvus, the most distinguished Atticists, found occasion to criticise him as redundant and over-elaborate.[9] Quintilian says that the Atticists characterized him as "timid, Asiatic, redundant, too fond of repetition, loose in structure of sentences, tripping in his manner, and almost effeminate in his general style."[10] It is probable that Julius Caesar wrote *de Analogia* to refute statements made in the *de Oratore* relating to the importance and means of attaining *Latine.*[11] A number of criticisms that must have been made of Cicero as a stylist during his lifetime have been lost and we know of them only through mention and reference in later writers. Petronius describes at length a controversy between the Ciceronians and the anti-Ciceronians on the merits of the new educational method called *declamatio.*[12] Seneca refers to the criticisms of Asinius Pollio.[13] Quintilian says that the Asinii, both father and son, attacked the blemishes of Cicero's style with vehemence in several places.[14] The younger Pliny mentions in one of his letters that he had read a book by Gallus Pollio where he compared Cicero unfavorably with his father.[15] And we have answers to Gallus Pollio's attacks mentioned by Suetonius.[16] Aulus Gellius also speaks of the criticisms of Gallus Asinius and of one Largius Licinius who wrote a book entitled *Ciceromastix* in which he criticised Cicero for lack of precision and inaccurate use of words.[17] Aulus Gellius further defends Cicero against the rhetors who charge him with solecisms, and says that Cicero is undoubtedly the most eloquent of all.[18]

---

[8] De Oratore, iii, 53.
[9] Tacitus, Dial. de Orat., c. 18, "Satis constat ne Ciceroni quidem obtrectatores defuisse, quibus inflatus et tumens nec satis pressus, sed super modum exsultans et superfluens et parum Atticus videretur, legistis utique et Calvi et Bruti ad Ciceronem missas epistulas, ex quibus facile est deprehendere Calvum quidem Ciceroni visum exsanguem et aridum, Brutum autem otiosum atque diiunctum; rursusque Ciceronem a Calvo quidem male audisse tamquam solutum et enervem, a Bruto autem, ut ipsius verbis utar, tamquam fractum atque elumbem."
[10] Inst. Orat., xii, 10, 12–14.
[11] Hendrickson, *Classical Philology*, April, 1906.
[12] Satyricon, chapters 1–5. *Declamatio* was the speaking in private on fictitious themes.
[13] Suasor., vi; vii. vi,—"Namque Cicero nec tam timidus fuerit, ut rogaret Antonium, nec tam stultus ut exorari posse speraret, nemo dubitat, excepto Asinio Pollione, qui infestissimus famae Ciceronis permansit, et is etiam occasionem scholasticis dedit."
[14] Inst. Orat., xii, 1, 22.
[15] Epp., vii, 4, 4.
[16] Noctes Atticae, v, 41.
[17] Ibid, xvii, 1.
[18] Ibid, i, 4, 1; i, 7, 1; xvii, 13, 2.

Livy, the one great prose writer of the Augustan age, whose style was characterized very unjustly by Pollio as smacking of Patavinity, can be said to a considerable degree to perpetuate the Ciceronian ideal. Quintilian quotes him as advising his son to study Cicero first and diligently;[19] and Livy's style is as good an example of *copiose et ornate dicere* as a writer of history could furnish.

Toward the close of the first century of the Christian era Quintilian stands out as the first great and ardent advocate of Ciceronianism. It is fair to say that Ciceronianism as it developed in later times really began with him. All his influence at Rome in court and school was exerted to establish a system of technique which recognized Cicero as the model. In his *Institutio Oratoria* he follows very minutely the theory of the *de Oratore* and *Brutus,* acknowledging Cicero at every point.[20] There are the same divisions of rhetoric,[21] the same function of oratory,[22] the same stress on *copiose et ornate dicere*[23] and the same preparation in general culture. There comes a difference in the definition of general culture however, and here he lays the foundation for the later Ciceronianism. He says Demosthenes and Cicero should be read first and afterward those who resemble them;[24] that there may be individual virtues in the several great orators of history;[25] but that Cicero has furnished us the only model of speaking and of teaching the art of speaking.[26] We get in the first books of the *Institutio Oratoria* the formulation of rules for good usage in spelling and grammar, based on Cicero's authority, marking the beginning of one of the strongest traditions of Ciceronianism which assumed very great proportions in the development of the doctrine in the sixteenth century.

Tacitus and the younger Pliny were pupils of Quintilian and naturally were supporters of the ideal. Pliny in his letters acknowledges Cicero as his ideal of oratory, declaring that he desires to emulate him,[27] that eloquence has degenerated,[28] and that

---

[19] Inst. Orat., x, i, 39.
[20] ix, 4, 1.
[21] iii, 3, 1, inventio, dispositio, elocutio, memoria, et actio.
[22] iii, 5, 2, docere, delectare, et movere.
[23] i, 5; iii, 4, 5.
[24] x, 1, 39.
[25] xii, 10–12.
[26] iii, 1, 20.
[27] Epp., iv, 8, 4, "M. Tullius, quem aemulari studiis cupio."
[28] Ibid, i, 5, 12, "est enim," inquam, "mihi cum Cicerone aemulatio, nec sum contentus eloquentia seculi nostri. Nam stultissimum credo ad imitandum non optima quaeque proponere."

Cicero's *copiose dicere* is better than the Attic *brevitas*.[29]   Tacitus
shows a studied imitation of the master in the *Dialogus de Oratoribus* which teems with balanced periods and elaborate figures;
but in his maturer style he departs from his early practice and
can no longer be called a Ciceronian.   It may be seen from
Tacitus' Dialogue that Ciceronianism was a matter of discussion
at the time; for the conversation is between Julius Secundus,
Vipstanus Messala, and Curiatus Maternus, who were professed
Ciceronians of the preceding generation, and Marcus Aper, an
anti-Ciceronian.   Aper voices the criticism of the time by declaring that he cannot abide the lengthiness and tediousness of the
Ciceronians; while Messala offers the defence that the practice
of Cicero's day was much better when boys went to the forum
to learn oratory instead of to the rhetors.[30]

There were two elements that militated against the adoption
of the Ciceronian style by the Church Fathers, who, after the
immediate successors of Quintilian, were the sole representatives
of Latin letters for many centuries.   The first was the general
antagonism of the new faith to any learning and most of all to
pagan learning; and the second was the influence of the African
school of stylists that had lately sprung up, who advocated what
was called the *New Latin*.   In spite of these influences however,
we can follow quite clearly the thread of Ciceronianism down
through the centuries until in the Revival of Learning it comes
again into brighter light.   The Church Fathers were divided in
their allegiance but Cicero found able followers.   Minucius Felix
was so much of a Ciceronian that he wrote an argumentative
dialogue[31] persuading to Christianity without using a single Christian expression; Lactantius won the title of the " Christian
Cicero "; St. Ambrose introduced into the church a manual of
ethics based on *de Officiis;* and St. Jerome, after having satisfied
himself that there was no contradiction in being a Ciceronian
and a Christian, devoted himself enthusiastically to the study of
the great orator.

During the Middle Ages, the New Latin was preeminently in
the ascendency, yet school texts in the department of rhetoric
were based on Cicero as is very clearly shown by Abelson.[32]   For

---

[29] Pliny Epp. i, 20, 4.
[30] c. 22–36.
[31] Octavius.
[32] pp. 52–59.

example, in Capella's *Satyra de Nuptiis Philologiæ et Mercurii*, Cicero's aim of rhetoric is quoted[33] and the divisions—*inventio, dispositio, elocutio, memoria, pronunciatio*—are enumerated with illustrations from Cicero;[34] while throughout the book all examples of good usage are from Cicero. Professor Sandys also states that Cicero was not only known but was most influential during this entire period.[35]

At the beginning of the Renaissance in Italy it is evident that the philosophical works, some of the speeches, and a mutilated text of the Rhetoric were in circulation.

Petrarch (1304-1374) describes what delight he got from the marvelous harmony of Cicero's periods long before he was old enough to understand the sense;[36] and how he wept when the Rhetoric barely escaped the flames at the hands of his irate father who found him poring over that instead of studying law.[37] Though Petrarch's literary reputation to-day does not rest upon his Latin works, he was much more concerned about the writing of Ciceronian prose than of Italian verse. He definitely accepted Cicero as a model and set himself the task of recovering the complete works of the master. His labors were rewarded by the discovery of two Speeches, the Letters to Atticus and Quintus, and the correspondence with Brutus. Immediately upon the identification of the Letters he wrote as follows to Cicero:

" Father supreme of Roman eloquence: I yield you hearty thanks, and not for myself alone, but for all of us, who adorn ourselves with the flowers of the Latin language. Yours are the springs from which we water the meadows, you are the leader that marshals us; yours are the suffrages that support us, and yours the light that shines upon our path."[38]

By such devotion as this from the great leader of the Revival of Learning we may easily measure the prominence into which Cicero was destined to come.

The *ad Familiares* was discovered by no less an ardent Ciceronian in the person of Collucio Salutati, Latin Secretary of Florence, in 1389, who used it as a model of style so precisely and

---

[33] v, 167.
[34] v, 163.
[35] Classical Scholarship to the End of the Middle Ages, 623-7.
[36] Hallam, i, 84 (Epp. Rerum Senilium, xv, 1, 946).
[37] Sandys, Classical Scholarship, ii, 5.
[38] Sandys, Harvard Lectures, 149.

successfully that Villani says he could properly be called "the ape of Cicero."[39]

An impetus was given to the movement by the recovery of the *de Oratore* and the *Institutio Oratorio* of Quintilian in complete form about 1417. Immediately scholars turned to copying, annotating, emending, and imitating these works. Quintilian was used as the guide in the concrete organization of school curricula and Cicero was the model for style in composition. At Padua and Florence many prominent Ciceronian stylists could be found in the first half of the fifteenth century. Leonardo Bruni, Guarino da Verona, Giorgio da Trebisonda, Francesco Filelfo, Antonio Panormita, Aeneas Sylvius and Ambrogio Traversari might all be cited; but it is sufficient to take as the most perfect type and probably as the most influential advocate, Gasparino Barzizza, who lectured at the universities on Cicero and who according to Hallam was the only writer before 1440 who had the reputation of attaining a correct style. Hallam says further that Barzizza is truly Ciceronian in his turn of phrases and sentences which never end with a wrong arrangement of words as is habitual with his contemporaries.[40] Professor Woodward, estimating the early humanists, gives to Barzizza the credit of definitely establishing the Ciceronian tradition in the revival of classical learning and of being the first to approach Cicero in a thoroughly scholarly spirit bringing to bear upon the text an analytical and comparative method to which no ancient author had hitherto been subjected.[41] It is generally accepted that Barzizza studied Cicero constantly as a guide for style and as a source of general culture, and that the group of men he represents inaugurated a conception of Ciceronianism which stood for the study of the model for spirit as well as for form.

The development of the other conception of Ciceronianism, standing for the literal imitation of Cicero's vocabulary and construction and making him the exclusive model of style, had reached such proportions toward the end of the fifteenth century that the rational Ciceronians of the type of Barzizza came to be considered enemies of the cause while the servile imitators were

[39] p. 19, "Epistolae, quas emisit quae loquor esse. In textu insuper prosaico tanta iam valuit dignitate, ut Ciceronis simia merito dici possit. Publicavit iam complura volumina, quae possent dictis meis testimonia perhibere."
[40] i, 88–89.
[41] Vittorino da Feltre, 10.

counted the only true disciples. Out of this difference of interpretation grew those famous controversies of Poggio Bracciolini
and Lorenzo Valla, Angelo Poliziano and Paolo Cortesi, Gianfrancesco Pico and Pietro Bembo, as well as that long line of
charges and defences instituted by the famous *Ciceronianus* of
Erasmus.

CHAPTER II

CICERONIAN CONTROVERSIES IN ITALY: POGGIO AND VALLA; POLITIAN AND CORTESI; PICO AND BEMBO

I

Poggio and Valla

The first of the Ciceronian controversies originated in the criticism of Poggio's diction by one of Valla's pupils. Lorenzo Valla (1406-1457) had been educated by Vittorino da Feltre and had thoroughly imbibed the doctrine of the school of Barzizza. He had won distinction in the field of grammar and rhetoric by the publication of his *De elegantia Latinae linguae,* a critical study of ancient and contemporary writers. He had dared to advance somewhat beyond the position of the rational Ciceronians and to declare that one could imitate Cicero very effectively by following Quintilian. He had established a school in Rome with the avowed purpose of exalting Quintilian over Cicero. Poggio Bracciolini (1380-1459), on the other hand, was the advocate of the growing tendency toward *servilitas* in imitation. Though he was but an indifferent imitator he considered himself a perfect stylist and attributed his success to the adoption of Cicero as an exclusive model.[1] The defence of this position, as incidentally embodied in five invectives against Valla, will outline his argument in the controversy; while Valla's answers in the form of four *Antidoti* and two Dialogues will present the other side.

As we have said, the immediate cause of this quarrel was the most trivial incident of a school boy's annotation. A Catalonian youth from the school of Valla at Rome found occasion to write in the margin of a volume of Poggio's letters a correction of a grammatical mistake. The volume later happened to fall into the hands of Poggio who immediately accused Valla of being the author of the annotation and of thereby casting reflection upon

---

[1] Epp., xii, 32.

his perfect Latinity. This accusation, instigated no doubt more by jealousy than by a sense of justification, took the turn of personal abuse and scurrility of such kind as only Poggio, the most scurrilous writer of an age where scurrility was the fashion, could write. In the first invective there is little effort to prove that the marginal notes were ill-founded. The pages teem with disgraceful epithets which so far as we can discover were in no way merited by the life and character of his opponent. Valla is called a fanatical and crazy dreamer vomiting forth insanity, a most stupid ass, a beast grazing in the field of stupidity, an ignorant, incongruous, awkward, absurd writer of a book full of verbosity and stupid loquacity which ought rather to be called *de Ignorantia* than *de Elegantia,* a most stupid man with no power, no influence, no training, a mad dog, a raging reviler, a wrangling pettifogger, a misshapen hideous monster, a drunkard, a bastard, a prostitute, the worst kind of old sly-boots, a cook, a stable-boy, a braggart.[2] Every page is full of these epithets repeated time and again and woven into pictures; nor is a translation of them adequate, for, as Nisard has said, the language of decency has not the richness of that of obscenity.[3]

Poggio makes the charge that Valla despises, criticises, finds fault with and spurns the ancients who have been so highly honored through all the ages, as if he held the wheel of fortune and turned it at his will; further, that he considers Cicero ignorant of the art of speaking and prefers Quintilian. With equal stupidity Valla thinks that if he drives all others off the stage he will be reckoned the most learned and will receive the palm of eloquence,—saluted in the forum and in the theater as the only son of Minerva, brought up in the lap of the Muses. (189-190.) Poggio cites examples from Cicero to justify usages which Valla has noted in his writings. (191-193.)

The criticism of the " Elegances of the Latin Language " is so flippant that it does not seem worthy of quotation, but it is pertinent and therefore will be inserted: " That very childish book is full not only of no elegance but of the highest absurdity, boldness and crudeness. The whole speech is on the force of words and is an insignificant dispute of a stupid pedagogue or little grammarian at the cross-roads on childish and empty questions so that he who

---

[2] In Vallam invectiva prima; Opera, 188–243.
[3] Gladiateurs de la république des lettres, i, 129.

would become most stupid and wholly ignorant of the Latin language may commit these books to memory. And that silly gabbler, in order that his words should be considered of some value, selected all the early writers for objects of criticism. He chose a difficult province, indeed, from which he will carry back a triumph of stupidity and madness. I have read recently his books, devoid of all elegance, for the sake of laughing at them. . . . There are some things in them compiled from the authors whom he has criticised which are worthy of approbation. . . . He says that he will imitate Camillus; and as that one restored the City taken by the French so he will restore to the City Latin letters, exiles and wandering fugitives. . . . Our Valla is like the ridiculous man who promised that on an appointed day he would fly from a certain tower, and who, when the people had assembled to see him, kept them waiting till dark with various displays of wings; and, when all were eagerly expecting him to fly, he ran away. So Lorenzo, after many magnificent promises of words, after great expectation, at length shows not his back as the other did, but the insanity of a flying brain and a strange store of ignorance." (194-195.) All who know the esteem in which this book has been held by critics since the fifteenth century will agree that Poggio gives here not a real estimate but an expression of his jealousy and spite. The book no doubt had errors but with all its errors it was a work of great worth and originality which Poggio must have known perfectly well.

The only other point in the first invective to be noted here is Poggio's unbounded rage at the presumption of Valla in criticising Cicero. "What can be a plainer and more open sign of stupidity," he says, "than for Cicero's eloquence to displease? than for one to dare to change his words thinking they can be said more eloquently? But no man up to the present has ever been found who would dare do this or try to do it. Valla, the mad dog, the railing reviler, the wrangling pettifogger, emerging from some hovel, attacks Cicero, whom all know to have been the golden stream of eloquence. What kind of a monster is this, after almost fifteen hundred years during which the name of Cicero has remained inviolate, who, drinking not apollonine but asinine nectar, alone presumes to correct Cicero in eloquence?" (197-198.) With raving of this kind he continues for some time, but this is enough for our purpose. We can see clearly that Poggio will be classed among those who exert all their influence toward literal imitation of Cicero in vocabulary and style.

Beyond these few instances the invectives give little material of value for our theme. They are made up almost entirely of the most vicious accusations against Valla's private life and honor. In the first a triumph is given to Valla where the great procession shows his stupidity and folly; at the end of the second he is consigned to the lower world convicted of almost every crime on the calendar; and then in the third he is brought back and made to bow the knee to Satan and swear that he will consecrate himself anew to even more hideous vices, after which he is sent forth with a guard of all the furies that no honest man may approach him; in the fifth a third triumph is given him. In the second invective there is a bit of reference to disputes in regard to the allegiance of certain contemporaries. Poggio here says that Valla presumes when he claims that Leonardo, Guarino, Aurispa, and others had praised him; for Aretino had lived on most intimate terms with him (Poggio) for many years and instead of praising Valla had always considered him a beast. What Guarino thinks his letters indicate. Francesco Barbaro showed his opinion by a smile when Valla's name was mentioned.[4]

Valla answers the charge by declaring that he did not make the annotation; that if he had wished to attack Poggio he would have done it openly; that Poggio had not enough material for attack in the annotation so he assumed the rôle of patron of the dead whom he declared that Valla had criticised. Then he launches forth into personal abuse but soon checks himself by saying, "What am I doing? Why do I imitate Poggio? Why do I draw my sword against an old man who could be not only my father but even my grandfather?"[5] Turning then to serious discussion Valla answers the points one by one. He says that he has not criticised the best Latin authors unjustly; that he has not spoken of Poggio with insolence; that Poggio has shown ignorance in his attempts at emendation of the *Elegantiae;* that no one can understand Quintilian unless he thinks very well of Cicero nor can he follow Cicero unless he obeys Quintilian; and

[4] Opera, 211, 230.
[5] Antidotus primus, Opera, 253–256.

there has been no eloquent one since Quintilian who has not imitated him. (257-266.) Then he introduces Poggio into a court and causes the judge to question them both, and thus proves again the points above claimed. (274-300.) In the Third *Antidotus* Valla takes up a series of mistakes in Poggio's letters and explains wherein they are wrong. This is in the form of a conversation between Poggio and Lorenzo and occupies twenty-five pages of the volume of Valla's works. The fourth *Antidotus* answers carefully the accusations made by Poggio in his second invective on Valla's private life which has no literary significance. Here and there are some reiterations that he did not mark Poggio's letter;[6] that Francesco Barbaro does think well of him and offers as proof a letter from him.[7] The two dialogues add nothing to the general discussion, so their analysis will be omitted.

II

POLITIAN, SCALA, AND CORTESI

About 1490 we find Angelo Poliziano engaged with Bartolommeo Scala and Paolo Cortesi in the same controversy but with a very different spirit. Here there is none of the hate and jealousy so evident in that of Poggio and Valla.

Politian was noted for his great scholarship in Latin and Greek but was an eclectic in style and particularly fond of uncommon words. Hallam estimates that his affected intermixture of obsolete words, for which it was necessary in almost every page of his Miscellanies to consult a dictionary, in an age of pedantry would increase the admiration of his readers.[8] Yet this was the very thing which brought on his quarrel with the pedant, Scala, as the opening letter in the controversy written by Politian to Scala will show:

" You said openly a few days ago and it has been reported to me by a number of persons that you did not like my style of writing, because I strove too much after foreign and unusual words; that I was a sort of *ferruminator*. You have used this word for some time to signify a person who employs uncommon words,

---

[6] Opera, 329.
[7] Ibid, 334.
[8] i, 197.

for I hear that you called Hermolao Barbaro a *ferruminator,* perhaps in jest, because he used that word.

But, my Scala, just as I readily grant you that an unusual word ought not to be rashly adopted, I insist that no one ought to be censured because he brings back into use words of good authors and desires to add novelty and charm to his writings and does not allow good words that have fallen into disuse to lie neglected, for if our language is confined to words common to all we shall use nothing but the tongue of the scriveners.

In regard to your recalling me to the standard of Cicero, whom I grant to be the most celebrated author of the Latin language but not the only one, I ask, How do you regard others whose authority has always been accepted by scholars? What about Varro, who though he yields the palm to Cicero in pleading holds it for himself in speaking pure Latin? Do you reject as barbarians, Livy, Sallust, Quintilian, Seneca, Pliny, and many others approved by the vote of the ages? And I ask this particularly since very different writers have attained equally high reputation, for example, among the Greeks, Herodotus in history and Thucydides; among the Latins, Livy and Sallust. In what respect is Cicero so unlike Demosthenes?—both equally perfect in his way, yet it is plain to see that they are unlike.

To return, why is that word *ferruminator* spoken of in derision? It is proper, unpretentious, well-sounding, not obsolete, and both Pliny and the lawyers use it. Is it a sufficient reason to laugh at it or to reject it because Hermolao Barbaro used it frequently? You yourself have written though you have not published much which the public generally read. You are now writing a history, I believe, a long and arduous work. What standard do you fix for yourself if not that we can use words of good authors? I admit that one must have a method suited to the subject, the characters, and the times; that the same method would not have fitted Cicero's cases at court and the Milesian fables of Apuleius; that we jest with one tongue, if you please, and speak seriously with another. We do not use the same language to boys and to scholars, nor do we write in the same way to friends and strangers, to princes and private individuals; and for this reason your Cicero, and mine too, is found to vary so much that he does not seem equally the author of all that he writes.

Though we readily accept you, a most successful writer with long experience, as the censor, and though we cannot think ill of those scholars who measure all by the taste of Cicero, yet it has happened often, to my disgust and amusement, that they have severely censured those very things in my writings which were found in well emended texts of Cicero; while they themselves used the very worst kind of barbarisms thinking them Ciceronian words which evidently those Teuton artificers of new books had at some time perversely fashioned.

That precept which teaches that we must shun a new word as a rock was of more force, perchance, in Caesar's time than in ours; for then all spoke Latin, while now Latin is unknown to the common people and learned only by masters who ought to accept and use any words found in the thesauri of great authors.

I have written this to you, my Scala, most freely and friendly, not wishing to defend myself indeed so much against your derision, at which I am not offended, as to defend in some slight measure Hermolao Barbaro, the most learned man of our age and deserving in letters and philosophy. You will be generous enough to allow me to differ from you in letters without any breach between us of love or mutual good will.

vii Cal. Ian, 1493."[9]

From this letter it is evident that criticism had been made against Hermolao Barbaro as well as against Politian and that Politian had not the highest regard for the would-be Ciceronians' knowledge of Cicero. His own words were found in standard authors and that was enough authority for him. Burckhardt says, " Hermolao Barbaro and Politian made a conscious effort to form a style of their own, naturally on the basis of their overflowing learning, though they failed to inspire their pupils with a similar desire for independence."[10]

The general temper of Politian toward imitation is further portrayed in a letter to Piero de' Medici, translated by Greswell:

" I acknowledge that the style of my letters is very unequal, for which I expect not to escape reprehension. But let it be remembered that the writer was not always in the same humour;

---

[9] Epp. v, 1; Poliziani Opera, 130. The answer from Scala is not inserted because it makes no reference of any importance to the points cited by Politian.
[10] p. 254.

and that one mode of writing is by no means suited to every person and every subject. On perusing letters so dissimilar (should any person think them worth perusal) it will probably be said that Politian has been writing his " Miscellanies," not letters. However, among so many discordant opinions of those who write, or who give rules for writing letters, I do not despair of finding an apology. One will say, for instance, ' These letters are very unlike Cicero's.' I shall answer, not without good authority, that Cicero is not regarded as a proper model in epistolary composition. Another will pronounce me the mere echo of Cicero. To him I shall reply that I feel myself highly gratified in being deemed able to express even a faint resemblance of such an original. A third could wish I had adopted the manner of Pliny, the orator, whose taste and judgment are so highly spoken of. My answer will be, ' I entertain a thorough contempt for all writers of Pliny's age.' Does my style, in the opinion of a fourth, savor strongly of that very author? I shelter myself under the authority of Sidonius Apollinaris, an authority by no means to be contemned, who assigns to Pliny the palm of letter writing." In this strain he cites authority for every possible criticism that could be brought against his style and ends by saying, " Thus I hope to provide myself with a subterfuge against the malice of critics. But to their censures I am comparatively indifferent."[11]

The controversy between Politian and Cortesi is set forth in two letters which follow, where Politian denounces, the superstition of the " apes of Cicero " and urges originality of style; while Cortesi[12] argues well for accepting Cicero as an exclusive model.

Politian's Letter to Cortesi

" I return the letters diligently collected by you, in which reading, if I may speak frankly, I am ashamed to have consumed good time. For except a very few, they are of no account at all, though they are said to have been selected by some learned man or collected by you. I shall not explain which ones I approve or disapprove. I am not willing that any one, relying upon my

---

[11] Lib. i, Ep. 1; Greswell, 123.
[12] Cortesi had written (c. 1490) De hominibus doctis "in no unsuccessful imitation of Cicero's De claris oratoribus, from which indeed modern Latin writers have always been accustomed to collect the discriminating phrases of criticism. He uses an elegant if not always a correct Latinity, characterizing agreeably and with apparent taste the authors of the fifteenth century." Hallam, i, 183.

judgment, should be pleased or displeased with them.   Yet there
is some disagreement between us in regard to style.   For you,
as I have understood, are not wont to approve of one unless he
paint the outline of Cicero.   But to me the features of a bull or
a lion seem more honorable than those of an ape, even though an
ape is more akin to man.   Nor are those who are reputed to have
held the chief place of eloquence like one another, as Seneca has
set forth.   Quintilian ridicules those who considered themselves
Ciceronians because they ended a period with *esse videatur*.
Horace exclaims against imitators who are merely imitators.   To
me indeed those who rely entirely upon imitation are like parrots
or magpies; for what they write lacks force and vitality, action,
sympathy, and native genius; it lies, it sleeps, it snores.   For
there is nothing true, nothing genuine, nothing effective.   ' You
do not portray Cicero,' some one says.   Why should I?   I am
not Cicero; I portray myself.

Further, my dear Paolo, some beg style as they do their daily
bread and unless the person is at hand from whom they can make
extracts, they cannot put together three words and they contaminate the quotations even with stupid connections and barbarisms.   Their speech therefore is uncertain, vacillating, weak, and,
as it were, unkempt and ill-fed; and these creatures, whom indeed
I cannot bear, dare to judge boldly of men whose style has been
fomented by deep study, much reading, and long practice.

But to return to you, Paolo, whom I love deeply, to whom I owe
much, whose genius I praise,—I beseech you not to ally yourself
with the superstition that nothing which is entirely your own can
bring delight, that you must never take your eyes from Cicero.
When you have read, learned, assimilated Cicero and other good
writers, studying them long and carefully and when you have filled
your heart with the knowledge of many subjects and are ready to
compose something of your own, then at length I should expect
you to swim, as they say, without cork and to take counsel and
lay aside that discouraging and anxious care of fashioning only
Cicero and put to the test your entire strength.   Now those, who,
inspired, gaze only upon those ridiculous things which you call
characteristics and do not adequately reproduce them, believe me,
retard in this way any impulse of their own genius, stand in the
course, as it were, of a runner or, if I may use a Plautan phrase,

remoram faciunt. But as one cannot run well who wishes to place his foot in the tracks of another, so one cannot write well who does not dare to depart from a prescribed rule. Finally, be convinced that it is a characteristic of an unfortunate mind to produce nothing independently and always to rely upon imitation.
Goodby."[13]

Cortesi's Answer to Politian

"Nothing has ever surprised me so much as the return by you of my volume of letters for I was thinking that it had escaped your notice in the midst of so many duties. But now, as I read your letter, I see that it not only has been tasted but completely devoured by you, though you write that you are ashamed to have used your good time doing so and that none of the letters except a very few seem at all worth reading. I shall not dispute your word nor shall I express my opinion since it is not becoming for me to differ from you and since I am a person who, as M. Tully says, would not judge another if I could and could not if I would; but I shall come to the point where you say you differ from me very greatly.

You write that you have understood that I approve of no one unless he reproduce Cicero. I cannot remember ever to have said that nor do I wish to. What stupidity it would be, when the talents of men are so various, their natures so manifold, their desires so different, to wish them to be held to the limits of one mind! But since you invite me into this dispute, perchance it will not be an inappropriate time to state my position and to defend myself, for I see very plainly that your words are those of a friend and not a critic.

First then, as to my expression of judgment, I will acknowledge willingly that I have often in public declared (when I have seen the study of eloquence being so long neglected and forensic exercise given up and all native speech lacking in our men) that no one can at present speak with elegance and variety unless he place before him a model to imitate, just as strangers ignorant of the language cannot travel in a foreign country without a guide and children a year old cannot walk without the help of a nurse. And I remember from the ranks of many learned men who have flourished in every branch of eloquence to have chosen

---

[13] Epp. viii, 16; Poliziani, Opera, 251,—no date, probably between 1480 and 1490.

M. Tully as the only standard to which I thought the study of
all capable men ought to be referred, not because I did not know
that many others had gained great reputation in speaking who
could incite to industry and foster genius, but because I saw
that he was the only one of all the ages recognized by all as the
chief, and because I had learned when a boy always to choose the
best, thinking it a characteristic of a disordered and sick stomach
to choose less nutritious food instead of the more healthful and
better. I may dare also now to declare the same thing which
I have often declared, that no one since M. Tully has gained distinction in writing except a few who have been trained by him.
Furthermore, there was then a fixed method of imitation which
discouraged slavish likeness and had a piquancy of its own but
now that is either neglected or unknown. By likeness, my dear
Politian, I mean not as an ape is like a man but as a son is like
his father; for in the first instance the ridiculous imitator reproduces the deformities and faults of body only, on account of his
misconception of likeness; while in the other he reproduces the
face, gait, posture, carriage, form, voice, and figure and yet he
keeps something individual, something natural, something different so that the two, when compared, seem to be unlike.

I will repeat that the wealth of the divine man is so lucid
that, when considering him, he shows himself easy of imitation
but when attempting to imitate him he baffles the hope. All run
to him and each thinks that he can speak in that way; for men,
naturally prone to flattering themselves, measure the most difficult task by their desire rather than by their ability to accomplish
it. So while they imitate, as they themselves say, the language
and fluency they fail in the strength and piquancy and thus fall
very far short of Cicero. Furthermore, it profits nothing to fill
our writings with the ornaments of another unless we can do it
elegantly and aptly; for a kind of monstrosity is the result where
members that ought to be together are widely scattered. There
is no reason, presuming that I speak of myself, Politian, why
you should hinder me from imitating Cicero, but rather you
should criticise my ignorance because I cannot imitate him well,
granting that I prefer to be a sycophant and an ape of Cicero
rather than the son of another.

But it is of the greatest importance whether one seems to
wish to imitate some one or no one. I maintain that imitation

is necessary, not only in eloquence but in other arts as well; for all knowledge is obtained from antecedent knowledge and nothing is in the mind which was not before perceived in the senses. From this it is seen that all art is the imitation of nature but nature brings it about that both likeness and unlikeness are born of the same seed. Though men are unlike they are bound by likeness; though some are florid, others pale, others comely, others tall, yet all have the same form and figure. Again, as those who lack a leg or hand or arm are not to be excluded entirely from the human race but must be called imperfect or lame; so the art of eloquence has one form and image and those who turn aside from this form and image are found to be distorted and lame. Look at those men who have chosen M. Tully as a model, how different they are from him and from one another! Livy attained in a measure his richness but not his modesty; Quintilian his pungency; Lactantius his tones; Curtius his smoothness; and Columella his elegance; and though all these men had about the same idea of imitating, nothing is so unlike as they to one another or to Cicero. And from this I have very definitely decided that the matter of imitation must be considered carefully and that he was a wonderful man from whom so many and varied geniuses have flowed as if from a fount. Surely, Politian, definite authors ought to be chosen to form and foster genius for they sow seeds in the mind which grow later of their own accord. But those who wish to attain reputation by imitating no one, believe me, show no strength in writing. And those who say that they depend upon their own genius take the sense from the writings of others to aid them and from this form a very faulty style, since at one time they appear stupid and uncultured and at another brilliant and showy, and their writings are like a field into which have been scattered many antagonistic seeds. Or this medley of words so poorly mated might be compared to different kinds of food which do not assimilate, or the clashing of sounds to the collision of falling stones or racing chariots. What pleasure can ambiguous words, misplaced verbs, abrupt sentences, rigid structure, poor translation, and ill-measured rhythm afford? Yet this must be the result when thoughts and words are culled from various authors and no one is imitated. Surely their speech will resemble the house of the pawn-broker where all kinds of garments are found hanging together. I think that there is as much difference between the man who imitates no one and him who follows a definite leader as there is between the one who wanders at random and him who sets out with a well-defined plan. The first wanders from the highway and tumbles about among the thorns, the second hastens directly along the road mapped out to the appointed goal without slip or mishap.

Consider too, Politian, that no one has attained reputation in eloquence who has not employed some kind of imitation. Among the Greeks, not only the orators, Demosthenes, Hyperides, Lycurgus, Aeschenes, and Demarchus, but also those illustrious philosophers and teachers of virtue wished to be imitators of some one. I shall not mention our own writers, lest I seem to boast of a certain school, the most learned of all; nor is any defence of Cicero needed. It has already been proved that he who sets himself to imitating M. Tully, if he does not gain some reputation by his imitating, is at least honored by the good judgment of choice.[14]

Goodby."[15]

III

PICO AND BEMBO

The type of Ciceronian described by Politian in his letter to Cortesi is the final result of the pedantic worship of Cicero. Men as narrow in their conception of correct style were now the leaders of letters in Italy. Padua, the home of the *humanitas* of the early fifteenth century, had degenerated into a seat of *servilitas* controlled by Bembo, Sadoleto, Longueil, and Villeneuve. At Rome a society of *literati* was formed so exclusive that they bound themselves by oath to use no word except such as could be found in the works of Cicero.[16]

Pietro Bembo (1470-1547) stands as the preeminent leader of the stricter sect. He was the inspiration at Padua and at Rome. As papal secretary his letters are examples of Ciceronian style. Hallam describes his method as follows: " He kept forty portfolios into which every sheet entered successively and was only taken out to undergo correction before it entered the next. He was an exclusive Ciceronian, keenly feeling the beauties of Cicero's eloquence, and rejected every phrase not justified by the

[14] Quintilian, Inst. Orat., x, 1, 112.
[15] Poliziano, Opera, Epp., vii, 17.
[16] Erasmus, Opera, iii, Ep. 820.

golden age but even insisted upon Cicero as the only perfect model."[17] Burckhardt says that his " History of Venice " is an example of the perversions resulting from the application of the Ciceronian canon where the municipal councillors are called *Patres Conscripti,* the nuns *virgines vestales,* the saints *divi,* and the cardinals *Senatores.*[18] It was through Bembo's influence that Christophe de Longueil (1490-1522), " the only Ciceronian north of the Alps,"[19] took the oath of the society of *literati* at Rome and promised to read nothing but Cicero for five years.[20] It was Bembo who received Longueil at Padua a few years later when he came to lecture on eloquence, where he was estimated as one of the most successful representatives of the cult, winning a reputation that was jealously guarded by Ciceronians later and praised even by the bitterest opponents. It was Bembo who urged Sadoleto to refrain from the reading of the Epistles of St. Paul on the ground that they would contaminate his style.[21] This criticism not infrequently heard against Bembo that he was too much of a Ciceronian to be a Christian has considerable justification. It is very certain that he was much more interested in Cicero than he was in the writings of the Church Fathers. From his biography we trace that his interest in the church and the Christian religion was but perfunctory and limited to the period of service as papal secretary.

Gianfrancesco Pico (1469-1533) was the nephew of the celebrated Florentine, Giovanni Pico. His early life had been spent at Florence under the influence of Politian and Ciceronians of this type; so that, when the doctrine of Bembo and the cult at Rome was presented, he set to work to answer their tenets in formal style. This answer, in the guise of a letter or pamphlet addressed to Bembo, along with the lengthy response constitutes the only surviving literature on the theory of Ciceronian imitation of the early sixteenth century. Pico's article seems to have been instigated by some oral discussion which had been held between him and Bembo. Both articles were written at Rome, the first bearing the year date of 1512, the second that of 1513. The translation of these two letters in full may be found in Part II of the present volume, pp. 1-18.

---

[17] i. 330.
[18] p. 252.
[19] Ciceronianus, infra ii, 22.
[20] Burckhardt, 254.
[21] Cambridge Modern History, i, 564.

CHAPTER III

THE CICERONIANUS OF ERASMUS

The Renaissance spirit in its various phases had, up to 1512, wielded little influence upon the countries north of the Alps. Occasionally scholars from the north had gone to the universities of Italy to study and here and there an Italian had found his way to France or Germany or England; but the general attitude of Italy toward these countries was that they were barbarians, incapable of practicing or appreciating any form of culture. Among those few who had been alive to the Renaissance movement and who had reproduced the spirit of Dante and Petrarch was Erasmus of Rotterdam. He had broken the shackles of authority and had advanced into the free field of thought and expression. His writings were many and popular not only in his own country but in Italy as well, where they created no small stir on account of their avowed disregard for the authority of the Ciceronian canon. The fact that he scoffed at their so-called purity of style, declaring that any reputable Latin was standard and that matter was more important than form, brought him into conflict with the sect of Ciceronians. The controversy continued for several years, as shown by his letters, before it took formal shape in his famous Dialogue on the Ciceronians early in 1528.

The general theme of this Dialogue is not unlike that of the discussion on imitation between Pico and Bembo[1] while the method is very similar to the *De hominibus doctis* of Cortesi. It is a criticism of the Ciceronians' conception of imitation and an estimate of the chief literary men of the period. Hallam[2] is authority for the opinion that Erasmus, being entirely ignorant of Cortesi's work, went over the same ground in rather inferior language. Whether he knew of *De hominibus doctis* we cannot say; but upon his own confession he did not know of the discus-

---

[1] Infra ii, 1–18.
[2] i, 183.

sion between Pico and Bembo; for he says, " Long after the *Ciceronianus* was published I found that this very subject had been treated in three³ letters between F. Pico and Bembo."⁴ The evolution of the *Ciceronianus* in the mind of Erasmus can be traced in his letters. As early as 1519 Longueil, then at Rome, writing to a friend, made a comparison of the styles of Budé and Erasmus to the detriment of the latter.⁵ Erasmus wrote Longueil in answer, stating that he had seen the letter and that his style was justified on the basis that he could not take the time and the trouble, when writing upon serious and important subjects, to revise and polish as the apes of Cicero did.⁶ In 1524 we find him protesting to Jerome Aleander against the criticisms of the Italians: "As if your writers, I will not say Pico and Beroaldo but Hermolao Barbaro and Poliziano, have never made mistakes! They paint me as an enemy of Italy, though no one praises the Italian genius more frankly than I."⁷ And again, " At Rome there is a pagan fraternity of *literati* who have murmured against me. The leaders are, as I hear, Aleander and Albert, Prince of Carpi.⁸ . . . There is another sect of Ciceronians, an old sect indeed, revived by Longueil and not less furious than the Lutherans. I must stand the shock of these hosts alone and unarmed, for I have little or no aid from the court."⁹

Though these extracts would indicate that the quarrel with the Italians grew out of personal and religious enmity; yet there were other elements promoting the resentment that culminated in the Dialogue. Erasmus felt keenly that such purism and pedantry was dangerous, even deadening to the development of letters. He had appealed to Budé to protest; and though Budé had expressed his willingness, " I so perfectly agree with you regarding the sect of Ciceronians that I am ready to join in a charge against them when opportunity offers,"¹⁰ he did nothing; so Erasmus conceived the clever *Ciceronianus* to show the world how absurd their tenets were. In a number of places are found specific statements of this altruistic motive. Writing to his friend, de Brie, after the publication of the Dialogue, he says he under-

---

³ Only two letters are published in Bembo's works.
⁴ Ep. 1008 (January 24, 1529).
⁵ Longolli epistolae selectae, pp. 116–120. (January 29, 1519.)
⁶ Ep. 402 (April 1, 1519), Jortin, i, 152.
⁷ Ep. 693 (September 2, 1524).
⁸ These were two theological enemies of Erasmus.
⁹ Ep. 820 (May 16, 1526).
¹⁰ Ep. 842 (December 26, 1526).

took this little task of a few days to dispel superstition from the minds of youth, because the plague of Ciceronianism had arisen in Italy and was spreading into France and polluting letters and the free expression of Christian doctrine; that he did not under-estimate the value of Cicero as a master of style, but only their conception of imitation.[11]   And again, " In my *Ciceronianus* I do not condemn the style of Cicero. I have always attributed to him so much that others, compared to him however eloquent, grow dumb. But I have condemned the foolish affectation of Ciceronian diction."[12]   While in writing to Egnazio he says, " They rail at me because my *Ciceronianus* attacks the foolish apes of Cicero and exhorts to true imitation."[13]   A long letter sent to Vergera just before the publication shows that he believed the time was ripe for a definite protest. It exemplifies the char-acter of the war then being waged and is a forecast of Erasmus' position as more fully expressed in the Dialogue on the question of the value of the classics and their adaptation to modern needs.

" . . .   In the arena Erasmus must die, by nature fitted to anything more than fighting. Now for a long time I have fought a war by no means bloodless with those phalanxes who think that as a result of their tyranny more polite letters flourish. Nor is it a unified army: some oppose the revival of any polite literature because they fear an exposure of their ignorance; others, somewhat milder, seem to be willing to accept Latin but think that in no way Greek or Hebrew must be accepted. It offends the ears of these for the name of Christ to appear in letters as if nothing were elegant that is not pagan, to whose ears Jupiter Optimus Maximus sounds more pleasing than Jesus Christ, the Saviour of the world; Conscript Fathers sounds more agreeable than Holy Apostles. They laud Pontano to the skies, they scorn St. Augustine and St. Jerome, but I should prefer a single ode of Prudentius singing of Jesus to a ship full of Pon-tano's verses whose learning and ability I do not however dis-parage. In their estimation it is almost more disgraceful not to be a Ciceronian than not to be a Christian, as if Cicero would not talk differently about Christian themes than he talked in his own age if he were alive now,—since the especial province of eloquence is to speak fittingly. No one denies that Cicero excelled in ora-

---

[11] Ep. 981, (September 6, 1528).
[12] Ep. 1003 (1528).
[13] Ep. 1149 (1530).

tory but oratory does not fit all characters and arguments. What does this distasteful display of Ciceronian name signify? Let me whisper it to you? Under this cloak they hide paganism which is dearer to them than the glory of Christ. It does not grieve me at all to be erased from the roll of Ciceronians if only I remain on that of the Christians. If any one will unite in us the virtues of Ciceronian speech and Christian piety, him will I prefer to ten Ciceros. Even if I could attain perfection in portraying the figure of Ciceronian phrase, I should prefer a style of speaking more genuine, more concise, more forceful, less ornate, and more masculine. And yet, though ornamentation has been lightly considered by me, I should not spurn elegance when it comes of its own free will. However, I have not time to polish what I write. Let them be Cicero's brothers who have leisure to spend three months on one short epistle. I must sometimes finish a book in a day. Lastly, if we acknowledge the truth, not one of those who admire no one but Cicero has successfully reproduced him. For I do not regard a thin coating of *oratio* and ten words borrowed here and there from Cicero a reproduction. I insist upon the whole spirit. The trouble is, my dear Francis, that they do not see that what I say is not said to condemn Cicero as a standard of eloquence but to ridicule those apes to whom nothing is beautiful except what reproduces Cicero, although no form has ever been so fortunate as to be absolutely perfect. I maintain that the rhetorician, like the painter, must seek his model from many. . . ."[14]

The letter was written in October, 1527, but a few months before the publication of the Dialogue. References to the use of Jupiter Optimus Maximus for Christ and Conscript Fathers for the Holy Apostles was a protest against the character of the imitation which has been observed in Bembo's " History of Venice."[15] This was an offence in the eyes of Erasmus—that they perverted Christianity and really were pagans in their worship of antiquity. There seemed from the beginning of the Revival of Learning a recognized breach to cover between Christianity and the Classics. Lactantius and St. Jerome were examples of churchmen who found it consistent to be Ciceronian and Christian; Barzizza and his friends at Padua, in the early days, consciously aimed to

[14] Ep. 899 (October 13, 1527).
[15] Supra, p. 23.

teach that there was no contradiction; and Sadoleto, by his writings, exemplified the possibility of harmony; but, on the other hand, it will be remembered that Sadoleto was urged by Bembo to avoid the reading of St. Paul for fear of contaminating his style, and that Bembo is the type against which Erasmus directs his satire, a type of a large and influential school that wrote and rewrote, polished and adorned, yet reproduced finally the merest shadow of Cicero.

But the reader may turn with much more profit to the Dialogue itself, a translation of which will be found in Part II of this volume,[16] where he will find Nosoponus such a hapless Ciceronian that it will make his heart glad to frolic with Erasmus over the devotee's foibles and fancies; and surely he can but be persuaded that though ridicule is a poor weapon it is used here in a worthy cause and with telling effect.

The result of the publication of the *Ciceronianus* justified Erasmus' prediction that he must die in the arena. Straightway there went up a cry from Italy and from France. Every possible avenue of attack was thronged. The Italians professed that Nosoponus represented Bembo; the French stormed that their idol, Budé, had been mentioned in connection with Badius, a printer; the friends of Longueil took up the cudgel in his behalf; those who had not been mentioned were as angry as those who had. The whole situation is characterized by Erasmus in the following letter to Vlattenus:

" What fate or what genius has willed that such malignity be joined to human affairs, my dearest Vlattenus, that what pleases the majority should so intensely displease some! I sent forth recently two books: one on Pronunciation, the other on the Imitation of Cicero. The first offends no one and finds few admirers; the second is offensive to many and much sought in the shops. It is criticised because some who should have been mentioned were left out, because others were attacked unfairly, and because some were praised less than they deserved and others more. For the purposes of argument, which was the object of the treatise, a few examples of the ancients sufficed. It was furtherest from my intention to enumerate all writers, especially since the enumeration was but a secondary matter. . . . I

---

[16] pp. 19–130.

should have more justly deserved the name of foolish for enumerating too many rather than omitting some and I should have been more foolish if I had attempted to estimate the style of all who have won reputation by their writings, seeing that to-day Germany, France, England, Poland, and Hungary have so many young men who can write and speak elegantly. That I omitted no one because of hatred or forgetfulness can be seen from the fact that I made no mention of some whom I love well and see daily. . . . If I had done nothing but praise those whom I named and had praised without exception, I should have lessened the value of the work. . . . Although the argument was carried on under the rôle of Nosoponus, yet the title was not meant to give offence to any. I scattered much praise to individuals yet with such moderation that no one could accuse me of flattering and each one could see what belonged to him. I was not actuated by malice to omit the names of enemies, for I included Hutten and Stunica nor did I deprive them of praise due to them. Those who are angry because they say Budé was treated with too little honor are mistaken in their judgment. Not less impudently did some murmur that I slighted Longueil and yet I might fairly have taken vengeance upon him, for he scattered through his writings some things that showed a suspicion that he did not hold my genius in the highest esteem;[17] but that liberty of judging living writers never offends me. If they judge rightly they teach, if not it is a human fault and of little account. I should wish for many such as Longueil to ridicule the Batavian orator if only they stand high in the disciplines and in the Christian religion, which I think he would have done had he lived longer. . . .

But let us return. Long after the *Ciceronianus* was published I found that this very subject had been treated in three letters between F. Pico and Pietro Bembo,[18] the latter of whom differed widely from me, the former not so much. . . . I have revised the book[19] changing a few passages, also adding some names, for when it was first published there arose at once a slanderous braggart who somewhat interrupted the course of attention, as some are born for no other purpose except to give trouble to

[17] Supra, p. 25.
[18] Infra ii, 1–18.
[19] Io. Casp. Orellius in Ciceronis Opera, vi, 435, gives an edition published at Basle in 1529.

those who try to be honest, busying themselves with nothing but dice, prostitutes, revellings, and boasting.

Goodby."[20]

Many times Erasmus insists that the storm first broke in Italy and then traveled to France; but tracing through his letters and observing the dates of books and pamphlets published in answer to the *Ciceronianus,* we find that France showed prompt resentment. De Brie, writing in August, 1528, says that he has been compelled to defend Erasmus constantly against the tumult arising among his people from the publication of the *Ciceronianus.*[21] Erasmus the next month writes to Danès, " The tumult arising from my *Ciceronianus* has somewhat lessened my feeling of congratulation that France is a tranquil and happy home for the Muses ";[22] and a few days later to P. Decamerius, " The *Ciceronianus* which is eagerly read by every one is causing much ill-feeling against me in Paris."[23]   In 1530 Erasmus tells de Brie that the storm has reached Germany, Brabant and Italy.[24]   When the first lengthy answer was published in 1531 by J. C. Scaliger, Erasmus felt sure that it had emanated in Italy at Venice by the hand of Aleander.[25]   Perhaps he was much more ready to believe this because Italy was the home of those pedants and purists in style at which he had aimed his criticism; and undoubtedly there were many contributions to the controversy by word of mouth and by pen which lived but for the hour and therefore are not accessible to-day.

Erasmus describes the strife as follows: "   .   .   .   But against me there are so many phalanxes conspiring everywhere that the army of Caesar would prevail with difficulty.   I seem in the words of the old proverb an ass among bees, or better, among hornets.   The angry swarm increases daily.   Now some Pelusian fellows with gladiatorial minds are attacking me.   I see no end unless perchance like leeches when they are filled with my blood they will fall off of their own accord.   .   .   .   Libels fly everywhere from Italy, France, Spain, and various parts of Germany.[26]   .   .   .   At Rome there has been published 'A

[20] Ep. 1008 (January 24, 1529).
[21] Ep. 968 (August 12, 1528).
[22] Ep. 978 (September 5, 1528).
[23] Ep. 982 (September 16, 1528).
[24] Ep. 1135 (September 5, 1530).
[25] Epp. 1241, 1205, 376, 370, 1288, 1299.
[26] Ep. 1224 (June 22, 1532).

Defence of Italy against Erasmus,'[27] . . . Another book
has come out, ' Cicero Banished and Recalled from Exile,'[28] which
does not especially refer to me but which attacks Cicero harshly
and defends him indifferently. Another still is in preparation
whose title, 'A Civil War between the Ciceronians and the Eras-
mians,'[29] suggests that I am an enemy of Cicero. There is a re-
port that a certain Dolet is writing against me, and J. C. Scaliger.
These young men are poorly occupied who conspire against me as
an enemy of Italy and Cicero. Nor are schemers wanting who
urge them on, partly from hate of me and partly that they get
pleasure out of the madness of others. At Rome they are circu-
lating a letter[30] full of scurrilous jokes purported to have been
written by me. . . ."[31]

Quarrel with Budé

As we have said the storm broke in France immediately upon
the publication of the *Ciceronianus*, and the letters of Erasmus
between 1528 and 1532 are full of a personal quarrel with Budé
and his friends. The quarrel does not hinge upon the subject of
Ciceronianism nor upon any vital point in the plan of the book
but upon the collocation in the text of the names of Budé and
Badius. Badius was a printer of no great reputation while Budé
was recognized as the most distinguished scholar of France. He
was not a man of generous spirit nor was he on very friendly
terms with Erasmus, if one may judge from their correspondence
prior to this time; but he was the idol of the French people and
they could brook no reflection upon him. The position of common friends was especially trying: Jacques Tusan lost for a
time the goodwill of Erasmus; Jean Lescaris cast his lot in
with the Budaean faction; de Brie acknowledged that his sincerity was questioned because he did not break with Erasmus.

To follow the steps of this controversy is not wholly satisfactory because material is accessible only through the letters of
Erasmus and that is both fragmentary and one-sided. But on
the supposition that the profit will justify the effort I shall review
the substance of what can be gleaned from them.

---

[27] P. Curtius, (1535). This was an answer to statements made in the Adagia.
[28] Ortensio Landi, Leipsic, 1534. See also infra, p. 85.
[29] This was perhaps never published.
[30] Jortin (i, 61) thinks that the letter is a spurious one to Curtius.
[31] Ep. 1279 (May 21, 1535).

On August 12, 1528, de Brie writes a long letter to Erasmus
telling him how furious the French people are that he not only
has coupled the name of Budé with Badius but even has Budé
after Badius. ' They could not have been more angry if Achilles
had been compared with Thersites. Budé is the god of letters
in France as Erasmus is in Germany. It would have been better
not to have mentioned him at all in the *Ciceronianus* or to have
joined his name with another. He has, since the publication of
the Dialogue, constantly tried to defend Erasmus against the host
of critics. It is rumored that Budé feels offended. Erasmus
would be wise to change the passage in the book[32] or add an appendix with explanation or write a letter to some one which could
be published afterward and thus show that no insult was meant.'[33]
Erasmus answered in September, saying by way of justification
that the Budaeans could not be offended at the argument of the
book because Budé himself had signified his intention to attack
the Ciceronians when an occasion offered;[34] they could not say
he had spoken ill of Budé when Nosoponus would not accept
him as a Ciceronian because Budé did not aspire to that honor.
'As for comparing him with Badius, the names had come together
by accident because they were both French and both lived in
Paris. Other friends as well as de Brie had urged that some
letter be written by way of apology but it did not occur to him
what or to whom to write.'[35]

L. Berquin must have been one of these other friends, for
Erasmus addressed him thus:

" If I mistake not you write that you were offended at only
one thing,—that I compared Budé with Badius when there was
no resemblance except in the letters of their names. Then when
you urged me to write an apology to Budé, you indicated that
you feared that he was offended. I am well aware of his disposition yet I cannot believe that he was offended. My letter
written to you, I am sorry to say, was read by others. However
there was nothing in it uncomplimentary to Budé, or if there was
it slipped in without my intention. I did not think it necessary
to warn you. I had advised de Brie to keep the matter quiet that
no tragedy might arise from our correspondence even though

---

[32] There were changes in the next edition which I have not seen. See Ep. 1008 cited
supra p, 28, also infra i, 34.
[33] Ep. 968 (August 12, 1528).
[34] Ep. 842 (December 26, 1526).
[35] Ep. 981 (September 16, 1528).

I felt that no caution was necessary. But the outcome is after the fashion of mortals. The matter has been carried to the notice of the King."[36] In another place he mentions that the case was brought to the court and when the King inquired the reason for the dissension he was told that Budé had criticised Erasmus in a certain passage and that Erasmus had sought revenge by comparing him with Badius.[37]

Letters were sent about this same time to three other friends: Vives,[38] Danès,[39] and Hermann, Count of New Eagle,[40] all of which use practically the same phraseology of defence. The one to Vives is dated September 2, 1528; to Danès, September 5; and the other bears only the year date, 1528. It is interesting to note that the letter already quoted[41] to de Brie is dated September 6. The defence runs as follows, quoting from the letter to Danès. " All the Budaeans rage against me because I have compared Badius with Budé, not in all respects, but in that one thing merely which Budé plainly condemns and which I am showing at this point in the Dialogue to be worthy of condemnation. Nor do they notice that this speech is made by Nosoponus and not by Erasmus. At the end, in order that no evil-minded person could criticise the collocation, I added that Budé deserved admiration for many other great gifts." In the letter to Hermann, Count of New Eagle, he specifies that the thing worthy of condemnation is the Ciceronian affectation.

A sort of apology is sent to Budé soon after where Erasmus writes: " See what a high opinion I have of your justness since I wish no other advocate in the present case than the one offended. So far have I been from nursing ill-feeling or jealousy against you that when I heard of the publication of your work I congratulated letters in general and myself in particular as well as you, for it is under your patronage that Greek and Latin letters are beginning to flourish in France. . . . I think that you have laid aside the suspicion which you seem to have conceived about me, most false, that willingly I cast reflection upon the name of the French. Though that displeasure of yours aroused no small feeling against me among the French, I am aware it

[36] Ep. 999 (1528).
[37] Ep. 1003 (1528).
[38] Ep. 975 (September 2, 1528).
[39] Ep. 978 (September 5, 1528).
[40] Ep. 1003 (1528).
[41] Ep. 981 (September 6, 1528).

was engendered through inordinate zeal for your fatherland rather than hatred, and in consequence I bear what happened more moderately. In a letter which I wrote to L. Berquin I unwittingly made a false statement and was very much afraid it would get out of his hands; by me certainly it will not be published. It is one thing to write to friends, another to write for the public. I have confidence to believe that if your judgment does not grant the friendship I ask, it will not refuse tranquillity to letters. But such is your goodness that you will make me your debtor by both."[42]   I have called this a sort of apology and so it seems to me, for there is no direct reference to the point in question. Erasmus' disposition to cast reflection upon the name of the French had been the occasion of dispute between them for several years. The false statement in the letter to Berquin here mentioned cannot be traced. No doubt it was expunged before publication as suggested, but there is no reason to suppose it bore directly on the quarrel. In various letters, hints are found of overtures and apologies but nothing is clearly put. Erasmus, for instance, writes to Egnazio on March 31, 1530: " In regard to the collocation by which some suspicion he was offended, I am sending a letter, which if it satisfactory to you, there is no need of further words. However, this misfortune of the collocation has been done away with in a later· edition.[43]   Indeed it was farthest from my mind to wound Budé."[44]   The suggestion here of a letter of apology is not verified by letters extant and it is quite likely that the two men were never reconciled. Erasmus all the time pretends that he is entirely innocent and if Budé is offended he is ready to do his part toward making reparation. Budé must have written spiteful things about Erasmus to account for many expressions of forbearance in Erasmus' letters, but it seems that he did not write any letter directly to Erasmus after the publication of the *Ciceronianus*.

Quarrel with Tusan

The quarrel with Tusan, which grew out of that with Budé, begins to figure now in the correspondence. Jacques Tusan was a professor of Greek and Latin in the University of Paris and a

---

[42] Ep. 1001 (1528).
[43] This would seem to suggest that the passage had been changed, yet we find the names together in the editions of 1643 and 1703. See supra, p. 32, footnote.
[44] Ep. 1015 (March 31, 1530).

friend of Budé. Influenced by the first violent outburst of indignation against Erasmus in France, Tusan wrote the following
distich:

> *Desine mirari quare post ponat Erasmus*
> *Budaeum Badio, plus favet ille pari.*

It appears that he had no intention of publishing these verses
but they were soon circulated and came to the notice of Erasmus,
who writes to L. Berquin that he can scarcely be persuaded that
Tusan is a man of such stolid and uncultured mind as to wish
to revel in slanderous verses with such little provocation against
a man who has never wounded him by as much as a word,[45] and
then he addresses a letter directly to Tusan protesting against the
verses and declaring that he has never given him any reason for
such treatment and that he thinks as highly of Budé as any one.[46]
A month later he says he is pelted with little verses of the Grammarians at Paris for linking the names of Budé and Badius.[47]
Judging from the frequent reference to slanderous verses, epigrams, and libels flying everywhere, there must have been much
more of this than has survived. Lascaris is repeatedly accused of
writing scathing epigrams, but I have been able to find nothing
of the kind written by him against Erasmus. Nor indeed has
any epigram at all been discovered, only the two verses of Tusan.

De Brie used his influence to reconcile Tusan and Erasmus
with more promise of success than in the case of Budé; for Erasmus tells him January 30, 1530, that he has written to Tusan and
no one need worry about their sincere and mutual good feeling.[48]
However, Erasmus in his next letter explains that he thinks his
letter never reached Tusan and that Berquin suppressed it,—a
trick which he had played him once before in the case of Alberto
Pio.[49] In this last letter Erasmus seems puzzled to know whether
Tusan had written an entire poem against him or just a distich
at the end of a poem written by Lascaris.

The following letter written by de Brie in July, 1530, might
well have been written previous to the one of Erasmus dated in
January and if the date of this is correct some other of like nature
must have been sent; but I shall insert the one dated July:

[45] Ep. 997 (December 23, 1528).
[46] Ep. 1025 (March 13, 1529).
[47] Ep. 1035 (April 1, 1529).
[48] Ep. 1091.
[49] Ep. 1100 (March 27, 1530).

" Tusan loves you and respects you as much as he does any one. He is as zealous for your reputation as for that of Budé. If he has allowed himself to be carried on the same vessel in spite of the stormy sea, you must attribute it not to the lightness of the man but to the violence of the storm. I myself, to avoid shipwreck, have turned the rudder to one side to resist more easily the force of the waves. It was a strange wind that lifted the sea but the halcyons have brought back calm. . . . Though you have felt a little hurt you ought to show clemency and give Tusan your old friendship. Budé dreams of nothing less than of that which has been reported to you. From his mind and pen nothing can emanate but candor and moderation."[50]

The answer to this is one of the longest in the quarrel. It was written just one year after the first to de Brie. The style is rambling. He wanders with no coherence, talking of Budé, of Tusan, of the stupidity of the French, of the absurdity of carrying the matter to the king and of accusing him of jealousy, of the scurrilous epigrams and verses, of his repeated honorable mention of Budé and back again a second or third time to any of these at will. Many times he has declared that the storm began in Italy and spread to France. In this he makes an explicit charge against his personal enemies by connecting Aleander and Albert, Prince of Carpi, with the Budaean quarrel. He accuses them of being the instigators and scoffs at their recent development of friendship for Budé. An outline translation of the letter will suffice to show the content:

" How does it happen that he (Aleander) who the Louvanians tell me had such a dispute with Budé that they almost came to blows is so much interested in the defence of Budé's name? Perhaps he wishes to do us both harm. . . . He is quite equal to this. . . . And I am sure that Alberto Pio does what he can, for they say that all my books are read in Venice. . . . By what Italian trick has he excited the storm? Has he pointed out passages in my books uncomplimentary to Budé? I have never made mention of him except most honorable. . . . Shall we refer to Budé and Badius being named together on the same page? It is too silly to entertain. . . . You write of

---

[50] Ep. 1114 (July 6, 1530).

Tusan. . . . There is no need, for this whole matter of the little verses would have been forgotten if you had not reminded me of it. . . . Tusan and I have never been on intimate terms. . . . I have always thought most highly of him as a man of letters. . . . I have forgiven him. . . . You declare concerning Budé that I can hold in my heart no suspicion that is not worthy of an upright man. . . . I expected more dignity from men of reputation in France than that they should raise such a turmoil which should spread even to Germany, Brabant, and Italy about the names of Budé and Badius appearing upon the same page. . . . And to think that it has spread even to the court of kings! As if this collocation were worthy of the King's ear! Everywhere flies these words, ' Erasmus is jealous of Budé, Erasmus wishes to take revenge upon Budé.' . . . I'm not sure but that France seeks the reputation of being a synonym for stupidity and levity. . . . It is most difficult to believe that such inhuman tumults should arise among learned men. . . . Scurrilous epigrams have been written in the defence of Budé who has been mentioned most honorably in so many of my books. . . . These are written by insignificant fellows. . . . Budé is perhaps so busy with more serious things that he knows nothing of them. I have not even deigned to read them much less to seek revenge. . . . This quarrel is not becoming to men of letters. . . . You are tardy in your suit of Tusan, for some time ago I set my mind at ease toward him; and though I had no bond of friendship with the man, yet I am not unwilling to enter into one now if it pleases him. . . . I have always considered Budé an honorable and generous man, nor would I have suspected anything concerning his Commentaries if I had not been warned by letters of friends. . . . I think no less of you that you could not always keep your rudder straight in such a fearful storm. . . . I have scorned the nonsense of the Grammarians, not deigning to look at them. . . . As for Budé I do not need his help nor would I burden him with obligation. . . . He can forward my reputation, I acknowledge, and he can injure it, but I am accustomed to injuries though I fear nothing of the kind from him. If the offence is light I am human and can allow something to passion, more to friendship, and most to general peace in the field of letters. But I am not so dull as not to see the figures of rhetoric nor so unskilled as not to be able, if I wish, to employ in turn the same, and perhaps I should have subject-matter enough; but it would have to be an unusually atrocious insult to arm my pen against Budé. I should prefer to be fluent on another subject. Indeed I think Budé too great a man for one of my rank to envy. I freely grant him the chief of letters. I applaud him enjoying a brilliant triumph rather than desire to rob him of a crown which his brow wears with so much glory. But though he has virtues of the highest kind, others have theirs too. . . . If Budé wishes to correct the wrong impressions of the people, he will do the thing worthy of our friendship, already old, and of his character; but if for any reason he is unwilling, I shall take it in good part even if he publishes more books against me indirectly because of his great skill in writing. Greet Tusan for me. Also tell Budé what I have said if he cares to listen. If you can persuade both of them to express to me in writing what you assure me in their names, you will render us all a great kindness."[51]

Though we have no confirmatory letter from Tusan, the following two extracts prove quite conclusively that a complete reconciliation was effected between him and Erasmus. The first is a frank and urgent plea from Erasmus: and the second indicates that this plea was received kindly, for Tusan has assumed the rôle of mediator between Erasmus and Budé. The first, dated January 30, 1531, runs as follows: " For de Brie's sake, if not as our duty, we ought to come to an understanding. I had conceived no hatred of you because my nature could never allow me to hate men reputable in letters. Serious men wrote me of the distich and with most certain proofs persuaded me, I acknowledge frankly; but I interpreted that you had acted through immoderate zeal for Budé, and I wished I had such friends, though I was not jealous of him. . . . But before de Brie wrote about reconciling us my mind was already at ease to such a degree that no trace of this thing had remained in my memory. . . . To establish permanent friendship, so far as I am concerned, we need de Brie neither as hostage nor as witness after I have you bound by a signed tablet, and I wish this letter written by my own hand to have the weight of the same thing with you."[52]

[51] 1135 (September 5, 1530).
[52] Ep. 1157.

The second is to Tusan some two months later: " What you write about reconciliation with Budé shows admirable zeal and kindness; but I am unwilling for men of letters to think that I have returned into favor with him though there was never any hostile encounter and God forbid that there should be. There is no mortal friendship, however, which some cloud may not darken for a time. I shall never be persuaded that Budé, a man not less generous than learned, was offended at my *Ciceronianus*. If there was any offence, it was the poison of an evil tongue. . . . I have never been of a different mind toward Budé than is fitting toward an upright man and one learned and highly deserving in letters. . . . If the offence is such as often happens between friends even though the bond is strong, it is his to demand and mine to make reparation. Nor should I regard it as a burden to recede somewhat from my right if I knew certainly what grieved him. Since I cannot divine this I cannot make advances. If he is offended it is his duty to answer the two letters which, as you say, he has kept by him unopened for two whole years."[53] This letter as well as the one written the same day to Egnazio is very evident proof that the breach between Budé and Erasmus had not lessened. To Egnazio he says: " Do not mock at me with congratulations for I have never returned into the favor of Budé. God knows whether I ever shall, but I have never felt otherwise toward him than is proper toward a good and pleasing man and one illustrious in letters. If there is any offence it did not proceed from me but was managed by whisperings and witchcrafts of poisoned tongues. Budé is a man more upright than to wield his pen against any one through pique."[54]

Writers Slighted by Omission

I have found but few instances where protest was made against the omission of names, though Erasmus writes to Vlattenus, January 24, 1529, that his book is criticised because some who should have been mentioned were passed by in silence.[55] Velius must have reminded him of the oversight of Vives, for in a letter already cited which was written to Vives September 2, 1528, Erasmus says: " Velius expostulates because I left you out in

---

[53] Ep. 1166 (March 13, 1531).
[54] Ep. 1165 (March 13, 1531).
[55] Ep. 1008, see supra, p. 28.

the *Ciceronianus*,[56] though it happened, I assure you, from oversight and if it cannot be pardoned because of my age, it ought to be because of the press of my duties. And yet I was more fortunate forgetting you than remembering Budé, for the Budaeans are raging."[57] In another letter to Velius he says, " I see that the surest way is to write nothing. . . . I have not undertaken to praise the authors named in my Dialogue."[58] Vives himself, however, took no offence as is shown in the response to Erasmus: " . . . It is not astonishing that you forgot, busied as you were in gathering so many names of every rank and class; in fact in running through them there came into my mind what Atticus said of Cicero's making a review of orators. I did not think that you had forgotten me but attributed your action to another motive. . . . I am astonished that Budé or any other, knowing the art of dialogues, has been offended at what you have said. . . ."[59]

The following letter in answer to a complaint from Eoban Hess, written on March 12, 1531, gives a lengthy discussion by Erasmus of the accusations arising from omissions: " . . . You seem to be offended because in my *Ciceronianus* no mention was made of you. If you say with equal fairness, my dear man, that whoever is left out may bring me to court, more than two hundred may do so; for I did not make a list of those who had become famous by their writings but when ten examples would suffice for illustration of the subject under discussion, I used that number, which it seems was as unfortunate as unthoughted. I wish I had refrained entirely from using the names of those living or but more recently dead. Now, some complain because they have been passed by; some because they have been remembered; and others because they have been treated otherwise than what they would wish. There had to be an end of the list and that could not be without the omission of many. But you say you would have omitted the mediocre ones only. But those who are mediocre think themselves distinguished. Do not be offended that you are not named; Zazius and Beatus Rhenanus are not mentioned, for

---

[56] Vives is mentioned in the 1643 and 1703 editions of the Dialogue; but in Ep. 1008, (cited supra, p. 28), written January 24, 1529, Erasmus says that he has revised the book and added some names.
[57] Ep. 975.
[58] Ep. 946 (July 26, 1528).
[59] Ep. 990 (October, 1528).

which I cannot plead forgetfulness since I saw one of them often and from the other received letters. Yet they do not expostulate. I have always acknowledged what Filelfo proved, that there was hidden in you a wonderful faculty in both prose and poetry, but there is nothing that I know of that you have written except poems. Well, you say, there is in my *Ciceronianus* a list of poets. Perhaps, but incidental however, and only for the sake of argument, with the result that it ought to have been reduced rather than increased. And yet as I am writing I do not know whether you were in the list or not; and if you had not expostulated I should have believed that you were not left out, so far was it from my intention to purposely omit your name. Granted, however, that I had planned a catalogue of writers, it would be kinder to pardon the oversight on the basis of forgetfulness than to doubt my intention. . . . We have been such good friends that whether you were in the list or not I hope that I shall nevertheless enjoy your goodwill. Finally, if I have failed in any degree in my duty, it will be easy to make amends in some other place. Goodby."[60]

---

[60] Ep. 1164 (March 12, 1531).

CHAPTER IV

ORATIONS IN BEHALF OF CICERO AGAINST ERASMUS

BY

JULIUS CAESAR SCALIGER

Among those already mentioned as having answered the *Ciceronianus* was Julius Caesar Scaliger, an Italian by birth, who lived at Agen in southern France. Various reasons have been assigned for Scaliger's answer. Some say that he was an obscure person, ambitious to begin a literary career, and saw here an opportunity to get his name prominently before the public by attacking the most popular writer of the period.[1] This could be maintained easily because he had written nothing before and really made his début into the field of letters by this work. Others think that he was led to write in defence of the Italians of whom Erasmus spoke disparagingly; while others attribute the motive to offence at not being mentioned in the *Ciceronianus*. The last reason seems quite improbable; for Scaliger, though he may have considered himself a prominent Ciceronian, had written nothing and was quite unknown to Erasmus: indeed Erasmus could not be persuaded that any such person existed and insisted that the discourse had been written by Aleander.[2] Scaliger in his letters suggests that the motive was the defence of eloquence[3] and in the discourse itself he states that he wishes to defend Cicero.[4]

Whatever the motive, he sent a messenger to Paris in April, 1529, with the manuscript of "An Oration in behalf of Cicero against Erasmus,"[5] dedicated to the students of all the colleges of Paris. Along with the manuscript he sent a letter to the Col-

---

[1] Christie, 194; Nisard, i, 319.
[2] Epp. 1241, 1205, 376, 370, 1288, 1299.
[3] Schelhorn, vi, 512; viii, 554.
[4] Oratio I, 1–12.
[5] Nisard, i, 345.

lege of Navarre urging the students there to espouse his cause and circulate the oration.[6] The messenger returned with reports of favorable reception and promises of a speedy reply from the students. After waiting some time for the answer Scaliger sent again and found that his appeal had been treated with contempt and the manuscript lost.[7] This brought forth a series of invectives against the colleges in the form of letters, full of resentment and boasting. In these he said ' he had hoped that the defence of the honor of Cicero would touch the students. Perhaps they considered him of low birth and beneath their notice but the Scala family was one of the first of Italy.[8] Perhaps they were disciples of Erasmus and the new eloquence. Any way they would find out that his oration would be universally read in spite of their insolence.'[9] ' For some reason,' he continues in another letter, ' the manuscript had been purloined. Was it jealousy, or a desire to carry it to Erasmus?[10] or a hope that Erasmus would be cleared by intercepting the charges? or for the purpose of plagiarizing? If it had not been stolen, he did not understand why they did not return it with congratulation or criticism.'[11]

The loss of the manuscript, however, occasioned no inconvenience, for either he had another copy or this same was returned to him; and after much delay and bickering with publishers and friends it was printed at Paris by Pierre Vidoue under the supervision of Noel Beda and with the permission of Lieutenant-Criminel Morin bearing the date of September 1, 1531.[12]

Analysis of Oration I

As the name indicates, the content of the first Oration is argument to show that the strict Ciceronians were justified in their imitation of Cicero and that the aim of Erasmus was to condemn Ciceronian style and to substitute a loose and careless one of his own. Scaliger treats the *Ciceronianus* as strictly serious in all its charges.

It is not impossible to analyze his oration and get a fairly consistent line of argument; but it requires culling and rejecting a

[6] Ep. 3, Schelhorn, vi, 513.
[7] Nisard (i, 349) says the manuscript was returned the following September.—See Schelhorn, viii, 566.
[8] Ed. 13, Schelhorn, viii, 574.
[9] Ep. 9, Schelhorn, vi, 526.
[10] Ep. 12, Schelhorn, viii, 564.
[11] Ep. 11 and 12, Schelhorn, viii, 559, 566.
[12] Nisard, i, 349; Christie, 194.

very great deal of irrelevant matter in the form of personal abuse. He furnishes arguments and answers objections, but mingles without reason or provocation that scurrility and personal abuse which brings upon him general censure. Scurrility was seemingly a necessary setting for controversy not only in the time of Poggio and Valla but in the sixteenth century in France, and Scaliger uses it most freely. Yet we must bear in mind that it was not so unpardonable then as now. The abuse was brutal and unjustifiable but largely verbal and perfunctory. The analysis included here follows the suggested plan and, though not as satisfactory as a complete translation, it may show, I hope, the outline of Scaliger's argument for Ciceronianism.

After excusing himself for answering Erasmus, on the ground that Cicero could not and the more learned scholars of the age would not, Scaliger states that his aim is: (1) to speak of the design of Erasmus, (2) to prove that he has not carried out his design, and (3) to refute his objections. (1-10.)

The design was to destroy the memory of Cicero by having the characters in the Dialogue discuss his imaginary faults but " I am going to show you that he has not succeeded in his design, and that many times he has arrived at a very different conclusion after proposing to snatch the palm from Cicero. . . . Erasmus criticises the verses of Cicero or attacks his manners or brings against him the old calumnies that have long been refuted. ' Cicero,' he says, ' was so tormented with the desire for empty glory that he annoyed people with his boasting.' See the impudence! he does his best to disgust us with the style of Cicero and when he cannot do that, he says that Cicero had dissolute habits and unpolished manners." Then attacking Erasmus directly for pretending to write better and more popular books, Scaliger continues, " Illustrious rhetor, whom do you call inconsistent? And you who wrote ' The Praise of Folly,' you so good, so perfect an orator, so just an appreciator of the faults of Cicero, who praises you? Others or yourself? What Rome has your courage saved from the furies of Catiline? In which of your Consulates have you snatched the fatherland from the jaws of fierce monsters? . . . Cicero speaks well of himself, he boasts to excess; but all the Latin and Greek historians have not found that he has said enough and they vie with one another in saying more." (11-13.)

" You may see how the attacks which he (Erasmus) has made

upon Cicero's eloquence turn into abuse of his manners and habits. 'Cicero,' he says, 'strokes his chin with his left hand.' Unlucky man! He stroked his chin with his hand! I wonder if in Germany one strokes one's chin with one's foot." Then turning again to Erasmus he continues, " You speak of his long and slender neck. If you had a neck of that kind would you cut it off? You reproach him for defects of voice. A man who must make himself heard in the noise of crowds, amidst the shouts of the populace, must have vigorous lungs; and nature gave Cicero a voice suited to the use he had to make of it. You remark that he trembled at the beginning and that this trembling was the index of mediocre courage. Wretch! Are you troubled because you have not found him as bold as yourself? Who, pray, pleading in the presence of Caesar and the people and the tribunal, in behalf of the life of a friend and his own life and fortune, would not at least have the air of trembling, even if he did not actually do so?" (15-16.)

Satisfied with the proof that Erasmus had failed in his design, Scaliger advances to the third part of his speech. " In order that his depravity may be evident to you I shall come to the third part of my oration in which I shall set forth many of his sayings, many inconsistencies, many foolish objections,—all arising from malice and none from reason. In order that you may see this as easily as possible I shall answer briefly the individual objections from the beginning of the letter to the end of the Dialogue." (16.)

The third part is really the body of Scaliger's answer occupying about fifty of the sixty-nine pages and it takes up, with considerable regularity, the points of the Dialogue.

Beginning, as he promises, with the prefatory letter[13] he quotes where Erasmus says he will mingle a bit of foolishness with his friend's serious business by sending him the *Ciceronianus*, and declares that this speech has unwittingly characterized the book. " What God, what fate," he says, " what chance of fortune has foreshadowed that whole unhappy tragedy?" He answers the charge that the imitation of Cicero has done injury to letters and to young Christians by declaring that letters, on the contrary, have been saved from destruction by the monuments of the Ciceronians and that many Christians by the imitation of Cicero have pleaded their cause much more eloquently. The criticism of the Italians

---

[13] Prefatory letter to the Ciceronianus.

brings forth a long defence and a tirade of personal abuse. " The
Italians employed you as a corrector of proof; and because they
had no patience with you for your gluttony and drunkenness, you
take your spite out on them by making fun of them for their
peculiar taste for Cicero. These things have been told to me by
men of high station and serious minds. You misjudge the literature, the inventions, the ability of the Italians, but you are not the
first among your countrymen to proclaim this proud disdain. Unwilling to imitate Cicero yourself, you follow the example of those
who despise and consider all nations barbarians but their own."
(16-18.)

Against the Dialogue, Scaliger uses, as his first weapon of defence, the charge of *ignorance* and *malice*. Referring to the
humorous picture of Nosoponus sick with Ciceronianism:[14] " In
matters of medicine, Erasmus shows deplorable ignorance. He
says phthisis is in the liver and not in the whole body; he attri-
butes jaundice to the liver when it can come from the spleen. He
showed ignorance when he pictured the doctor hesitating between
diseases so different. If he had tasted the least bit of Galen he
would have known perfectly the difference between a pettifogger
and a scholar. Another absurdity in medicine is the division of
the parts of man into brain, flesh, veins, nerves, intestines, blood,
spirit, phlegm." (19.) The fact that Scaliger was a physician
may have made him resent the use of medical illustrations. When
Erasmus later in the Dialogue says that precise imitation is not
more desirable than excess of health which brings illness sooner
or later,[15] Scaliger answers: " I see whence you have taken this,
it is from the Aphorisms of Hippocrates. But I am going to
make you see as clear as day how you have misunderstood them.
Come, do you know what distinction Galen has made on the
subject of health? Do you know that according to him, some are
healthy who are such actually, others because they are most of
their lives, others because they pass for being so always; but
there are few whom he calls altogether healthy. To what
category do you wish to belong? Would you gainsay that
the condition of those who are perfectly healthy is not the best?
Have you not wished that good health were yours? You have
the fear of falling into some illness in spite of the witness of

---

14 Ciceronianus, infra ii, 19.
15 Ibid, 55.

Galen who says that perfectly healthy men never fall ill. As for the maxim of Hippocrates upon which you lean, you ought to understand it thus, that there is no excess of health where health actually finds itself. This excess, in order not to become a malady, ought to be regulated by a potion, a bloodletting, a dieting. What a disgrace for you, what a danger for your reputation to receive lessons of a young man, an untrained orator, not even an orator but a soldier, an Italian, a man who above all wishes to be a Ciceronian and to be called a Ciceronian! The ignorance of Erasmus is just as deplorable in philosophy where he says that earth is never turned into fire.[16] It is no less deplorable in rhetoric. Nothing could be more absurd than to call Cicero a bad poet, citing *O fortunatam natam me Consule Romam* with its repeated syllable as proof, in order to show that he was not a good orator.[17] Was Virgil a bad poet because he wrote prose indifferently? or Horace because he did not plead cases?" Addressing Erasmus directly, he continues, " You have professed Horace to be the chief of poets. Yet in the first book of his *Satires* he says, *Cum dicas esse pares res.* You are trapped. If you criticise Cicero you must criticise Horace and therefore yourself, and then Cicero is proved innocent. You show impossible ignorance in regard to the occurrence of two molossi at the close of a sentence.[18] Every writers uses this." Scaliger proceeds here to cite instances from Terence, Caelius, Caesar, Plato, Demosthenes, Virgil, calling Erasmus an old parrot and asking if he is not grateful for this information, and finally as last proof of the point says : " Omitting all whom you condemn I shall bring one to you whose judgment you have always admired above all others, a certain Erasmus by name, to whose authority all the host of authors bow the knee ; at whose nod religions tremble ; and before whose censure institutions wane. He published some remarkable dialogues which I think you have not read and in one was written, *Liberi datis dextris aegroto jurant se servaturos quod recepissent.* When I read this I felt that by the judgment of such a man your most impudent assertion was instantly throttled." (20-24.)

To the pleasantries of Erasmus on the methods of work and the superstitions of the Ciceronians, his refutation is vigorous

---

[16] Ciceronianus, infra ii, 76.
[17] Ibid, 45.
[18] Ibid, 45.

denial and personal abuse with little or no attempt at proof. Nosoponus asks, " Who would not rather be celebrated in the eyes of posterity as a Ciceronian than as a saint?" Scaliger recognizes the sarcasm and grows angry. Erasmus accuses the Ciceronians of touching nothing for seven years but Cicero's books; Scaliger is satisfied with calling him a liar. But when it is suggested that they think more of Cicero's picture than of those of the saints he rails out: " If your picture is found everywhere, if the sensual face of Luther, your accomplice, dishonors so many canvasses, if they are fools who are smitten with such furies as you, why refuse more illustrious men the same privilege?" The humorous picture of the Ciceronian working at night in a chamber, shut off from the wind and noise of the street, whose walls are sealed with pitch and plaster, where not even a fly can enter, provokes the declaration that these accusations come from Erasmus's disposition to measure others' fortune by his own. The jibe at the Ciceronians for taking three to seven days to compose a letter to ask for the return of a manuscript or one whole night to compose a single period causes Scaliger to ask if there was ever a pleasantry duller than to suppose the human race so stupid or idiotic as to do this. Yet he acknowledges in part the justness of the jibe by proceeding to defend their slowness in composition, saying that Euripides took four days to compose one verse, that Virgil composed slowly, and that Horace recommended holding back from publication till the ninth year. That the Ciceronians will use no word except from Cicero, Scaliger denies and claims that they try to avoid words condemned by Cicero but accept authentic words wherever found. " What Ciceronian," he asks, " ever rejected Caesar? or Cato? or Caelius?"[19] (25-30.)

Coming to Cicero himself, he defends him against the charges of Erasmus and argues to prove him a perfect model of style. When Brutus and Cato are cited against Cicero, Scaliger answers that Cato was not without faults and that Brutus does not necessarily handle a case better because he handles it differently, just as he (Scaliger) need not be better than Erasmus because different. That Cicero should be called arid brings out expression of disgust and Scaliger tells him that no one but a vain, lightheaded and inconsistent fellow would in the same dialogue call a man

---

[19] Ciceronianus, infra ii, 23-32.

arid and then redundant and Asiatic.   He defends Cicero's
brevity by saying (1) that brevity has been defined as setting
forth the whole argument in the fewest words possible; (2) that
all authors have taken Cicero as a model in this; (3) that Erasmus lies when he says that brevity can best be sought from
Brutus whose only extant work can be shown to be verbose; that
he lies when he says that Sallust is a good example of brevity,
citing examples where he is prolix.   He closes his defence by
saying: " If I show Cicero to be brief, there is no case except
that Erasmus does not know what he is talking about.   I prove
that Cicero is the best exponent of austerity by asking, '.What
laughter did *pro Milone* excite?   What jokes in *pro Marcello?*'
Erasmus is wrong in ranking Hortensius before Cicero in partition, as the *de Officiis* and *Topica* prove.   Erasmus certainly has
not read these or he would not lie so openly." (31-37.)[20]
He ridicules the objection that a lifetime would not be enough
to imitate Cicero perfectly, by asking if a lifetime is too short
to imitate one would it be long enough to read and imitate many,
as Erasmus recommends.   He answers the argument that we
cannot be Ciceronians because all Cicero's works are not extant[21]
by replying that with just as much logic one could say that Erasmus cannot be a Christian because all that Christ did has not
been written. (37-38.)

The next general division of the discourse deals with the
solecisms, mistakes in facts, and the arbitrary rejection of expressions acceptable to reputable authors.   In the *Ciceronianus* Erasmus cites these as proof that Cicero was not perfect and that the
cult of Ciceronians, to be consistent, must imitate his very faults.
Scaliger denies that Cicero has faults or has been guilty of solecisms.   Some of the examples cited he admits are mistakes of the
scribes; while others he defends as good Latin.   *In potestatem*
for instance was used by reputable authors among the ancients.
Gellius said *in medium relinquere*.   That Cicero incorrectly attributed Hector's lines to Ajax in quoting Homer, Scaliger considers a matter of the least importance.   It cannot be considered
a fault of consequence since any number of writers have done the
same.   Nothing seems to irritate him more than this.   He rails
out: " Does this lessen Cicero's claim to eloquence?   The accusa-

20 Ciceronianus, infra ii, 35-37.
21 Ibid, pp. 41-69.

tion sprung from envy and malice. As if it mattered which of
the heroes made this speech! It is not, O most learned calumniator, Ajax or Hector who move philosophers, but Homer. What
matter if he had interchanged Phoenix and Ulysses? Plato made a
like mistake in attributing one of Euripides's verses to Sophocles;
Gracchus did the same. What if in history I show you one name
substituted for another? Does not Valerius call the man Nicia
whom C. Claudius calls Tynocharos? Does not Cato ascribe to
Q. Ceditius what Claudius ascribes to Laberius? Homer calls the
father of Procnes, Pandoreus; while others call him Pandionis.
. . . The mother of Romulus himself has several names,—
Rhea, Ilia, Silvia. You see, old crow, who try to scratch out the
eyes of authors, whom you have criticised?" In answer to the
accusation that Cicero rejects *piissimus, facere contumeliam,
novissimus* and *novissime,* used by reputable authors, Scaliger
says that the Senate condemned *piissimus;* that Cato and Plautus
who used *facere contumeliam* are not always to be followed; and
that Laelius, who rejected *novissimus* and *novissime,* is a better
authority than Cato or Sallust.[22]   (38-47.)

The usual answer is given to the claim of Erasmus that neither
the style nor the vocabulary of Cicero was adequate for the
handling of Christian themes and that the conception of the
Ciceronian in regard to this was absurd:[23] " You ask if for Jesus,
we should say Optimus Maximus; for God, Jupiter; and for the
Virgin Mary, Diana? What a silly question. Let us say also
Lucian for Erasmus. That name would be appropriate for you;
since you have imitated him in the style of his History, have
followed his despicable method of criticism, and you like him
have jeered at our religious orders. Shall I call you Timon?
Why not? You seem to hate supremely the human race and to
love yourself. Or Porphorus? You know that your Commentaries are known to all our sacred colleges and are unanimously
condemned for their impiety. . . . Would to God, Erasmus, when you introduced Jesus in the midst of a crowd, sporting
as if he were a peer and a companion of drunkards and peddlars,
he had suggested to you not to pronounce his name." (53-54.)

When Erasmus slips from the needs of Christian eloquence
and from the protest against paganism into ridicule of that wor-

---

[22] Ciceronianus, infra ii, 43–47.
[23] Ibid, 66–68.

ship of antiquity which causes us to "gape and stand stupefied if we find an image or even the fragment of an image of the ancient gods,"[24] for the purpose, in the opinion of some critics, of making a side thrust at Budé and his work in archeology, Scaliger declares that for him the coins, the inscriptions, and the monuments have served better than books. He has compared the faces of emperors on the coins and recalled their deeds, their habits and their lives. He has enjoyed the beauty of the vase, but has read history from the inscription at the same time. The statues are ancient witnesses of human history and the tombs are reminders of men whose lives are worthy of emulation. All serve to teach history and patriotism and stand as open books to the busy man. (58-60.)

Scaliger does not agree that one cannot express himself as Cicero because we have no senate, no empire, no consuls, no praetors, no forum.[25] "Modern countries have senates. Catilines plot to-day as formerly and brave men, such as Roscius, need defence. One cannot use the language of Cicero before the indiscriminate crowds of ignorant people, but before learned bodies it is wholly desirable. Longueil, who is ridiculed by Erasmus for speaking in his own defence at Rome, was not at all ridiculous but most praiseworthy and most successful."

The argument that all cannot hope to be successful imitators of Cicero because one cannot succeed in lines which do not accord with his natural bent of genius is answered thus: "Cicero was not perfect at birth. He became what he was by dint of work and development. An infinite number of Ciceros can be born and an infinite number of geniuses like his."

After reminding Erasmus of some of his inconsistencies where, for example, he says that we must emulate rather than imitate when by his own confession it is impossible to surpass whom we cannot hope to equal, where at one time he says that Cicero must be imitated but not wholly and another time he rejects all imitation, where he says a lifetime is not enough for imitation of Cicero and yet we must imitate many more than Cicero, he comes to the beginning of his conclusion by saying, "Such are the things that have compelled me to detain you, O excellent youths, in long and tedious speech." (66-67.)

---

[24] Ciceronianus, infra ii, 74.
[25] Ibid, 112.

The conclusion is in the form of a résumé, in which he ironically compares Cicero to Erasmus, and an appeal to the students to arouse themselves to preserve Ciceronian Latinity which is the only hope of letters: "You, Erasmus, when you had decreed that all imitation of Cicero should be discarded, why did you not so arrange as to say the same thing always? If you were ashamed of this calumny which you uttered so many times why did you not desist? Or why did Cicero seem to you of so little account? If he did not compare with Caesar in jokes, in that he was moderate in speech; if he was surpassed by the force of Demosthenes, in that he by more gentle gliding failed to hold the minds of the hearers; if he was inferior to Brutus in brevity, in that he was carried away by wealth and empty richness; less than Pollio in austerity, in that he wished his speech to be more ornate; if he is not modest, in that he says what has been written in histories of him; if no memory is for one who has allowed a solecism in the name of Ajax such as all ages have approved in Latin speech; if he inserted borrowed verses after the fashion of Lucian, Plato, Aristotle, and especially Quintilian and even you yourself; if he alone of all men is inferior, surely he is not worthy of defence. If, on the contrary, you are a vile man, a very great slanderer; if you have made false, fictitious, and empty statements for true, certain, and accepted ones; if so many times you have contradicted yourself; if you have destroyed all imitation so that we are compelled either to seek eloquence under cover or to have none at all; if you preferred those whom you have never seen to that man who had deserved best from you; if you have cut the throat of him whom you called your parent, whose offspring you acknowledged you were in your extant writings against yourself; what kind of a man may we think you are who criticise him instead of judging him and who equal him only in the number of volumes you publish?" (68.)

"Wherefore, O best and most humane and most learned of young men, who have always sought real fame, who have declared yourselves enemies of arrogance, of vanity and of envy by your virtues and by those of your predecessors, by the hopes of eloquence attained, I pray and beseech you to take care that by your negligence it may never deteriorate. Not only must you check the boldness of this calumniator but you must destroy the fancy of others to imitate him. Avenge the most excellent of men and his beneficent memory against the railleries of so evil spoken a man whose jealousy cannot be satisfied with insulting so illustrious a name. Some day this beast, if you allow him to rage against the Prince of letters with impunity, will hurl himself at you; and then the rage which he has employed against you he will not give up till he has more bitterly attacked others. Challenge his intemperance, dispel his influence, bring to naught his boldness, blot out his criminal decrees in order that Latin letters may owe more to you for having saved Cicero than they owe even to Cicero who, not being able to defend himself against a scoundrel and full of confidence in your humane and generous sentiments, commits his person and his eloquence into your hands, the hope and the support of letters." (69.)

Erasmus disdained to answer this attack. In some of his letters slight reference is made to the oration, but he always maintains that Scaliger is not the author and that it is unwise to notice such attacks. Writing to Goclenius he says: "Jean d'Eck has gone to Paris and also Aleander. Now I suspicion that this last has busied himself especially to contrive my destruction. I know that Scaliger's book is his as well, as I know that I live."[26] In a letter to D. Balivus he speaks of Aleander as the author though no mention is made of the name: "I am astonished that by any artifice they have pressed upon your name a book teeming with scurrilous attacks and most impudent lies and evidently full of madness at every point—a not less dangerous example to the most celebrated University than pernicious to aspiring youths. . . . What is easier than to write what one pleases under a fictitious name? Far be it from me to imitate his madness. This unnatural offspring was conceived at Venice and has an Italian father. They did not dare to bring it to light there so it was published in Paris under the patronage of theologians. . . . I can hardly believe that Beda approves of the deed, yet they write me that he not only approves but adds a bit of venom of his own. If this is true he is almost a demon. It would be great sport if I attempt to return like for like which would be quite proper and easy for me to do. I have material at hand and could paint that mad-cap author in his own true colors without lying, but I prefer to consider my own dignity rather than his deserts."[27] The following

[26] Ep. 1205 (December 14, 1531).
[27] Ep. 1241 (1532)

short letter to Viglius Zuichis is a re-statement of the same
opinion: "Briefly, my most learned Viglius, the book of
Scaliger's is so furious that Orestus would not write more in-
sanely. I could easily believe that some poison has been added by
Beda; for he does this in all works published in Paris against me.
And may be Camillo helped some. But the real author I know
as surely as I live. I could repay in like, but the affair runs
absolutely into madness. I have not been able to divine why they
are enraged at me. Those who make up that cult of Ciceronians
do not know what a pest they are to letters, for what will happen
in the future if they carp at all things that do not copy Ciceronian
phrase? Scaliger's book I have not read through."[28]   Again
to Viglius in the following year: "Scaliger pretends
that he is a Frenchman and names some obscure place.
From his Aldine style of phrasing and by other things too I am
persuaded that this work, at least the greater part of it, is that
of Jerome Aleander. I have lived with him and I know him
through and through as well as any one could. I have expostulated with him by letters; but he swears that he has always been
my friend and always will be. He wishes to avenge my attacking
him in the Apologies against Pius."[29]   In another letter: "Scaliger
has published at Paris epigrams selected from three thousand. He
prefaces that there is no illwill in them because he always shrinks
from all biting criticism. He awaits my response and has already
prepared another invective. But I have not yet read his book,
I have only glanced at it."[30] Mention is made of Scaliger's name
in connection with that of Dolet in a letter to D. Damanus a Goes
where he says: "These young men are poorly occupied who
conspire against the enemy of Italy and of Cicero. Nor are
schemers wanting to urge them on partly from hate of me and
partly from the pleasure they get out of this madness."[31]

All through these extracts it is seen that Erasmus never aban-
dons the idea that Aleander is the author of Scaliger's work. We
have a letter written by Rabelais to Erasmus from Lyons in December, 1532, in which there is an endeavor to convince Erasmus
that there is such a person as Scaliger and that the work is
genuine. Rabelais writes: "I have learned recently through

---

[28] Ep. 369 (November 5, 1532).
[29] Ep. 370 (1533).
[30] Ep. 372 (May 14, 1533).
[31] Ep. 1279 (May 5, 1535).

Hilary Bertulph, with whom I live very familiarly, that you are preparing some answer to the calumnies of Jerome Aleander whom you suspect of writing against you under the assumed name of Scaliger. I cannot allow you to be longer in suspense and mistaken in your suspicions. For this Scaliger does exist. He is a Veronese, of the exiled family of Scala, and he himself an exile. He is now practicing medicine at Agen. He is a man whom I know very well but not to my advantage, I am sorry to say; for he is a slanderer who, to define it in a word, has some knowledge of medicine but in other respects shows himself the most depraved of men. I have not yet been able to come across a copy of his book and, though it has been many months since its publication, no copy has arrived here; the reason I think being that it has been suppressed by your friends in Paris."[32]

The immediate occasion for the writing of the second oration, published in Paris in November or December, 1536,[33] was the following letter written by Erasmus to Merbelius and Laurentius March 18, 1535, and sent to Scaliger by these friends without comment:

" To my two friends of kindred spirit I am writing a single letter, though I must be brief on account of the gout in my hands and feet which has seized me industriously and is in full swing. Some days ago I wrote you sending the letter as you suggested by the tradesman. This will perchance reach you before that. I should be inhuman if I were not grateful to you for your friendly interest; but I think it wiser to pay no attention to the nonsense of the young men. Their tumult will have no other effect than to retard studies and destroy culture. The book you sent me I had received many years before. In it I see nothing that fits my case. If they make me an enemy of Cicero they are entirely wrong. The only ones I can call to witness are my best friends,— Pietro Bembo, Giacomo Sadoleto, and Andrea Alciati. This I can prove from their many letters written to me in the most loving way. They say that at Lyons a harsh book has been composed against me by Etienne Dolet, whose Orations and Letters are in circulation. There is a certain Longus, whom I have never seen, who continually censures me, not with the pen but by

---

[32] Nichols (i, 472) says there is no evidence that Erasmus ever received this letter. For the identification, see Revue de Études Rabelaisienses, iii, 12–44. Paris, 1905.
[33] Christie, 196.

word of mouth. My friends write me that by him another Vatrislaniensis has been instigated whose book flies through all Italy. It has not yet, as far as I know, been published but was sent to me in the manuscript. I have never read anything more stolid. Julius Caesar Scaliger has published against me at Paris an oration full of the most impudent lies and insane abuse, of which he is not the author, however, as I have found out by many certain evidences. This has been patched together by another not unknown to me. With such minds it is not my intention to wrestle, nor is it wise. I would have you take the same course. They will seek antagonists. If August Scapinel is with you, who recently wrote me from Ferraria, give him my regards. I wish you all success.

Erasmus with his own hand."[34]

The content of the letter along with the action of his friends in forwarding it without comment so enraged Scaliger that his second oration proved little more than an invective.

Analysis of Oration II

He begins this discourse by saying that though the friends have sent him the letter rather at the instigation of Erasmus than to gratify him personally yet he considers it his duty to answer it openly and publicly. ' The feeling of anger against him had come to light after five years of anxious waiting on his part. Erasmus had not considered the Oration worth answering and was unwilling to make him famous by mentioning him, since by silence he could condemn any one he pleased to oblivion. At length by the advice of friends and the probing of enemies he had thought it consistent with his dignity to call him an impudent liar. Learned men would not be satisfied with that. Proof is necessary for persuasion. He ought to have given proof.' (1-12.)

Scaliger proposes to show that he has not lied and that Erasmus therefore has. ' In what part of the Oration has he lied? About the private life of Erasmus? Surely that will not need witnesses. About his mistakes, some most impudent, others most foolish? Surely these do not admit of defence or excuse. About the calumny of Cicero? Every one agrees that he has attacked not only the style, but the person, the manners and even the bodily

---

[34] Ep. 1277 (March 18, 1835).

defects of Cicero. The charge of libel cannot be brought, for that is not considered libel which emanates from an upright man against one who has attacked him first.' (12.) The method of Scaliger throughout this invective is abuse of Erasmus and boasting of himself. To Erasmus he turns with abuse like this: "Concerning your life, did you not correct proof in the office of Aldus? Were not the errors in books there due more to your wine than to the printers? Trustworthy men in the presence of witnesses have told me of your gluttony and drunkenness. . . . Aldus Manutius told me that you did more work in one day than another could do in two and then you dissipated, . . . and he said this in no malice. If a good man and your best friend could say this, you would better correct yourself instead of Cicero. . . . Will you, the instigator of lies, dare to convict good and honorable men of lying? Is he a liar who says that he saw you in the court of Philip as a teacher? who says that you ran through Italy maligning all men, exhausting the libraries in plagiarizing? You who did not hesitate to steal and put into your Colloquies what had been sent you to be read before it was published by the author. My old teachers, Joan Jucundus and Jerome Dominius, warned me in my youth against your religion. Those men who, though they may not have made me acceptable to you as a scholar, made me a more honorable man." (14-15.)

This is but a preface to further boasting. One is loath to believe Scaliger when he promises modesty in speaking of his own virtues; for, while he promises it, quotations do not verify his promise as will be seen by his answer to some slight remark presumably made by Erasmus about his being a soldier. "The most honorable office of soldier[35] which has raised men to the rank of gods ought not to exclude one from the profession of letters which oftentimes has been received and enriched in the bosom of arms. Indeed the little that I have indulged in letters has not hindered me from fighting at times with much glory. If the glory in battle has not taken from me the fame of letters, how could the reverse be true? How do you know, Erasmus, but that this habit of enduring heat, cold, hunger, fatigue, and all the hardships which I have suffered in the rude profession, where fortune has served me so cruelly, has not been the first rudiments

---

[35] *Scaligerana*, 73.

or rather the foundations on which I have built to gain other laurels?" He goes on to claim that endurance and military training has created in him what the ancients called *prudentia,* while on the other hand the close application of Erasmus to study has caused him to lose vigor. Then follows a long paragraph of comparison between the virtues of himself and Erasmus: "While you were laughing at philosophers," he says, "I was learning the charm of Aristotle and was comparing him with Plato; while you were running about the provinces, I was correcting the treatises of Euclid and Ptolemy; while you were reading to your disciples the Publian Mimes, I was studying Virgil; while you were criticising Cicero whom you could not equal, I was imitating him whom I was going to defend; while you were snoring in drunken stupor, I was sweating at work; while you were drinking, I with my supper untouched before me thirsty, hungry, forgetful of self, pale, and red eyed was fed with the hope of glory of letters which was of so much importance that all else seemed sordid." (16-18.)

'In vain Erasmus defends himself against being an enemy of Cicero by taking as witnesses his illustrious Ciceronian friends. If he praised Bembo, Sadoleto and Alciati it was because he was led by their great popularity. Bembo, Sadoleto and Alciati by their failure to answer the *Ciceronianus* have shown that they have taken no more notice of Erasmus than Erasmus took of Scaliger. The boon companions of Erasmus have been turning away from him lately.' (18-22.)

Scaliger assumes that it is his duty to rid the republic of letters of the instigator of all kinds of discord. "See how Scaliger is the first and the only one among the flower and nobility of Italy who has flown to the rescue of eloquence in distress. Longus has followed him, they say, and some one from Insumbria whom I do not know, and Dolet has vied with him. It is I, Scaliger, who come as an exile from the remotest corner of the world, carrying as another Aeneas, my penates and the gods of my fatherland in the face of I know not what barbarians, under a troubled sky. A new Marcellus, I have been the first to show how a more than Punic Hannibal could be conquered not by borrowing his ruses from him but by using my own. (28.) I called this enemy *coenum* because he has defiled the fountain of eloquence; and *parricida* because he has sought the destruction of him whom he has claimed as his father; and I called him *triparricida,* for, as the ancients invented new words and new punishments for crimes that Solon thought too horrible to commit, so I had a right to invent this new word for the new crime." (23-24.)

Dwelling with continued emphasis upon the lies of Erasmus he then speaks of his own life at Agen, his simple tastes and the distrust of Erasmus in regard to the authorship of the Oration. Erasmus has sent a messenger to Agen to learn if there is such a person as Scaliger. This touches the pride of the would-be celebrated man. To prove that he is the author of the Oration he asks why some one else has not come forward with an expression of resentment at the insults of Erasmus, and mocks at the idea that the person would be afraid to resent being called an impudent liar. He regrets that he cannot produce the manuscript but the rough copy has been burned.

Boasting of his learning further he now says: " He does not know that I have examined more than a hundred books of the ancients. He does not know that I most wisely of all have corrected the mistakes in manuscripts of the ancients in discovering simple remedies, and the imprudence of the moderns in correcting their elders. He does not know that in many dialogues I have called not only all the doctors but even Galen himself and Aristotle back to the correct principles of truth. He does not know that a long time ago I wrote another discourse where I show what he is and what I am, and that I did not publish it out of regard for my friends. Knowing that one gains sometimes more glory in pardoning than in punishing, they have begged me not to gain a bloody victory. But a victory I have gained. I have imposed the bond of silence upon that tinkling little bell of Dodona. What more could I desire? Shall I continue attacks upon a corpse? What could I answer to those who were anxious for my reputation? And so I readily allowed myself to be persuaded." (39.)

It seems from this that there must have been something written by Scaliger against Erasmus which was not published. Sarcastically yielding to Erasmus who despises his Poetics and considers them vulgar, foolish, schoolboy essays, as oracle and judge, he grants that the name of Scaliger must ever be obscure; then later exults that nothing better has ever been written than his first oration, that all read it and admit that in it no point can be gainsaid, that by this the friends of Erasmus have been persuaded to fall off, closing finally by saying that his modesty does not allow him to linger longer over these things.   (40-44.)

With a confident assertion toward the end of the speech that Erasmus is downed, he turns for a parting word to Merbelius and Laurentius, expressing his astonishment that they should send the letter without a word of greeting, but suggesting that they had even, as it was, been guilty of a breach toward Erasmus by as much as writing the superscription, " To Mr. Scaliger at Agen "; for it had been agreed by all Erasmus' friends never even to speak or to write the name of Scaliger. 'As for himself he had let the matter of dispute between them drop and it had slipped from his mind.   But he noticed that Erasmus had grown more careful in his attacks upon religion and more kindly disposed toward Cicero; and yet it seemed that he had spared Cicero merely to attack the advocate of Cicero.   He closes by saying that he would not have written it at all if it had not been in defence of truth, liberty, and his own reputation.'   (44-47.)

The second Oration was evidently circulated in manuscript before it was published; for on March 11, 1536, which is some months before the earliest date assigned to the publication, Erasmus tells Gilbert Cousin that Scaliger has vomited forth some sort of book against him,[36] which however he has not seen; and which most probably he never saw for he died in July of that same year.

Joseph Scaliger says that Erasmus and his friends sent out emissaries to collect and burn all copies of these orations.[37]   This action does not seem at all consistent with the general tenor of Erasmus' letters; and it is quite certain that he could have done nothing personally to suppress the second oration. Joseph Scaliger would have us believe that his father repented the writing of his first oration when he came to understand how great a man Erasmus was;[38] but such knowledge must certainly have come to him in time to have forestalled the second Oration had he wished.   This discourse so teeming with abuse and reviling was finished September, 1535,[39] but was not printed till

---

[36] Ep. 1296.
[37] Scaligerana, 73.   See also Le Clerc's note on Ep. 1205.
[38] Scaligerana, 73.
[39] Bayle, i, 2.

November or December, 1536.[40] There is a letter addressed to Omphalius, May 14, 1536, which shows a disposition to treat for the establishment of goodwill with Erasmus. In this Scaliger says that he will yield to his friend's importunity, influenced by the splendor of Erasmus' reputation, his erudition, and his unselfish devotion to letters. He will entrust his own interests to Omphalius but begs him to be careful that they do not suffer. " I have always admired Erasmus," he goes on to say, " for his many great literary gifts. I have respected his labors, vigils, and accomplishments; and for this reason I have regretted that institutions were led away from true eloquence by him, whom I should gladly have chosen otherwise as a guide for my youth and a goal for my old age. But I am acting now with a clear conscience, for Erasmus but recently in his preface to the Tusculans[41] returned to his allegiance to Cicero."[42] Durand says Omphalius persuaded him to write to Erasmus and in such a letter, dated May 14, 1536, Scaliger declared that he had always admired Erasmus. And he states further that this letter is found in the Maussac collection but that it is not known whether Erasmus ever received it, for he died seven weeks after, before there was a reconciliation.[43] Burigny makes practically the same statement.[44] I am inclined to think, however, that they are mistaken, that Scaliger did not write directly to Erasmus at all, and that the letter referred to by these writers is the one quoted by me and addressed to Omphalius.

If the letter to Omphalius was written in all sincerity and with no desire of self-aggrandizement by seizing the opportunity of comparing himself with the greatest literary genius of the age, which I am inclined to believe was not the case, why did he not forestall the printing of that vilest of harangues which was published six months later?

[40] Christie, 196.
[41] Preface to the Tusculans:—"What happens in the case of others I do not know but in my own case the reading of Marcus Tully, especially when he discusses a point of morals, affects me in a strange manner. Then it is that I do not doubt that some divine emanation controls that heart from which springs such beautiful thoughts. And I am more persuaded of this when I think of the immense, the immeasurable goodness of God, of that goodness which some minds try to limit, in measuring it without doubt with the narrowness of their own minds. Where at present is the soul of Cicero? Perchance it is not within the scope of human judgment to say. Yet let me be classed with those who hope that he is living in peace with the saints above."
[42] J. C. Scaliger, Orationes et Epistolae, 269.
[43] Durand, i, 689,—"Omphalius, ami commun d'Erasme et de Scaliger, essaya de les réconcilier. Il determina le second à écrire au premier, le 14 Mai 1536, une lettre dans laquelle il declarait qu'il l'avait toujours admiré. Elle se trouve dans le recueil de Maussac. On ne sait si Erasme reçut cette lettre, car il mourut sept semaines après, avant qu'il y eût reconciliation."
[44] p. 205.

'Tis true that he did write an epitaph after the death of Erasmus which is dignified and praiseworthy; but it is also true that even after that he spoke disparagingly of Erasmus when occasion offered.[45]

---

[45] Nisard, i, 369.

CHAPTER V

DIALOGUE IN BEHALF OF LONGUEIL AGAINST ERASMUS

BY

ETIENNE DOLET

Etienne Dolet published an answer to the *Ciceronianus* entitled, *Dialogus de Ciceroniana imitatione pro C. Longolio* in 1535. He was somewhat better known to the world of letters than Scaliger; for he had already published some orations and was associated with men of influence, such as Budé, Estienne and Bishop Langeac. He had become a Ciceronian of the most servile type through a residence of three years in Italy. In 1527 he had gone to Padua to study under the tuition of Simon de Villeneuve, the successor of Longueil as professor of Latin, at a time when Bembo and the Ciceronian cult were most influential there. Later at Venice he had attended the lectures of Battista Egnazio. Returning to France in 1530, he determined to devote himself to letters and began definite work on his " Commentaries of the Latin Language," which was but an elaboration of notes on Cicero taken while in Italy. The letter cited[1] to Guillaume Sceve shows his zeal and ambition for literary reputation.

Dolet's reason for writing against Erasmus appears to be exactly that stated in the title of the Dialogue, though some have said he took up the cudgel in defence of Budé. It is true that he knew Budé and joined all France in praising him; but small space is devoted to his defence here. As a Ciceronian he had reason to feel that no one had adequately defended Longueil whom he had learned to worship at Padua as the most perfect Ciceronian and against whom he felt all the attacks of Erasmus had been directed.

---

[1] Infra, i, 80.

Analysis of Dolet's Dialogue

The plan of the Dialogue is not unlike the argumentative symposia celebrated in history.

He has More carry the *Ciceronianus* of Erasmus to Villeneuve at Padua and pretends that he is present when it is delivered and when this dialogue takes place between the two men. After finding a pleasing spot in the fields, Villeneuve asks More to recite the substance of the publication to him and a group of students present and proposes to answer the arguments. Thus all More's conversation is an exact quotation from Erasmus and no little of that of Villeneuve is a repetition of the same. For this reason it does not seem necessary to include in the analysis any large part of More's conversation, since a brief of Villeneuve's argument will outline Dolet's answer to the *Ciceronianus*.

Dolet is very careful to inform the reader that this colloquy is to be one of pleasant relaxation after the manner of the Sophists, and not in any way a contention : but he scarcely keeps the humor of Villeneuve sweet tempered throughout ; for time and again he exhausts his vocabulary of ugly epithets against Erasmus, the friend of More.

Villeneuve, glancing over the *Ciceronianus,* grows angry and amused by turns, remarking that Erasmus seems to despise Cicero and to persuade the youth to despise him because he himself cannot attain to Ciceronianism ; and that, offended at some letter written by Longueil in his youth, he attacks him, ridiculing not only his method of work but his religious zeal. In answer, More maintains that Erasmus does not attack Longueil but praises him. Villeneuve denies this and says first that he will defend Longueil; second he will consider whether Erasmus, as he assumes, is more acceptable to the aspirants for eloquence than Longueil; and third he will show that Cicero alone must be imitated. (1-16.)

Then More recites the various criticisms of Longueil made in the *Ciceronianus*[2] to which Villeneuve responds in the following way :

"You say Erasmus praises Longueil. It is a beautiful mixture of praise and blame to say that letters suffered a great loss in his death and then to say that he died in a foolish attempt to

---

[2] Ciceronianus, infra, ii, 110.

gain the empty title of a Ciceronian. That elegant and prolific writer, Erasmus, would have Longueil belch forth whatever came into his mouth and fill libraries with nothings and pondrous volumes of proverbs, fit for grammarians and children. Longueil thought too much of his reputation for that. . . . One is forever ruined who reads Adages, Commentaries, dry Scholia, Annotations, and Epitomes, who writes standing on one foot, with garrulity and jokes pleasing to women and children. The careful study of Cicero and painstaking composition gave Longueil a polished and perfect work, and the assiduous reading of Cicero gave him a reputation for eloquence equal to Erasmus. If he were alive to-day he would seek no other praise than to follow Cicero. (16-20.) . . . Erasmus says that Longueil lacked the opportunity to plead cases at court which Cicero enjoyed.[3] Absurd and foolish argument. Is there no other material for eloquence? Longueil's writings show that fictitious themes are even better than real ones. (21.) . . . Erasmus acknowledges that Longueil wrote letters but adds that they were on trivial subjects and far-fetched.[4] Subtlety and weight are not necessary in letters, for their mission is to speak on private matters, to console or to congratulate, to chide or to promise, to praise or to blame. (23.) . . . The next statement is as absurd, that a good part of Cicero's letters have been lost because they have been written so carelessly that scholars did not consider them worthy of immortality. I presume the chief and god of Roman eloquence was ignorant of the art of writing letters, which is the least of oratorical and rhetorical art, though he knew the subtler parts. I pity the old man, More, turning to his second childhood. (24.) . . . The charge of being far-fetched like Pliny[5] comes from his desire to ridicule. Is there a law, fixed and presided over by Erasmus, which says that we cannot discuss all subjects in letters? (24.) The charge of affectation and lack of truth in many of Longueil's letters to Bembo, Sadoleto, and Grimoaldo,[6] no one has made but Erasmus. If Longueil wrote on all kinds of subjects to the edification of Grimoaldo, who would call this any more affectation than courtesy? He did write many things about wars in which he had

---

[3] Ciceronianus, infra, ii, 11 .
[4] Ibid, 111.
[5] Ibid, 111.
[6] Ibid, 111.

never been but of which he had heard from other friends; but
these were not idle rumors. You will find nothing of the kind
in his letters. All are full of truth, dignity, and wisdom. If
you deny this, compare the letters of Erasmus,—common, cold,
jejune, sordid, impure, badly composed. What has that censor
of others in his letters but abuses of monks, disputes, quarrels,
turmoils of theologians? He makes no discrimination between
the foolish and serious; he harangues, criticises religion, teaches
the principles of the Sophists, attacks the dead and the living,
ridicules Longueil, calls Albert, Prince of Carpi, insane, casts
reflection on the French nation. . . . However, it is not
my intention to criticise Erasmus but to defend Longueil. Erasmus's method is to flatter and then to disparage. (25-27.) He
says that Longueil delivered most beautiful orations in Rome
which won all and yet they were far inferior to Cicero.[7] Then
he says it was no fault of Longueil but of the times.[8] I almost
double up with laughter, More, at these unheard of follies. ' Longueil did not speak aptly because to-day there are no Conscript
Fathers, no authority of the Roman people, no tribes, no magistrates.'[9] Ridiculous! The essentials of apt speaking are to devote oneself to the case, to say what is fitting, to furnish abundant argument in refutation, to strengthen the weak points, to
teach, delight, move the feelings, discriminating what will make
for unity and conviction. I acknowledge that we do not have
magistrates, but I will not grant that the office and duties of the
Conscript Fathers is so obsolete that they cannot be invoked in
pleading cases. Rome, France, England have their senates.
Things have not vitally changed. Before a learned audience,
Longueil was able to use with propriety Ciceronian words.
He did not deliver his speech at Freiburg nor in London but at
Rome and he used these words aptly there. . . . Erasmus
has two tongues, one touched with honey and one with poison;
he mingles bitter criticisms and praise; he says Longueil speaks
so well that no Italian could surpass him;[10] yet he dares, the
impudent buffoon, to call the proceeding ludicrous." (28-33.)

When More recites that Longueil would better have spent his
time in exhorting to Christian piety than in praising Rome,[11]

[7] Ciceronianus, infra, ii, 112.
[8] Ibid, 112.
[9] Ibid, 112.
[10] Ibid, 113.
[11] Ibid, 115.

Villeneuve answers: " This opens up all the theological question. One person thinks there is virtue in labor and vigils, another in exhortation. . . . Erasmus arrogantly confuses the human and the divine, assuming to himself divine power. He thinks that by his efforts Christ's power is increased. Therefore he exhorts to religion, thinks we would not obey Christ if not for him, writes paraphrases of the Epistles of St. Paul. Many learned men differ from him. They think that talking and writing Commentaries kill our innate reverence and religious feeling. . . . What have such men as Luther done for religion? I hear some one whisper that they have done away with superstition and restored religion. An insolent speech! The result of their work is that people lose reverence, despise the teaching of Christ, deny that human affairs depend upon God, deny the immortality of the soul and declare that death ends all. . . . The complaint that Longueil contributed nothing to the Christian religion is answered by saying that he did more than Erasmus and Luther in that he cherished it reverently and did not try to teach as if he were Christ. . . . Interpretations bring nothing but difficulty and strife. . . . Christ left his teachings plain. . . . Though Luther publishes the gravest commentaries and Erasmus the most elegant paraphrases and Oecolampadius makes a great noise and Zwingli tells wonderful tales and Lambertus, throwing aside his cowl, speaks loud; yet Christ alone exercises the divine will. . . . Wrath and anger and reviling are not characteristics of the Christian, yet what more bitter than the expressions of Luther and Erasmus against the monks and bishops? I am not so stupid as to say that the monks and bishops lead blameless lives, yet I do not approve of the attacks of Luther and Erasmus. . . . Our fathers knew the duplicity of the monks and the faults of the priests and the bishops; yet they thought it better to pass them by in silence than to stir up a strife. But Erasmus, whose custom is to attack everybody, enveighs against the monks, rails, emulates Lucian, delights in facetiousness and thinks he serves letters and the state by this licence; while Longueil, who is modest and sensible, contributes in Erasmus's opinion nothing useful and attempts vain things because he does not busy himself with paraphrases and annotations." (35-40.)

In reply to the suggestion that the Italians praise the Orations of Longueil but read the Colloquies of Erasmus,[12] Villeneuve says that people enjoy a buffoon but soon weary of him; that no one would read the writings of Erasmus more than once. (42.) He takes this opportunity of making an estimate of the works of Erasmus and continues the comparison with Longueil. More enumerates the works and he estimates them as follows: " The Annotations are esteemed highly but they have no claim of eloquence. *De copia rerum et verborum* is good. ' The Training of a Christian Soldier ' is a work of value. ' The Praise of Folly ' and the Dialogue against Barbarians shows Erasmus's cleverness rather than his strength; for he laughs, sports, and jokes but uses poor arguments. The *Apophthegmata* is a work more worthy of a grammarian than of a man of reputation. ' The Complaint of Peace ' is a beautiful story but lacking in skillful argument, in proof, in fluency, in exquisiteness of thought, teaching, delighting, moving no one.[13] His Colloquies remind one of an ape which thinks its offspring easily excels all other animals. Surely no one but Erasmus could praise such silly stuff. You may say, ' The Colloquies are useful. They teach boys politeness. Nothing useful can be sought from Longueil or other writers to compare to the Colloquies. All should run to the Colloquies to learn to speak more politely, to live better, as Erasmus speaks and lives.' Wise advice! Bembo and Sadoleto, your wisdom is challenged for turning Longueil to the imitation of Cicero rather than to the Colloquies of Erasmus. Literature certainly has a right to call you to account. I maintain that more eloquence, rhetorical art, splendor of Latin, acumen, invention shine in one of Longueil's letters than in all the writings of Erasmus. Erasmus published prematurely, therefore his works are crude and barren; Longueil sent forth nothing unworthy, writing and revising all carefully. He yields to Erasmus only in the number of volumes, but quantity is not a virtue. Erasmus is arid, dry, jejune, barren: Longueil is polished, elegant, fluent, reliable; he fits his language to the theme and the occasion; he restores the ancient method of pleading and excels his contemporaries. . . . Erasmus wrote the *Ciceronianus* because he was jealous of Longueil, in order to ridicule his

---

[12] Ciceronianus, infra, ii, 114.
[13] Supra, p. 3.

method of study and his religious zeal and to cast aspersion upon his character. Or else why does he speak so often of Longueil's zeal for study and lament the emptiness of his labor? If you will grant that Erasmus is great only in the eyes of the uncultured, that he cannot approach Longueil in eloquence; and if you will grant that Longueil is not second but far ahead of Erasmus in reputation for learning and speaking, I shall say nothing further. If you will not grant this, the truth of it can easily be seen in the fact that the majority of the works of Erasmus have already perished while the writings of Longueil are sought by all." (44-52.)

At this point the discussion of imitation is introduced by More's rehearsal of the scene where Nosoponus is afflicted with the dread disease of Ciceronianism.[14]

" Is it not the extremest folly," says Villeneuve, " to interpret the desire of eloquence as insanity? And it is just as great a mark of insanity for Erasmus to offer himself as a physician. Is Quintilian to be bound because he urges us to that insanity? Is Erasmus worthy of peculiar honors because he cures us by urging us to avoid the imitation of Cicero and wander through all kinds of authors? Quintilian believes that a great part of art is based on imitation. Cicero in his *de Oratore* says there could not be a standard of writing for all unless there were a model, therefore the chief thing in the art of speaking is that we try to imitate one person. . . . Three things are necessary for imitation,—wealth of vocabulary, variety of thought, and smoothness of composition. No one will deny that Cicero is the chief in the wealth of vocabulary; for his name is the synonym for speech where no harsh, inappropriate, or obsolete word can be found. The reading of other authors may furnish information but it is of no value for vocabulary and style. I do not forbid the reading of other writers but I urge to the imitation of Cicero only. Imitation does not mean quotation, it means digesting and absorbing. Some few words peculiar to the arts and professions may not be found in his works but still he is the model. . . . Erasmus no doubt would like his proverbs copied instead of Cicero. In variety of thought, nature is of more value than imitation but the reading of Cicero is especially necessary

---

[14] Ciceronianus, infra, ii, 19–20.

here to arouse and inspire. Sometimes when we are struggling, a passage of Cicero comes to us directing and inspiring our thought. Though we may not put our feet in his tracks we advance with confidence. Harmony and rhythm produce the third essential, smoothness; and by this, one style is distinguished from another. No one looked more carefully after this than Cicero. 'Tis true that style depends upon natural ability but Cicero studied how to join words to produce harmony." (54-69.)

Then Villeneuve proceeds to answer the various objections made by More against accepting Cicero as the only model of imitation.[15]

" You say that Tullian phrase does not fit all themes and characters nor is it in accord with every one's bent of genius.[16] You judge wisely. It would not suit Erasmus. It does suit any one who aspires to speak Latin well. . . . It can be used for any theme, just as the painter may use the same paint for the picture of Achilles, of Hercules, or of a mountain; for Tullian phrase and good Latin are the same thing. . . . Our age is not so different from the ancient. Do not we have the same themes? Do not crimes like those of Clodius and Catiline exist to-day? Do not you find men as full of virtue as Milo? . . . If a Ciceronian treats of religion where words are lacking, he may get them elsewhere but he still imitates Cicero in style. (69-74.)

Listen to Erasmus, most excellent young men. Salute him! ' The Ciceronian strives at the expense of health, even of life. Do not attempt Ciceronian imitation. Do not read Cicero, that foulest pest and plague.'[17] With these words I dare say Erasmus fed his long cherished hate. But he does not mention the name of Longueil. He shrinks from that. Who would believe that Longueil died of imitation? or that any one could? that life could be shortened or health injured by reading Cicero? When we follow Cicero as a model do we need then more than at other times to take medicines, potions, to fast, to give up joking and become recluses? Jealousy is the cause of these charges. (74-75.) Cicero cannot be a model for theologians, I admit; but I deny that he cannot be a model for piety. Hardly would he be lacking in the principles of piety who embraced philosophy

---

[15] *Ciceronianus, infra,* ii, 120-121.
[16] Ibid, 120.
[17] Ibid, 121.

with such zeal. 'Tis true that he did not use the word, Christ, but his writings are not different in spirit from Christ's. By his exhortations to the cultivation of philosophy he instilled in us more religion than Erasmus with all his theological garrulity. (78.)

What Erasmus says about the Ciceronians throwing out of their libraries authors who prefer to express themselves rather than wear a mask of Cicero[18] is not true. No one would exclude from his library those deserving of immortality for some other reason, if they were not Ciceronians. He must have made the charge to frighten his inferiors so that he might not be wholly scorned for not using Tullian phrase. Then, one does not put on a mask by the imitation of Cicero. Men change and borrow what they like and are still themselves. It might not be amiss to ask what mask Erasmus wears. A double one, intolerable enough to scholars,—a mask of words from Horace, Apuleius, Beroaldo, and a mask of thoughts from Lucian, the most vicious of men. (88-89.) Erasmus ridicules the Ciceronians when he makes Nosoponus say that he would use no word not found in Cicero and that he has set phrases for compliment, congratulation, condolence.[19] No one considers such a one a Ciceronian nor does one who has learned Cicero's force and richness indulge in those follies because he is overflowing with wealth of vocabulary, variety and smoothness. A word from Terence is not rejected if it adds to harmony and style. (93.)

What shall I answer to jealous enemies?[20] You say that Brutus disapproves of Cicero. Brutus follows his own bent, Cicero his. Shall we condemn Cicero on the judgment of Brutus? The judgment of posterity is better, therefore let us cast Brutus aside and decide ourselves. Erasmus will say that we are not as exact as the ancients, and that it is difficult to judge now, and that the judgment of Brutus is better. But we would decide in favor of Cicero. How absurd that Cicero feared the criticism of Atticus, his friend to whom he submitted his writings for criticism! (97-99.)

The charge that Cicero is dry, jejune, sapless, bloodless, disjointed, weak and unmanly, bombastic, Asiatic, redundant, is answered by calling Caesar, Verres, or Antony, to witness

---

[18] Ciceronianus, infra, ii, 122.
[19] Ibid, 33.
[20] Ibid, 35-37.

whether he was weak when he attacked them. Philosophy bears
witness that he is not arid. Scholars laugh at the idea of his
being redundant. (100-101.)

The argument that others excelled Cicero in various elements
of style is not well sustained. An example of wit cannot better
be found in another. Cicero's wit is the most delicate and refined. He used it when he saw that it would be effective and
was careful not to fall into scurrility. (103.) . . . Every
one acknowledges that Cicero excels in *sententiae*. You say
that Seneca ranks the Publian Mimes first in this. Seneca is a
writer of little reputation. (104.) Cicero is certainly a better
model for brevity than Brutus or Sallust. What is there in
Brutus either of brevity or richness? And Sallust wrote history where brevity was not essential. (105.) . . . No
witness can be brought that Demosthenes was a better rhetorician
than Cicero. . . . If the works of Brutus and Pollio were
all extant we might tell who was the best model of the three in
austerity but as it is we do not believe they excelled Cicero.
(105.) . . . The partitions of Hortensius were famous.
Those of Cicero were not famous though they were as simple and
clear, unless you say that Cicero used partition less elegantly because he did not give detailed headings of the case, gesticulating
and enumerating on his fingers. (106.) . . . Aristides, Phocion, Cato, or Brutus were not better models of the perfect orator because as you say they were honest men.[21] Though a reputation for honesty is valuable because it gives an orator a more
sympathetic reception, yet it is not essential to the art of speaking. I do not agree that an orator must be a good man. Fidelity does not make a man eloquent nor does integrity make him
learned and clever. Work and practice make the orator. The
ancients defined an orator as a good man because they believed
eloquence consisted in probity. They thought that if probity
were lacking the orator would not work for the common weal.
Will any one say that Cicero did not work for the common
weal? Was Demosthenes unworthy of the name of orator because he was not always trustworthy? Compare Phocion and
Demosthenes. Phocion was honest. Which of the two will
discharge thunderbolts? Which will win his hearers? or dispute more cleverly? Your claim of probity falls. I do not dis-

---

[21] Ciceronianus, infra, ii, 38.

parage probity, but it is not vital. We seek first natural ability and wealth of vocabulary and knowledge of the subject, then practice, good voice and gesture. If probity be added his reputation will be greater. Take Erasmus for example, he writes one thing and thinks another; he cries out against Luther but secretly connives with him; he loves brawls, dissensions, altercations but pretends to be a Christian; he flatters, lives as a parasite, filches money from bishops for some letter or inscription; yet if he merits any praise of eloquence we will praise him for that, regardless of his habits of life. (107-111.)

You say that it is not possible to be a perfect Ciceronian because we must treat of themes unknown to Cicero; because his works are not all extant and among those that are extant there are mutilations and forgeries; because Cicero has condemned some of his work himself.[22] Erasmus would not have deafened us with his garrulity if he had known that imitation does not consist of words so much as expression of art and that he is not a Ciceronian who borrows words rather than follows Cicero's other virtues. If we must write of subjects of which Cicero did not speak or furnish the vocabulary, we shall imitate him no less if we get his good Latin, his eloquence, his smoothness, his order and acumen. . . . The writings of Cicero are extant enough for this. Many of his best works have perished I know, but we can express him entire nevertheless. . . . There are few mutilations in Cicero to-day. French and Italian scholars have corrected with great pains the faults of the scribes. Gellius, Valla, Poliziano, Budé, and Longueil have worked so well that if Cicero should come to life he would change nothing. . . . As for forgeries, who would not know the difference between Cicero and the Germans? The authorship of the books of Herennius is still a matter of dispute, but the majority of scholars are inclined to assign them to Cicero. No scholar places the oration *pro M. Valerio* among Cicero's writings. No one considers the speech of Procius Cicero's, therefore we shall not torment ourselves with imitating Gothic terms. Nor does the dog scent the game nor the bee the honey-laden flower more wisely than do those who read Cicero discern his elegance and charm. (119-127.)

---

[22] Ciceronianus, infra, ii, 38-42.

Quotations are made from Erasmus of solecisms found in Cicero and poor translations, of grammatical forms rejected which are used by other good authors.[23] There are no faults in Cicero. *Potestatem esse* was a mistake of the scribe. There was no slip of memory. He condemned with good reason the words *piissime, novissime,* and *novissimus.* In all countries there are words which candidates for eloquence shun because they are harsh or inappropriate or newly coined. So at Rome formerly, words acceptable to the common people and sometimes to Cato or Sallust were rejected by Cicero. . . . Whether he used a double or a single *s* or whether we do does not affect our imitation of him. . . . I detract no more from the name of Cicero when I deny him the name of poet than I do from Virgil when I deny him the name of orator. In answer to the charge of poor translations, it was not Cicero's chief concern to translate verse correctly. He used the thought but adapted it. From the same fount of insanity Erasmus says that Cicero put the uncouth verse of Ennius, Naevius, Pacuvius and Lucilius in his works. Whom else could he have quoted? . . . I might call *O fortunatam Romam me consule natam* a mistake of the scribe but I prefer to say that this is not without charm. Virgil has made like collocations. It is foolish to suppose that this came from the ignorance of Cicero. *Invissae visae sunt* is a fault of the scribe. I think that Cicero wrote *Invissae mihi res visae sunt, Brute,* and if he did the trouble is removed. But even if he did not he justifies the clashing of vowels in *de Oratore.* (130-137.)

What a slanderer Erasmus is when he argues that a true Ciceronian must not let it be known that he is imitating, on the basis that Cicero taught that the height of art was to conceal art! It is a very different thing. In pleading cases it is the chief thing to deceive the judges, but in imitation we desire to do it so perfectly that all may know that we are imitating Cicero not Apuleius. The more manifest the imitation, the more truly a Ciceronian; and yet this does not mean that we are seeking eloquence for display and not for utility as Erasmus suggests.

Perhaps if we tempt the old man with money he will tell us whence we may drink eloquence. He may say, ' Read my Scholia, my ' Epitome of Valla,' my ' Complaint of Peace.' Let these

---

[23] *Ciceronianus,* infra, ii, 44-45.

divine writings, not the cold works of Cicero, furnish power to acquire fame as an orator.' Surely this seems to be the aim of his book.

He says he will acknowledge him an orator who copies Cicero successfully but he must copy him as a whole and his very faults too—the stroking of the chin, the long and slender neck, the straining of the voice, the nervousness at the beginning of his speech and so on.[24] It is not necessary to express his faults even if we should admit that what you enumerate are faults, which we do not. The straining of the voice was becoming to Cicero as was the hesitation at the beginning of a speech and the stroking of the chin. No one has called them faults before. Yet we shall not try to express these and shall still express him entire.

Erasmus ridicules the Ciceronians, calling them apes and saying that their conception of imitation is to use only Ciceronian words, phrases and tropes, to end periods with *esse videatur,* and to refuse, on this basis, to use any Christian salutations in letters.[25] Who would refrain from these salutations if they occurred to us in writing simply to avoid the ridicule of a Batavian buffoon? It is nonsense to consider it a fault to add S. P. D. to a name as a title of dignity. Longueil did it but with a different motive from Erasmus; for he did it as a mark of dignity, while Erasmus made it a means of flattery. . . . Erasmus is in his element when he can talk of theology. He says it is far from Ciceronian to begin a letter with *Gratia, pax, et misercordia a Deo Patre, etc.* He puts peace at the head of his letters and then, forgetting, rages and fights and brawls. (154-157.)

Argument is advanced to show that Cicero is inimitable,—that even if the words and phrases and tropes are copied, the soul and flesh and blood and life of Cicero will be lacking as it is in the picture which can reproduce nothing but color and outline.[26] Everybody knows that the painter cannot express anything but color and outline; the same is true of oratory. These criticisms are foolish and malicious. Natural ability is first in art as in all things and Cicero as a perfect model will train our natural ability and teach us by example. We do not fear the warts and scars. . . . The argument that slavish imitation is likely to

[24] Ciceronianus, infra, ii, 47.
[25] Ibid, 48–51.
[26] Ibid, 52–55.

overleap itself and produce something very different from its aim is merely an opportunity for Erasmus to attack Cicero. He calls Cicero so fluent that he seems loose, and so free and exuberant that he seems redundant. He says that Cicero balances his faults and his virtues, thus insinuating that he has faults. He recites these faults to make us flee from reading and imitating Cicero. He says if you try to add to Cicero's wealth you become redundant, if to his freedom you become petulant, to his jokes you become scurrilous, to his composition you become a declaimer instead of an orator; if you try to equal, you are in danger of becoming inferior. (55.) He hopes by thus slandering Cicero to turn us to Erasmus, to the ' Complaint of Peace ' and the Colloquies. But he cannot persuade the Ciceronians. Imitation has nothing in it of danger. We do not fear becoming redundant, petulant, scurrilous. Cicero is our perfect model and we can safely follow him. (162-170.)

The various reasons offered that the imitator of Cicero can not speak appropriately[27] to-day are easily answered. He says that style in speaking changes as it does in dress, and that what was appropriate a hundred years ago is not so to-day. We do not agree. Is not the same cloth used in different dresses? So we may use the same words. What was elegant and beautiful in Cicero's time is still beautiful. It is absurd to think of painting God as Jove, but the painter will use the same colors whether he paints Jove or Christ or the Virgin Mary. If one writes in Latin or Greek, he will not take language different from that used at Rome or Athens; and yet he will speak appropriately if he adapt his language to his theme. . . . The eloquence of Cicero does not consist of such little words as Senate and Conscript Fathers. The Latin language is not bounded by these expressions. (174-177.) . . . His objection is of no account that all things are changed, that we stand on another stage and in another theater and that we cannot speak on Christian themes in Ciceronian style.[28] If we speak on Christian themes we shall take words and thoughts from the Sacred Writings and shall speak both Ciceronian and Christian. We shall not then be ridiculous if we speak of fasting and prayer and the sanctity of marriage. Erasmus thinks that because he cannot treat these

---

[27] Ciceronianus, infra, ii, 56–60.
[28] Ibid, 61– 2.

subjects in Ciceronian fashion no one can. . . . He calls
the Ciceronians apes of Cicero to whom all words are dull except
those of Cicero. If the old man can cite a Ciceronian who shuns
words which are especially fitted to our age, we will laugh with
him and condemn the Ciceronians. . . . We are aware
that Cicero coined words such as *beatitudinem, finem bonorum*
and we do not shun such words as *church, apostle* and *bishop.*
Ciceronianism does not depend upon these. . . . But can
one imagine a Ciceronian delivering an oration on a Christian
theme before a promiscuous crowd as ignorant of all the arts
as of the Latin language? Would his speech be more pleasing
because he constantly used *Christ, church, faith?* And suppose
before a learned audience he did use *sacred assembly* for *church,*
or *faction* for *heresy,* or *sedition* for *schism,* would he be less
clear or pleasing? They would say his figures were admirable.
(177-180.) . . . Who hearing Erasmus attack Ciceronianism as paganism[29] would not think it a drunken man talking
rather than Erasmus? But we all know his propensity for talk on
theological subjects. He first attacked Longueil, then Cicero,
and when he found that he could not move us he calls imitation,
paganism. He seems merely to be satisfying his taste for garrulity. . . . One thing we shall stop to answer. He says
that paganism persuades to the imitation of Cicero and that we
do not dare to profess paganism so we plead Ciceronianism. I
wonder how such an evil-tongued man as this Batavian jackdaw
could have been created by nature or how we have so long
esteemed him. Sadoleto, he accuses you of paganism, you who
reproduce Cicero so beautifully; and you, Bembo, he reviles, whom
he pretends to love. He attacks Longueil by the name of paganism who is invulnerable in eloquence. Compare the writings of
Longueil. Any one will call the style of Erasmus childish, weak,
absurd, unpolished, loose, while that of Longueil is eloquent and
Ciceronian. The Christianity of Erasmus is not above reproach;
in Longueil there is no suspicion of impious mind. With such
modesty he pleaded his case at Rome that he melted the hearts
of his accusers. He pleaded the case against the Lutherans for
which reason perhaps Erasmus accuses him of paganism. Bring
the case into court. Wiser judges than Erasmus will decide.
Find if you can in the writings of Longueil any sign of pagan-

---

[29] *Ciceronianus, infra,* ii, 75.

ism. He is full of impiety and paganism who pretends to bring a charge against an upright man. Though Erasmus should embrace the image of Mary and kiss that of Peter and Paul, worship the relics of the apostles, cling to the wood of the cross, and gabble perpetually on theology, I should believe him least a Christian because he attacks all so maliciously." (182-187.)

When More at this point interrupts by asking why he suspects that it is Longueil who is referred to by Erasmus, Villeneuve bursts forth with a reiteration of all the offences of Erasmus against Cicero and the Ciceronians: " But let him rave, show his jealousy, gabble, blab, indulge his second childhood, repeat the same thing time and again, call the imitation of Cicero a new kind of disease, deny to Cicero the name of perfect orator; let him say that Cicero is deformed by many faults, solecisms, collocations; that he is weak, loose, redundant, boastful, inconsistent, untrustworthy, a poor translator of Greek verse; let him cry that his works are not all extant, that granting him a perfect orator it is impossible to imitate him; that he is not a fit model for modern times and themes; let him laugh at the slow methods of composition of the Ciceronians and criticise them in every thing and in every way,—what else is it all but the fury and ravings of a reckless old man? what but the stutterings, the garrulity and humor of a buffoon? Notwithstanding all this we shall devote ourselves to the divine Cicero and shall go on as before striving to become like him." (187-188.)

Then turning to More, Villeneuve asks what remains of Erasmus's follies. More replies that there is nothing but the estimate of ancient and modern authors, to which Villeneuve responds: " Don't bother. I can easily recall these. I remember the passage when I ran through the Dialogue as you handed it to me. Erasmus shows his insolence in the estimate of Quintilian; and his desire to disparage in the case of the more recent writers when he speaks of Valla, Poggio, Hermolao Barbaro, Poliziano, Giorgio da Trebisonda, Theodore Gaza, George Merula, P. Leto, Filippo Beroaldo, Pietro Crinito, Antonius Sabellicus and Baptista Egnazio. These men were great though they were not Ciceronians. Had they devoted themselves to Cicero they would have been greater but they are not neglected by scholars because of this. Come to our times. Why did Erasmus discuss his contemporaries except to flatter some and disparage others? He rightly praises Sadoleto, Bembo, Pins,

Nicolas Bérauld, Lazare de Baïf, Germain de Brie, Francis Deloin; but not always without the suspicion of flattery and bribery. He abounds in jealousy and love of disparagement. An example of this is the joining of the name of Budé, the most learned Greek and Latin scholar, with that of a grammarian and versifier where he expatiates upon the endowments of the versifier and passes by the virtues of Budé. Erasmus excels Budé only in loquacity and volubility; Budé excels him in learning, dignity of style and uprightness of life. A certain Frenchman explained the action of Erasmus thus: ' Cease to wonder why Erasmus put Budé after Badius; he gives preference to the one resembling himself.'[30] You must accept this explanation unless perchance you say that Erasmus was influenced by an obligation to Badius for hospitality while he lived in Paris." (188-191.)

With a final exhortation to imitation of Cicero only, and an appeal to the young men who are represented as listening to this conversation, the dialogue between More and Villeneuve is ended and all the company return to the city. (191-192.)

The circumstances of the publication and reception of the Dialogue form even a more interesting part of the history of Ciceronianism than the content of the book itself.

The manuscript was sent to Guillaume Sceve in November, 1534, accompanied by the following letter: " On the 15th of October I arrived at Paris without fatigue and without meeting with any misadventure on the way. And as I fancy that you will expect me to write to you what I am doing, and how I occupy myself in cultivating and prosecuting my studies, I will in the first place explain this to you and then will inform you of what is passing here.

" My studies, my dear Sceve, become more serious daily. Indeed I can hardly express, and you will with difficulty conceive, with what alacrity, and inflamed as it were by a new love, I devote myself to literature. I both plan and write many things as to which, however, I shall not arouse your expectation until I perceive that I am able to complete them. I send you a dialogue concerning the imitation of Cicero against Erasmus, which you will hand to Gryphius. I shall be under very great obligation to you if you will see that it is printed as carefully as pos-

---

[30] Supra, p. 35.

sible. Do not allow your kindness to me, which has never yet
failed, to fail in this instance. The trivial crowd of grammarians who worship Erasmus as a deity, and place him before
Cicero, will scarcely refrain from attacks upon me. Moreover
I do not doubt that the old man (who is now almost childish
with age) will ridicule the young man with his usual and persistent scurrility. But nothing troubles me less than the scurrility of a buffoon, nor do I fear any sharper bite from the tooth-
less old food-for-worms; while as to those who may accuse me
of insolence and may cover me with reproaches because I attack
Erasmus, let them in the first place consider in what way they
can defend Erasmus himself from the charge of insolence and
scurrility in venturing to ridicule Cicero and those who strive
to imitate him.

" I spend my evenings in rewriting my ' Commentaries on the
Latin Language,' which I hope to complete by the beginning of
January. The remainder of the winter I shall devote to enlarg-
ing my orations and epistles for another edition. I should not
promise so many things if I had not determined on this, that for
once I would show what it was to be eagerly and studiously devoted to letters, and what it was to undergo labour for the sake
of immortality, and would also show that I hated idleness worse
than death.   .   .   .

" Yet however much study, labour, and diligence I devote to
literature, I refer whatever I compose to your judgment, so that
you may order my writings to be suppressed or may decide that
they shall be published, for I am certain that you will neither
desire that I should remain for ever unknown, nor, owing to the
premature appearance of the fruits of my studies, that I should
obtain a merely slight reputation rather than one which is firmly
fixed. I think that it is my duty, whilst my age and the abundance of my leisure allows, to devote myself as vigorously as
possible to literature, but only to publish such things as, without
flattery, I may understand to be approved as well by the judgment of other learned men as by yourself.

" My great devotion to study forbids me from setting foot out
of doors, so completely am I bound to literature. It thus happens that I have not yet visited your friend Aemilius; I have
however taken care to send him your letter. Nor have I yet
paid my respects to Budé, which may indeed be considered as

a great omission on my part. I shall visit him the first opportunity, and to this I shall for a short time postpone my work
and my present studies. .   .   . "[31]

As indicated in this letter Dolet expected Erasmus to take
some notice of his masterful protest but he was to be disappointed. Erasmus maintained the same silence that he had
toward the attack of Scaliger, briefly mentioning to a few of his
friends in letters that he had heard of the book but had not seen
it or that he believed Aleander had written it.[32]

Resentment did come, however, from a most unexpected
quarter; for J. C. Scaliger wrote immediately to their mutual
friend, Arnaud de Ferron: " I suppose you have seen Dolet's
dialogue against Erasmus, the author of which was not ashamed
when my writings were in print to steal everything from me by
giving my oration another turn and decking it out in his tinsel.
There appear the same extravagances as in his orations, a style
indeed a little rough, but for which he is indebted to another,
so that his loquacity seems to be supported by other people's
words rather than by solid arguments. But you will say he
praises Caesar.[33] He does so, for they say you advised him to
consult his reputation by doing so, he having already rashly and
foolishly ridiculed the Italian name. You had acquainted him
also that I was preparing a dialogue wherein I should expose
his malicious temper and empty arrogance, his petulance and
stupidity, his impropriety and loquacity, his raving expressions
and impudence. Having thus soothed me with the design to
divert me from my purpose, he praised me in such a manner that
he seemed unwillingly to follow the judgment of other people
rather than to express his own. Wherefore I have endeavored
that both he and others may for the future repent of their rage
and impudence. I hear that he is a corrector of the press at
Lyons; and if it be true that he was concerned in correcting the
books I bought which were lately printed by Gryphius, our very
school-boys have therein discovered faults for which he deserves
a severe whipping. I have reprimanded him in this second oration,[34] not by name indeed, but painted in such colors that he
may be known by the very children of Toulouse."[35]

---

[31] Translated by Christie p. 197.
[32] Epp. 1277, 1279, 1288, 1299.
[33] Julius Caesar Scaliger.
[34] Christie (p. 206) says that Scaliger must have cut this reference out of his second
oration upon the advice of Ferron.
[35] Translated by Christie, p. 205.

Only the year before there had been an exchange of letters[36] very complimentary between Ferron and Dolet looking toward the establishment of a friendship between the latter and Scaliger; but all this is at an end. Nothing could be too mean now to say about the impudent young upstart who dared to open again a controversy which a man of distinction had effectively and successfully closed. The change in attitude may be depicted by comparing the following excerpt from Scaliger's " Ode on the Death of Simon Villeneuve " to the letter just cited to Ferron: " Dolet may be called the canker or ulcer of the Muses. For besides that in so great a body, as Catullus says, there is not a grain of wit, fool as he is, he sets up for a tyrant in poetry. He has according to his own fancy set Virgil's pearls in his own resin in such a manner that he would have it pass for his. A wretched prater, who out of scraps of Cicero has patched up certain wild orations as he calls them, but which the learned judge to be latrations. He imagined that he had as good a right to make free with the divine words of Virgil. So while he was singing the fate of that good and great King Francis, his name met with its own evil fate, and the Atheist alone suffered the punishment of the flames which both he and his verses deserved. Yet the flames did not purify him, but he rather sullied them. Why should I speak of the filth which is to be found in the common sink and sewer of his Epigrams? They are dull, cold and witless, and full of that arrogant madness which, being armed with the most consummate impudence, would not even confess the being of a God. Wherefore as the greatest of philosophers,

---

[36] Christie, pp. 122–123, *Ferron to Dolet:*—"I am on terms of greatest intimacy with Julius Scaliger, a most accomplished man and devoted to all kinds of liberal culture. We have so many grounds of friendship that you would hardly find any persons more intimate than we are. In reply to a letter in which I made mention of your singular erudition, eloquence and culture, he wrote most pleasantly and gracefully that he had as great an esteem for you as I had, and that he had already heard of your eloquence; and although he is a man exceedingly averse to ingratiating himself with others, he especially desired me to salute you in his name. I do this most gladly, as well on account of the message itself, as in order to perform that duty to him which he imposed on me in this letter. I think you will highly esteem his learning, for he is of the number of Ciceronians, and well known to the learned men from the oration which he has published in defence of Tully against Erasmus of Rotterdam. At the same time the message is very agreeable to me, since it furnished me with an excuse for writing you . . . ."—*Dolet to Ferron:*—"That you should take the trouble of writing to me is, in the first place, agreeable to me, and I am greatly pleased by your extreme goodwill. That Julius Scaliger has, by your means, become friendly to me is something for which I confess I am greatly indebted to you; and if I do not immediately require so great kindness I shall yet strive by my thanks to imitate your friendly disposition. I beg you to be persuaded of this, that you have conferred a favor on one who will remember it, and to understand that I shall spare no pains if there is anything you wish for in which I can be of service to you. . . .

"Of my goodwill to Caesar Scaliger in return for his to me I shall not write you at length; this only I ask of you, first to bear in mind yourself, then to strive to persuade Scaliger that there is no one for whom I have a greater regard or a higher opinion. You will salute him for me, and will without hesitation offer him my services." Toulouse, January, 1534.

Aristotle, in discoursing of the nature of animals, first describes the several parts of which they are composed, and then takes notice even of their excrements, so let his name be read here, not as that of a poet, but of a poetical excrement."[37]

Scaliger had really little reason to be offended except as impelled by jealousy; for the Dialogue was not borrowed from his Oration. Critics can find resemblances; but in the method, matter and style Dolet's is much less like Scaliger's than Scaliger's is like the letter of Cortesi to Politian or of Bembo to Pico. The fact is that one can find a remarkable sameness in much of this literature on the merits or faults of Ciceronian imitation.

Dolet's Dialogue was a source of as much regret to his friends as it was of annoyance to his enemies. Sceve urged him not to print it. Gryphius would not allow his name to appear as printer of the first edition and wholly refused to allow the second edition to go through his press.[38] Jean de Boyssone in August after the publication writes to Dolet: " As to what is thought of your dialogue, *de Imitatione Ciceroniana,* though you will no doubt have heard everything from others before this, yet I must tell you that the bitterness of your style, which you once promised me that you would discontinue, has produced a bad effect upon many, because (as they say) you ought not to have attacked so violently an old man who has rendered such services to literature. The rumor is that the Germans are preparing a vigorous attack upon you in order to avenge the wounded dignity of Erasmus. Whatever happens, I trust that you will not be disturbed by these matters but will continue, as is your wont, to show an unshaken firmness of mind. This only I would beg of you, that you would so accommodate yourself to the time as that it should not seem inevitable for you to offend the good and pious. When I ask this of you, you will understand what I mean. . . . "[39] Dolet at once makes answer: " What you designate as the excessive severity of my Dialogue I have determined not to excuse to you at great length. I will excuse it, or rather defend it, with all my might against those who undertake the cause of Erasmus. You will scarcely believe how little account I make of the attack of that young German fellow, an attack which I attribute to the

[37] Christie, 207.
[38] Ibid, 201.
[39] Ibid, 210.

influence of wine and intoxication, or rather perhaps indeed to a childish ostentation of German garrulity and a love of chattering. I know what the fellow's strength is, excessive in relation to wine and women, but in respect to other matters weak and feeble. But I would have any one who defends Erasmus against me to know that I shall not write against him but against Erasmus. I am however about to treat of the whole matter in four orations and two books of iambics.

As to the one thing that you especially ask of me, namely, that I should so accommodate myself to the time as that it should not seem inevitable for me to offend the good and pious, this only is wanting, that I should understand what you mean; for I am so far from understanding it, that I have not even anything from which to form a conjecture. But we can talk of this matter hereafter when we meet, as you are thinking of coming to Lyons. . . ."[40]

Though Dolet had no epithet too vile to hurl at Erasmus living, it is creditable that he wrote a laudatory ode upon his death, which, perhaps in a sort of irony, he addressed to Scaliger: "Formerly the generals of Rome and Carthage engaged in a desperate conflict. As long as the enemy fought full of force and life, as long as he set his teeth, was it not good, was it not great to attack him hand to hand with the sword, to riddle him with darts? So be it! As long as he kept his strength and zeal for the fight, I caused the enemy of Cicero, the detractor from the good name of France, to feel my darts. Now he is dead. . . . I spare him and my embittered stilet shall not wound a corpse. Oh Muses, let us pay to this old man a just tribute of praise. The greedy tomb has swallowed him, the pride of Germany, greater than any scholar of Italy or of France, except you, Budé and Longueil. Yes, the pride of Germany and the glory of letters, the greedy tomb has devoured."[41]

Erasmus himself, as we have said, showed no disposition to answer this attack, but his friends felt somewhat different. Melancthon wrote to Camerarius (1535), " I have seen Dolet's book, and I am thinking of instructing some one to reply to it. Erasmus indeed is not altogether undeserving of the Nemesis which he has met with, but the impudence of this young man

----

[40] Christie, 211.
[41] Dolet, Opera, Carmen, ii, 20.

displeases me."[42]   Shortly after, writing to another correspondent he says, " Have you read that very impudent book of Dolet written against Erasmus?   I have taken care that it should be answered."[43]

·The following very interesting letter written by Odonus, October 29, 1535, from Strasburg to Gilbert Cousin, secretary of Erasmus, shows not only the attitude of Erasmus' friends but the prevalent conception referred to in the *Ciceronianus* that Ciceronianism was but a mantle for paganism.   As the early humanists had sought to harmonize classical antiquity and Christianity, so now the great body of criticism against the strict sect of Ciceronians is that such harmony cannot be attained by literal imitation.   Erasmus, Vives, Politian, and Pico perpetuate the spirit of the fifteenth century; Bembo, Sadoleto, Longueil, Dolet, and Scaliger pervert and subserve Christian doctrine to Ciceronian form and style.   The letter contains so much directly bearing on the whole question that I have concluded to quote it entire:

" I have just heard that it has been written from hence that the friends of Erasmus here wish that he should briefly reply to the rage and fury of that very mad fellow (Dolet), which those who have heard so great a croaking think is the roaring of some great animal (as the fable of the lion and the frog has it).   But I, who when at Lyons both saw the man (or rather the mindless thing in human form) and talked to him, know him to be a worthless beast.   He somewhere calls himself a young man, but he is nearer to his fortieth year than to his twenty-eighth.[44]   He is bald to the middle of his senseless head.   He wore a short Spanish jacket, coarse and much worn, scarcely covering his back-side. His countenance is of such a funeral and black pallor and has such a wretched air that you would fancy an avenging fury had fastened on his breast and was dragging him to the punishment of the wheel.   You will ask who introduced me to this portentous spectacle.   It was the other precious Ciceronian, that despiser of the Greek language and studies, who has published those dialogues, *Cicero revocatus* and *Cicero relegatus*.[45]   He indeed is banished from, but not yet recalled to Italy; where

---

[42] Epp. Melancthoni, iv, No. 180, p. 732, Ed. London, 1642.
[43] Christie (p. 211) says he has searched in vain for the answer here referred to.
[44] Dolet was then twenty-six years of age.
[45] Ortensio Landi.

(though his native country) not only did he fear to be recognized, but was so conscious of his own deserts that he even suppressed his name on the title page. I was however on terms of great intimacy with him at Bologna. At Lyons he repeated this saying to me, ' Let others choose other masters, I approve only of Christ and Tully; Christ and Tully are sufficient for me.' I saw nothing of Christ however in his hands or in his books; God knows whether he had anything in his heart. This however I know from his own mouth, that when he fled into France he brought with him as a consolation in the wretchedness of his journey neither the Old nor the New Testament, but only the Familiar Epistles of Cicero. Both the circumstances of this fellow, which are worthy of his life (yet the Phrygian has not yet undergone the stripes of God calling him to repentance; oh, that he might at length feel them!), and his levity, his effeminacy, and his irreligious conduct, I should have briefly described to you were it not that we know that all these apes of Cicero are characterized by the same depravity and impudence. This fellow took me to the bird of ill-omen. Outside his chamber there was a good deal of noise and untidiness, caused, as I suppose, by boys learning the rudiments of grammar. (By this means, as you know, banished tyrants are accustomed to earn their living.) Inside, I do not remember what books the exile had. In the course of the conversation he referred to a passage in his orations where he speaks of Erasmus, and as it seemed not so bitterly. And this passage he wished to be recited by Ortensio lest I should be shocked by his Gallic pronunciation; nor was there any mention made of the rabid dialogue which he was about to publish. He earnestly begged Landi however to write a preface to his orations, and offered to dedicate them to whomsoever he (Landi) wished; but the latter declined the proposal. Nor did Gryphius appear willing to undertake a new edition of them; indeed he complained to me of the vehement and unreasonable pressure which certain persons had put upon him to induce him to print them. Then as we were going away he offered me the poisonous trash of Carvailus[46] and Scaliger, which I had not seen in Italy. No doubt with books of this kind the wretch consoles himself for his banishment from Toulouse, and again inflames his mind,

---

[46] Ludovicus Carvailus, a Minorite, wrote against Erasmus in defence of his monks. Christie, 218

worn out as it must be by his quarrels. The next day I returned both books to him with certain pages turned down, and we had some conversation concerning the king and the theater of Guilio Camillo.

" Now, my dear Gilbert, I see no reason why this fool should be answered according to his folly. Perhaps I am in error, but as Alciat writes, he is still more in error who has so mean an opinion of the majesty of the name of Erasmus and of the veneration which men of letters have for him as to think he could ever be cast down from the citadel of learning and virtue, where he has for so long been established, by the calumnies and insolence of a fellow of this kind. He is no jester, to amuse one with his writings while making a great profession of piety, like Amsdorf; he has not the title of knight or count or monk; he is indeed scarcely human in his appearance. Moreover we do not know whether the University and Parliament of Paris have not taken care that he should be capitally punished by law at Paris. For it often happens to these atheists, when they are especially rejoicing and saying (as it is written in the epistle) peace, peace, let us eat and drink, then suddenly they are overwhelmed with a deserved destruction.

"Perhaps, however, friends from Paris may have sent you a more full account of the wickedness of this hornet or chameleon, who bawls out to the very breaking of his jaws, and for the sake of a slight breath of applause is rushing to certain destruction of body and soul. Yet who could ever carve in stone or paint in colors a better representation of a foolish, senseless, insane, furious, rabid, boastful, insolent, scurrilous, petulant, vain, lying, impudent, arrogant, impious fellow, without God, without faith, without religion, than this man has by his own words shown and expressed himself to be? To me he seems to be of the number of those whom St. Augustine and Erasmus himself order us to laugh at when they weep, and to weep over when they laugh, both which I certainly did when I read his book. It has indeed been a matter of great grief to me that a man should be found so well versed and baptized (so to speak) in polite letters, and yet of such brutality and impiety. God is my witness, my dear Gilbert, that not forwardness but affection has induced me to write these things to you.

" And now let me stop in the middle of my course, lest if I say more I may seem to wish to be wise overmuch. For even on this matter I do not profess to see all sides. Therefore whether Erasmus thinks fit to reply to Dolet, or thinks it not worth while to do so, I shall be satisfied. For whatever he thinks right I doubt not will really be so. So now I will conclude, commending you and Erasmus to God.

Strasburg, 29th October, 1535."[47]

The most formidable champion that arose to defend Erasmus was Francesco Florido Sabino, who made a formal answer to Dolet in his *Subcisivae Lectiones*,[48] a critical estimate of authors, published in 1539. Florido, curiously enough, had been private secretary and tutor in the family of Albert, Prince of Carpi, one of Erasmus's bitterest enemies; but he was moved to answer Dolet because he opposed the Ciceronians and because he admired the literary attainments of Erasmus.

" Ciceronian imitation," Florido says, " has so taken hold of the minds of literary men in Italy and in all countries where letters are cultivated that the most bitter strife exists among them, some contending that no author but Cicero should be imitated, and others that all should be read and the best culled for imitation." " I had for a long time intended to write," he continues, " so when Dolet's book came out against the *Ciceronianus* of Erasmus it impelled me to insert in my *Lectiones* a long chapter entitled ' What Authors Should be Read and What Imitated.' By the very caption I testified that I would show not what ought to be observed in imitation, for that had already been done by others, but who of all the host of ancient writers ought to be imitated. Inasmuch as a school of imitators recently sprung into existence among us declare that Cicero is the only model not only in oratory and philosophy but also in history and poetry, I saw that I had to cover the whole field or discuss only a part of imitation. I therefore declared that all authors should be read by orator, historian, or poet; that Virgil was a fit model for poetry; Livy and Sallust for history rather than Caesar; and when I came to Cicero I took up the particular headings of the Erasmian

---

[47] Translated by Christie, p. 216.
[48] i, ch. 2, ed. Gruter, p. 1007.

Dialogue and refuted Dolet partly by reasons and partly by testimony from the ancients."[49]

The refutation[50] of Florido follows the line of argument common at that time,—abuse, sarcasm, and a bit of reasoning. In the main it runs briefly thus:

Florido's Criticism of Dolet's Dialogue

" Cicero would have been more modest than Dolet in his answer a few years ago to the *Ciceronianus* of Erasmus where he warned the reader at the outset that all the speeches of More were taken from the *Ciceronianus* lest some one might think that Dolet was sometimes forceful and sometimes weak. Was there ever such conceit? He speaks of himself here as if he were a Cicero or a Demosthenes. He fears that some one will mistake Erasmus' style for his. Who has ever read your writings, Dolet, that he could detect the differences? How is it ever possible for any one to think Erasmus' style weak and yours strong? When the style of the two is compared, we find in Erasmus supreme erudition, in Dolet only empty sounds,—no thought, no knowledge. Let him clear himself of this charge if he can.

He calls the Adages of Erasmus a farrago. (*Respon.*) Let him compare them not to his Commentaries nor his Dialogue but to Longueil's Letters and Orations. Wrinkling his brow he says, ' There is more eloquence, rhetorical art, and splendid Latinity in one of Longueil's letters than in all the works of Erasmus.' (*Dial.* 48.) Is it not truer that in one page of the Adages there is more doctrine than in all Longueil? He says that Longueil imitated Cicero more perfectly. (124.) What if he did? In Longueil there is nothing but the cold name of imitation, in Erasmus there is erudition and good Latin if not Ciceronian.

Let me explain briefly the plight of the Ciceronians. They reject all Latin which is not in Cicero. Nothing could be more impudent. Who of the ancients ever attributed this authority to Cicero? He was, they say, the most eloquent of all the Romans. Quite right, but he was not the only eloquent Roman. The Greeks and the Latins always admired his eloquence but did they confine themselves to him as a model? Because Virgil and Horace did not imitate Cicero, must we consider them barbarians? You say they were poets. Well, take Caesar, Livy, Sal-

---

[49] Adversus Doleti Calumnias Liber, 4.
[50] Subcisivae Lectiones, i, ch. 2, pp. 124–136.

lust. They have not written in Ciceronian Latin. You protest
that they are historians. Then must orators only be read? Why
does Quintilian teach that the candidates for oratory must begin
by reading the poets? If the poets, historians, and all except
Cicero furnish nothing to the orator, the author of *de Copia Verborum* need not have mentioned any one but Cicero. On the
contrary, does not his lengthy examination of poets, philosophers,
historians argue that the reading of one author is not enough?
I should not present this so confidently if Cicero himself did not
in the *de Oratore* urge the reading of all kinds of authors and
the culling from them. (125.) If the writings of the ancients
should be read, how much more those of later writers? Cicero
did not take Demosthenes alone but followed Plato and Isocrates
and read every one. So we must acknowledge that this superstition of imitation was unknown to the ancients. If the writings
of Asinius Pollio, Licinius Calvus, Caelius, Caius Caesar, Brutus, and all the ancient orators were extant, I am sure that I
should use from them anything that fit my theme and no law
of the rhetors would forbid. What of the fact that Cicero has
not treated all subjects? If in this article I follow another author, shall I be less Latin? No, but I shall not be Ciceronian.
Dolet rejects from his list those who use the formulas and are
ignorant of grammatical principles, accepting only those who
thoroughly digest and absorb, citing Longueil as a perfect
Ciceronian. (*Dial.* 63.) But tell me, in good faith, Dolet, what
Longueil has except the lifeless form of imitation? Where is
Cicero's genius? his learning? his pure and divine phrase? I
should place Pontano, Valla, Politian, Theodore Gaza and many
others before Longueil. (126.)

Dolet objects when Erasmus says that Tullian phrase does
not fit all minds and that those that have not natural ability
are foolish to strive after the impossible. (*Cic.* 120; *Dial,* 71.)
He does not agree with Horace that we can accomplish nothing
against the will of Minerva. Will it profit one with literary
ambitions to imitate Cicero? Shall we follow Cicero or Caesar
or Livy or Sallust in history? Dolet says *Cicero,* but I have
never been so astute as not to wish rather to be like Livy or
Sallust. 'What is the use,' says Dolet, 'of reading other
writers? They may give information but they can furnish nothing for imitation more than Cicero has furnished.' He thinks

we can fashion everything from Cicero's vocabulary as a painter can paint all kinds of portraits with the same colors. (*Dial.* 73.) He has not told us how we can imitate Cicero in history when we have no examples of that from his pen. Is it the same to write history and to deliver an oration? I think we pervert Cicero so that if he should come to life he would not recognize himself. Dolet after his fashion calls all Latin writers off-scourings except Cicero. Is Virgil such? or Caesar? or Livy? You dare to publish your silly Commentaries and then to tell me all the Roman authors are off-scourings! Such a person would be capable of venting his wrath against not only Erasmus but all Germany and France too. (127.) All will see how mean he is when I show why he attacked Erasmus. He was unknown and insignificant and hoped to gain reputation by attacking some very celebrated man. Though men who choose letters as a profession are supposed to love and praise the scholars of all nations, Dolet rejects all except Bembo, Sadoleto, and Budé, the latter of whom he tries to win by servile flattery. He is stupid enough to ridicule all Germans without discrimination. He must know that he has not increased his reputation at all by trying to blot the name of Erasmus from the memory of men.[51]

But let us return. He says we must imitate Cicero only and then is inconsistent enough to grant that we may choose words from any source we will in writing on sacred themes, provided we retain the strength, wisdom and acumen of Cicero. (*Dial.* 119.) Perchance we might preface and explain when we use such a word. Then will our whole work be prefaces. (128.)

Wishing to persuade us that some semblance of the Ciceronian age remains, he says that Rome, France, England and Spain have their senates where we may imitate Cicero; and that there are not lacking Pompeys, Caesars, Catilines to-day to praise or to condemn. This is nothing but a pure figment of Dolet's. Which of these senates has senators who can convince by the art of eloquence? Is it not rather true that they will not listen to Latin and that Bartholdus and Baldus, who are anything but orators, have set the style for forensic pleading? And there is no place for *deliberatio* either, unless we wish to exhort the Pope or

---

[51] Another reason is added in *Subcisivae Lèctiones* i, ch. 4,—"If the judgment of Erasmus should prevail, the Commentaries of Dolet would have no value, compiled from the Thesaurus of Étienne and the Observations of Nizzoli on Cicero."

Carolus Caesar or the King of France to take up arms against the Turks. Thus, the two exercises in which Cicero excelled are closed to us. *Demonstratio* is left. Let Dolet exercise his strength in this and fashion his productions after a mutilated model. And when he runs out of epithets he may say there is in Erasmus only a desire to pour forth foolishness on all occasions. He may drag forth the old Batavian and prove him weak and arid by making Longueil equal to Cicero. (129.)

Dolet does not approve of reading all authors. He says that if we read them we profit only by seeing what they have borrowed and by a desire to return to Cicero, after wandering through all the bypaths of literature, to sharpen our dulled palates. (*Dial.* 62.) This is an illustration, not of mistaken judgment but of stupidity. (130.)

Nothing more dreadful or baneful has ever been sent from the lower regions than Dolet. I do not see how he is tolerated in France, where among men of letters a certain modesty reigns, and in whose cities modern writers are respected as well as ancient and the youth is taught to give Cicero first place but to consider others as well.

No one disputes him when he advises care in the choice of words and says Cicero is the highest authority. But he offers no argument that Cicero is the only one to be read or imitated. He compares the age of Cicero with the one previous, concluding that the previous age was crude and antiquated while the age of Cicero, which boasted of Hortensius, Caesar, Domitius, Brutus, Calvus, and P. Lentulus, introduced a more elegant and splendid style. Of all these Cicero was the chief and greatest whose name is a synonym for eloquence in which there is no harsh, uncouth, or obsolete word. (*Dial.* 58.) Let me ask. Did the contemporaries of Cicero speak Latin? Were they superior men? If this is evident, we are compelled to admit that they ought to be imitated in many ways. What of the writers after Cicero? Dolet does not mention Pollio, Virgil, Livy, Horace and their contemporaries. Was it because they did not retain purity of Latin? (131.)

He who has not talent or erudition of style equal to Cicero cannot, in my judgment, choose a more unhappy plan than to devote himself to this superstition of the Ciceronians who represent the class that Horace addressed,—' O imitators, servile herd, how often your clamoring has moved me to anger, how often to mirth!'

I ask again how any one can express Cicero, when his works are not all extant. Dolet's statement that they have been so well amended by French and Italian scholars that if Cicero were alive he would wish nothing changed (*Dial.* 126.) is manifestly false, as all know who have read Cicero with care. This shows that Dolet knows so little about it that he cannot tell when there are mistakes. (132.) I do not understand why he mentions Gellius in connection with Valla and Politian, as if they were all engaged upon similar work in relation to Cicero. Valla, Politian, Budé, Erasmus, and above all Aldus, have been diligent, but still Cicero is not perfectly restored. Therefore we shall never be able to reproduce him entire.

Hear what Quintilian says on imitation. ' Is it enough to say all things as Cicero said them? It would be enough for me if I could follow the copy in all respects; but what harm can there be in copying sometimes the force of Caesar, the severity of Caelius, the carefulness of Pollio, the discernment of Calvus? Further, it is wise to make your own as far as you can the best from all. It would hardly be possible for any human to express any model exactly; therefore let us place before us at the most the good things, taking one thing from one and another from another, whatever is appropriate for our theme.'[52] These words confirm our opinion as manifestly as they show the Ciceronians to be mere praters.

How insane Dolet is to spurn all authority. The rhetoricians before him have said that an orator must be a good man, but he thinks eloquence is not aided by a reputation for integrity. (*Dial.* 107.) We must express our greatest thanks to the Gods because, when all the ancient and modern writers have been mistaken, they have sent us Dolet as an interpreter who, after deliberation, has decided that the ancients joined honesty to eloquence not as a help to eloquence but because an orator so furnished would not injure the state through hatred or desire of revenge or ambition. (134.)

How absurd and ridiculous his rejection of *novissimus* and *novissime!* (*Dial.* 130.) He criticises Sallust, calling him a bold architect of words as if he were a Pollio. He refers to the

---

[52] Inst. Orat., xii, 10, 10.

distich of Tusan. (*Dial.* 191.) We see here an epigram worthy
of Dolet's commendation. Who would ever be so stupid as to
think that Erasmus would compare Budé with Badius? What if
Badius had aspired to the honor of the Ciceronian name by writing a few letters and Budé had not? (135.) Would any one
accept the judgment of Erasmus if he had declared that Badius
was a greater scholar than Budé?

I shall say nothing further about Erasmus or Longueil; but if
Dolet thinks that he has been criticised too severely, let him remember how he has criticised Latin authors in general. If, as
is his custom, he answers me with denials only, offers no reasons,
no testimony, he shall reap as he has sown; and if he takes pleasure in reviling he shall listen to the same in turn." (136.)

Dolet published in 1549 an answer, entitled *Liber de imitatione Ciceroniana adversus Floridum Sabinum,* consisting of a
defence of his theory of imitation and a separate response to
particular insults. The defence is a quotation, with appropriate
introduction and conclusion, of pages fifty-seven to seventy of
his Dialogue, omitting the complimentary references to Scaliger
and the criticisms of Erasmus.

The response (pp. 23-48) has much repetition and no new
argument but presents sufficient individuality to warrant some
slight notice. Dolet here reiterates that Cicero is the only model,
that Longueil is the most perfect representative, far excelling
Erasmus whose works are either dead or dying. He repeats a
third time his theory of imitation that wealth of words, variety
of thought, and smoothness are the essentials in history, poetry,
or religion, and that though individual words may be chosen from
others writers the phrasing and style must be confined to Cicero.
There is no lack of bombastic display of conceit through it all.
At the outset, he accuses Florido of being angry because the
Ciceronians have placed their confidence in him and boasts that
they had not been disappointed, for his writings showed how
he had profited by reading Cicero. " If he did not write Latin
more purely, more ornately, with more careful rhythm, more
weight of thought, more dignity, judgment, and wisdom than
Erasmus he would think native ability lacking, life bitter, and
all his zeal for eloquence in vain. Granting Erasmus and his

coterie the privilege of indiscriminate imitation, if he could show in his writings the Ciceronian characteristic of purity, splendor, and harmony, he had proved his case. The comparison of his style with that of Erasmus scarcely made him call Erasmus weak. But how weak Florido seemed when he opposed his style could be plainly seen. Indeed when Florido said that his Dialogue had only empty nothings and wearisome desire of garrulity, it was as if Homer had been called untaught, Aristotle crude, Plato ignorant of philosophy, Cicero barbaric, Virgil ignorant. He would advise Florido in a friendly way to strive after pure Latin and give up obsolete and antiquated words. Yet he would not have it thought that he had read all the works of Florido. He would not use his time so poorly. But when he glanced through the *Lectiones* he had noticed *obsequelam* and *singularissimus,* whence he guessed that there were many more mistakes of like kind. Then Florido must be careful not to wander so much, for his work was not rhythmical, not compact, not orderly; and he had no power of writing clearly and forcefully."

He takes up the following charges and refutes them one by one: "He had not written his Dialogue for self-aggrandizement but to defend Longueil and save the youth from the teaching of Erasmus. He had not derided the Germans indiscriminately but had given them credit for illustrious minds even if they did not speak Latin well. He had justly called Bembo, Sadoleto, and Budé the lights of the age but had not in any way sought to obtain favor of Budé by flattery. Instead of despising Terence he had admitted that any word could be used from his works if it added to the brilliancy or fluency of the style. He had not been guilty of plagiarism or of impiety."

He adds at the end of his volume containing these answers a number of epigrams against Florido.

Early in 1541 Florido went from Bologna to Rome. Soon after, he received a letter from France saying that Dolet's book had been published against him. He said at first that he would not answer because he had work of more importance to do; but, when the volume came into his hands, he changed his mind, led by the feeling that the uneducated people would misinterpret his silence and that Dolet would boast that he could attack him with impunity! Therefore he published at Rome his *Adversus*

Stephani Doleti Calumnias Liber. It is a small volume of forty pages consisting ·largely of taunting ridicule as may be seen by the brief here given:

" Dolet had seemed stupid enough in the Ciceronian Dialogue but more stupid still in this answer. How unbearable was his boasting! He considered his opinions on imitation valuable and interesting if read ten times over, so he had simply repeated here what he had written against Erasmus in the Dialogue. He had taken up the fight in defence of imitation as if there was any argument about the value of imitation *per se.* The anti-Ciceronians did not object to imitation, but to the exclusive use of Cicero as a model. He had declared that he would not waste his time reading the works of Florido. He had no doubt taken refuge under this subterfuge to avoid defending mistakes in his Commentaries that had been pointed out there. Boasting would be excusable in Cicero or Pontano or Accius Syncerus or Erasmus because they would have reason, but not in Dolet. Let it be observed that in an age full of most excellent critics not one had praised Dolet and that the most generous patron of letters, the King of France, had not recognized his ability by granting a stipend. He praised himself because no one else would. His verse was so fine that Greece and all her poets might well hang themselves; for Dolet alone had excelled Homer, Menander, Sophocles, Pindar, and Callimachus. ' O Great Dolet! What would have happened to Latin letters if you had not been born? Surely they would have completely perished if they had not found you, so great an advocate!' His Commentaries on the Latin language were worthless and would never have been sold at all had it not been that they had been issued from the most excellent press of Gryphius."

Dolet's criticisms of the style and purity of Florido's Latin was one of the strongest motives for retaliation. Dolet had said that Florido was neither forceful nor clear, that his style was rambling, without order, halting, and loose; that he had used the words *singularissimus* and *obsequelam* and he did not know how many more such barbarisms. Florido declared in answer that he had always been most careful about any words that were not in common use. He said that *singularissimus* was a mistake but that it was the fault of the printer; that he had never intended to use a word which any school boy would know was wrong; that the other word was acceptable according to Terence and therefore not objectionable Latin. He ridiculed the fact that Dolet had not read his writings, asking him how he knew enough about the *Subcisivae Lectiones* to accuse him of stealing the three books on C. J. Caesar from Battista Pio if he had not read them. Then he must have read the " Apology against the Calumniators of the Latin Language," for the two words pointed out were in that and not in the *Subcisivae Lectiones*.

CHAPTER VI

OTHER PHASES OF THE CONTROVERSY UP TO 1600

While the *Orationes* of J. C. Scaliger and the *Dialogus de Ciceroniana imitatione* of Etienne Dolet were long and violent answers to the *Ciceronianus* of Erasmus, their publication did not close the controversy.

Guilio Camillo, the celebrated Italian Ciceronian who was in France working upon his great amphitheater of knowledge under the patronage of the king, wrote a *Trattato della imitatione* which was addressed to Erasmus, though it contains little serious argument. In it he suggests that Erasmus must have written in jest for he could never have seriously condemned Cicero, the most perfect model of eloquence of an age when the Latin language was in its flower of perfection. Most of the thirty-five pages is taken up with fantastical dreams about his theater and elaborate similes. The closing words would indicate that he considered he had been personally attacked by Erasmus.

Pontanus is said to have replied to the *Ciceronianus,* and Julius Pflug in writing to friends took issue in some slight measure;[1] but the direct answers to Erasmus practically ceased with his death.

Cicero relegatus et Cicero revocatus, which Erasmus mentions in one of his letters[2] as containing " a harsh attack upon Cicero and an indifferent defence," was not a direct answer but was no doubt instigated by the *Ciceronianus.* Ortensio Landi, the author, was an Italian exile in France on intimate terms with Dolet at the time the book was published (1534).[3] Odonus in his letter to Gilbert Cousin describes Landi as a " precious Ciceronian who brought with him into France as a consolation in the wretchedness of his journey neither the Old nor New Testament, but only the Familiar Epistles of Cicero."[4] The *Cicero relegatus*

---

[1] Walch, 728.
[2] Supra, p. 31.
[3] Christie, 183, 217.
[4] Supra, p. 86.

et Cicero revocatus consists of two very interesting dialogues
setting forth the arguments *pro* and *con* in the question with the
purpose of exalting Cicero: A band of friends meet at the home
of Philoponus to cheer him in his hours of ill health. Their
conversation turns upon Cicero and soon they find themselves
in a heated debate. Cicero's faults are set forth and fully discussed with the final result that by unanimous vote he is to be
banished on the charge of being barren, dry, bloodless, colorless,
and weak. When the question arises as to where he shall be sent,
one by one the various countries are rejected. They will not
send him to England because Reginald Pole is there; nor to
France because Ciceronians are there and the French are too
humani; nor to Germany because there too are many Ciceronians; and Spain is too busy with foreign affairs. The decree
is at length drawn up, banishing him to Scythia and providing
a like treatment for any one who ever thinks of reversing his
decision. *Cicero revocatus* describes the situation when the decree is announced at Rome. Immediately there is great wailing
and lamentation. The equestrian order, the citizens, and the
pedagogues protest, and the women pray. Supplications are
ordered. A senate is convened to decide whether for just and
legitimate reasons Cicero has been banished. The accusations
are brought forward and answered most enthusiastically and eloquently. A long list of Ciceronians who have written most perfectly, headed by Sadoleto and Bembo, are cited as evidence of
Cicero's value. Guilio Camillo is given as an example of a Ciceronian who has quickly risen to prominence and Philip Melancthon
as one who can speak *ex tempore* with great success. When the
vote is taken at the close of the discussion, it is decided that
Cicero shall be recalled. Six splendid young men are chosen
to invite him to return in the name of the senate; and six others
meet him at the gates, loose the horses, and draw him into the
city in triumph. Led to the senate he delivers a most charming
oration.

On the side of the anti-Ciceronians, a disciple of Erasmus, a
prominent leader, and a valiant fighter stood out in the person
of Peter Ramus. He was a Protestant in the world of letters.
He protested against scholastic methods when a student and defended as a master's thesis the proposition that everything which
Aristotle taught was false. As professor in the Colleges of the

University of Paris he inaugurated an independent method which
brought upon him no end of censure—a method which embodied
humanistic pragmatism, relating philosophy to eloquence as an
art to a science. In 1546 he pronounced a public discourse on
the union of philosophy and eloquence.[5] From the material of
lectures delivered later he published the *Brutinae Quaestiones in
Oratorem Ciceronis* (1547) and the *Rhetoricae distinctiones in
Quintilianum* (1549), in the first of which Cicero was criticised
and in the second, Quintilian. His criticisms and his method
caused the greatest turmoil in the University of Paris. Cicero
was defended in *Pro Ciceronis Oratore contra Petrum Ramum
Oratio* by Jacques Perion, where " all rhetors and orators who
cherish Cicero as the father of eloquence are implored to resist
Ramus who denies him art and judgment."[6] Quintilian found
an advocate in Pierre Galland,[7] once rector of the University and
principal of the Collége de Boncour, whom Ramus calls the
" evil genius of the Academy of Paris." Waddington says that
the debate between these two champions divided the university,
engaged the parliament and amused the public.[8] The views of
Ramus on Ciceronian imitation were given in a series of lectures
correlated with the reading of *Brutus* while he was regius professor in the College of France. He delivered these lectures
to show practical reforms and made the text of this discourse on
practique the much mooted question of what constitutes a Ciceronian. The lectures were collected and published (1557) under
the title, *Ciceronianus*. The brief analysis which I append will
show the general aim and tenor of the lectures:

Analysis of Peter Ramus's Ciceronianus

" My aim is to show who may justly be called a Ciceronian.
To do this I shall trace the history of rhetoric from the Greeks
up through the time of Cicero, outlining the various theories and
schools. My first thesis is that a Ciceronian must take Cicero
not only as a basis for Latinity but for virtue and praise, not
only must he consider the effects but the causes, not only Cicero's
Latinity but his *prudentia* in handling themes and in private life,
not only his letters and orations but his methods and processes.

---

[5] Oratio de studiis philosophiae et eloquentiae conjungendis.
[6] p. 4.
[7] Edition of Quintilian, Paris, 1549, in fol.
[8] Waddington, 90.

I accept the definition that an orator must be *vir bonus bene dicendi peritus.* (1-11.) The early period of youth is very important. Latin and Greek first. Cicero had Greek first. Schools of French vernacular must be incorporated with the Greek and Latin. This will be surprising to some but Cicero had Greek masters for Greek and Latin masters for Latin. Why not then French teachers for French, if we are to follow Cicero, or how pray will the likeness of our imitation otherwise be perfect? Our Ciceronian will exercise in *grammatica* and will imitate the best authors in each language. This differs much from the Ciceronians. They think Cicero must be imitated wholly and exclusively. (17-18.) He who confines himself to words found in the editions of Cicero's works extant to-day is not Ciceronian. I call that Ciceronian which is consistent with good usage, for Cicero followed this rule. Let us define a Ciceronian as Cicero defined an Attic,—one who speaks well. We are not justified in using all Cicero's words for he found mistakes in his own writings. We are justified in using words which he did not use, for he coined new ones. Innumerable words peculiar to the arts Cicero would have used if he had had occasion; therefore such words found in Plautus, Cato, Varro, and Columella are Ciceronian. (20-21.) The Roman critics made the same objections against Cicero that the Ciceronians make against us. As Cicero justified himself in using new words we may justify ourselves. This will provide for the words of the Christian religion. (22-27.) Some things that are in Cicero are not Ciceronian, for instance, long and involved sentences. (31.) It is Ciceronian to imitate all the best authors, to gather *copia* and *bonitas* from all. The Greeks and Latins were similar because they followed the same model not in individual words nor in phrasing but in style of *elocutio* and *actio,* in cleverness of *inventio,* and care and accuracy of judgment. Cicero advocated wide reading but condemned verbal imitation. Therefore to take all from the best is certainly Ciceronian. (35.) Let the Ciceronians prove their tenets from the precepts of Cicero. He thought all good authors should be imitated, they only one. He rejected the imitation of words, they retain this only. (43.) We must do as Cicero did if we are Ciceronians. He put speaking before writing; he preferred public education and attended the public schools and law courts; he emphasized *virtus* and *auctoritas* more than *oratio.* Virtue plays an important part in his definition of an orator. (54-57.) Our rhetoric covers Cicero's *elocutio* and *actio,* our logic his *inventio* and *dispositio,* hence the necessity of the union of the two. Beginning with grammatical studies after the example of Cicero, our Ciceronian learns to speak and write acceptably, gains some skill in oratorical and logical thinking, then goes to the forum and temple to listen to orators in order to form his style from example rather than rule. They will say there is no forum, but ample opportunity for this is afforded in France to-day. (59-63.) After logic and rhetoric come philosophy and jurisprudence. If our Ciceronian imitates Cicero, he will take this order, for such Cicero followed in his own education (64-69) ; and such we have in the University of Paris to-day. (80-84.) The *ornate dicere* of Cicero is very Ciceronian; but his exercise in poetry, his inane repetitions and digressions are not Ciceronian. We will follow the one but not the other. (95-100.) The orator who pleases the masses will please scholars, which can be proved by quotation from Cicero. (113-120.) We accept the force of Caesar, the austerity of Caelius, the accuracy of Pollio, the discrimination of Calvus, which we may acquire by studying their works. (126.) By the example of Cicero we recognize travel as a valuable aid to education. (128.) In his imitation of Cicero, our candidate must seek a reputation for integrity, must show political and religious virtue, must manifest strength in adversity, and must be a lover of books and study ; so that to be a Ciceronian is something very different from what is commonly supposed and is nothing else than eternal vigilance and care in the government of the republic and in the intelligent use of leisure. (143-183.) Of Cicero's ideal orator, the chief glory was temperance, constancy, equity, patriotism. He who imitates these may be called Ciceronian. (200-209.) Therefore, my hearers, if you wish to imitate the eloquence of Cicero, recall the various reasons, from this whole biography, for his great virtue,—the studies of his childhood, boyhood, manhood, maturity and old age,—and you will find no portion of his life free from the labor and vigils of eloquence. As a boy he first learned Greek and then Latin grammar in which he surpassed all the other boys in his earnest application to speaking and writing well. As a youth he listened to all rhetors, philosophers, orators, lawyers, of every kind and place, ambitious to vie with the best in the fame of speaking well. And what a victory at length he won by forensic activity and by a long line of public offices, through great struggles of mind and genius, through sweating and danger! How many illustrious works did the wonderful keenness of mind and the vigor of his declining years compose! Native ability furnished Cicero the power to attain to the highest point in eloquence, and art assisted nature; but his remarkable industry in study and exercise contributed far more to his success than either. Therefore, he who would be a Ciceronian in truth and not in name merely may hope for talent and training, as good or better than this, but must especially cultivate as a companion and ally throughout his life that remarkable industry." (253-254.)

In perfect sympathy with Erasmus and Peter Ramus were their friends, Johann Sturm, Joachim Camerarius and Philip Melancthon; yet their writings and teachings show a disposition to imitate the letter of Cicero more minutely. It will be noticed that while Melancthon was highly incensed at Dolet's attack upon Erasmus, he was listed by Landi as a Ciceronian.[9] Camerarius in his edition of the Tusculan Disputations makes the following statement, " To one fixed example and one form let the mind and eye be directed and this example and form I should wish to be the books of Cicero. I consider these ancient classics the best, and any departure from them I count disgraceful, or turning to others worthy of censure."[10] Sturm expressed his opinion in a lengthy treatise, *De imitatione oratoria libri tres* (c. 1568), which is in no sense controversial but merely a treatise on rhetoric under the name of imitation, following very closely the doctrines of Cicero and Quintilian.

Controversies of another type grew out of the publication of lexicons, phrase-books and commentaries on Cicero. The center and material for these discussions were the Observations of Mario Nizzoli, the Commentaries of Etienne Dolet, and the Thesaurus of Robert Estienne. Nizzoli's Observations was an alphabetical arrangement of Ciceronian words and phrases bearing the title, *In M. T. Ciceronem observationes linguae Latinae*, published first in folio at Brescia, 1535. It was edited and en-

---

[9] Supra, p. 99.
[10] Walch, 748.

larged by Basilius Zanchus (Rome, 1541?), by Caelius Secundus
Curio (Basil. 1548), by Marcellus Squarcialupus (Basil. 1576)
and Christopher Cellarius (Basil. 1583) under the title of *Thesaurus Ciceronianus;* by Alex. Scot (Basil. 1588) with the title of
Apparatus Latine locutionis; by Barezzi (Venice, 1606)[11] and
Giacomo Faccialoti (Padua, 1734) under the title of *Lexicon
Ciceronianum.* There were also abridged editions by Aldus Manutius (Francof. 1590)[12] and by Antonius Schorus (Coloniae 1578),
the latter of which was published in 1580 with a preface by
Sturm.   The *Thesaurus linguae Latinae* of Robert Estienne was
an alphabetical arrangement of words based on the lexicon of
Ambrosio Calepino[13] (1502) which was in turn a transcript of the
Cornu Copiae of Perotti (1469).[14]   There were two editions
modified and enlarged by the author himself: the first (1531)
being barely more than a reprint of Calepino; the second (Paris
1536) in two volumes, folio, with the explanatory title, *Dictionarium, seu Latinae linguae Thesaurus, non singulas modo dic-
tiones continens, sed integros quoque Latine et loquendi et scribendi formulas, ex Catone, Cicerone, Plinio, Avunculo, Terentio,
Varrone, Livio, Plinio Secundo, Virgilio, Caesare, Columella,
Plauto, Martiale: cum Latina tum Grammaticorum, tum varii
generis scriptorum, interpretatione.*   Later and enlarged editions
were published by his son, Henri Estienne, in 1543 and 1573.
The Commentaries of Dolet were published in two folio volumes
at Lyons, the first appearing in 1536 and the second in 1538.
They differed from the lexicons of Nizzoli and Estienne in that
the words were not arranged alphabetically but in groups according to related subjects.   Dolet explains in his preface, " When
I have shown both in my own language and by examples drawn
from Cicero the primary and secondary meanings of the word
in question, I then subjoin other words of cognate meaning, and
so continue in a connected series as long as it seems possible
to do so."

Nizzoli and Dolet stood for the strictest kind of verbal imitation of Cicero and arranged their dictionaries for the use of the
youth who aspired to attain the perfect style.   In his preface to
the Commentaries Dolet says that he hopes, by the happy abun-

[11] Christie, 260.
[12] Walch, 380.
[13] Ibid, 337.
[14] Ibid, 339.

dance of Ciceronian examples, to allure youth to the reading of Cicero; and his active, aggressive support of the sect of Ciceronians we have already seen manifested in the answers to Erasmus and Florido.[15] The complete title of Robert Estienne's *Thesaurus,* on the other hand, would indicate that he was an eclectic and recommended words from any classical author.

Erasmus ridicules these lexicographers when he has Nosoponus relate that he has arranged all the words of Cicero in an alphabetical lexicon of three volumes. In the first are all the words, in the second all the phrases, and in the third all the meters and periods.[16] If it were not that the *Ciceronianus* was published in 1528, eight years before the three volume edition of Robert Estienne and the Commentaries of Dolet, one would think he was characterizing these. He may have heard of their preparation or he may have referred to the Observations of Nizzoli, though that was in two folio volumes.

The real fight on the lexicon begins (1541) when Florido taunts Dolet by declaring that he has dared to publish his silly Commentaries and to call all authors except Cicero off-scourings. When Dolet says that he has not read all of Florido's writings, Florido retaliates by telling him that he makes this statement in order to be relieved of the responsibility of answering the charges made there against the mistakes in his Commentaries, and that the Commentaries are worthless and would not have been sold at all if they had not been issued from the press of Gryphius.[17]

Henri Estienne wrote a most scathing criticism of the inaccuracies of Nizzoli's book in his *Pseudo-Cicero* (1577) and his *Nizoliodidascalus* (1578). In the first, a book of 228 pages, he represents some young men in the library discussing the authenticity of certain words. Through this kind of dialogue he shows that a true Ciceronian cannot depend upon lexicons but must go to Cicero himself and imbibe the spirit of the master. Much fun is made of Nizzoli when some one suggests that reference should be made to his lexicon as an authority in settling the dispute. The second has the same form and setting. One of the young men is looking for a book and is asked what it is. He answers, " The Observations of Nizzoli, which every one should

---

[15] Supra, pp. 63-97.
[16] Ciceronianus, infra ii, 24.
[17] Supra, p. 96.

study who wishes to become a Ciceronian." Objection is made
to the name, Observations, on the ground that it is a misnomer
since he does not annotate or explain. Further objection is made
that the book contains words which are far from being Latin
to say nothing of being Ciceronian. Examples are cited where
Nizzoli, the leader of the Ciceronians, has made mistakes by
mixing up passages of Cicero which show the use of the same
word but in different meanings, and by placing for synonyms
words which are far from being so, and by making explanations
which are plainly false, hardly Latin and not at all Ciceronian
and thus clearly distorting Cicero.

About the same time M. Antoine Muret (Muretus)[18] uttered
protests against the Ciceronians and Nizzolians. In an oration
delivered at Rome (1572) he says: " Do not think I accept the
word eloquence as it is commonly accepted. For to-day whenever
any one has learned the rules of the rhetors and can write a letter
or oration by the aid of Nizzoli's book he straightway assumes
the name of an eloquent speaker."[19] In the *Variae Lectiones*
xv, c.1 (1580), he repeats the same criticisms with more
elaborate illustration, the whole of which I shall translate because of its bearing upon the general movement as well as upon
this particular folly:

Muretus's Criticism of the Ciceronians

" *Conversation with Darius Bernardus on the folly of some
who call themselves Ciceronians:* Some young German nobles
had come to the Quirinal to see and greet me, who had traveled
over almost all Italy and had practically passed no one by who
had any reputation for learning without seeing and talking to
him, and they said they had desired to see me also for the same
reason and to talk to me. We spent an hour or two in conversation, they asking me about my studies and I in turn asking them
about the state of Germany and such learned men as were said
to flourish there at present, their age, personal habits, fortune and
condition in life, and especially about those who were constantly
trying to preserve the ancestral religion, and not to allow themselves to be carried away by the tide of pernicious doctrine.
With embraces and words of good cheer I dismissed them.

---

[18] Muretus was an ultra-Ciceronian himself previous to 1550.
[19] Oratio xxi, Opera prima, 169.

Darius Bernardus had been present during this visit and when the others were gone he said, ' It is certainly true that at the present time in no one except the transalpines can there be found a ready and free power of speaking Latin. They who have just left never seem at a loss in speaking, never hesitate, have all things in order and their speech runs on with no hindrance; while our men, even those who have become thin, pale, and peevish from over-study, if ever there is an occasion for speaking Latin, struggle and perspire and gasp. You would think that they were drawing big words from the depths of their lungs; while in the case of these men there seems to flow a kind of perennial stream of suitable Latin words, with no care or effort, from their lips.'

' It is indeed as you say, Darius,' I answer, ' but yet Italy has illustrious men who write most elegantly and speak most cleverly and fluently when there is need.'

' Manutius,' he says, ' perchance you mean, and Sigonius and Petrus Joannes Maffeius or that man of the same company at the news of whose death you recently were so greatly grieved I remember, Perpinianus.'

' Yes, those and others, although the one whom you mentioned last was a Spaniard, not an Italian, but he had so long lived in Italy that he might be considered an Italian. I wish that you could have heard him when he was teaching eloquence in this city, you would have accepted no other teacher. For never have you heard nor will you ever hear any one to whom in my judgment that passage of Nestor, *cuius ex ore melle dulcior fluebat oratio,* would fit more perfectly. But what was it, two or three times during the conversation, that you seemed to disapprove of ? '

' I ? ' he says, ' I was troubled that the older man sometimes used words that were not good Latin and by this the splendor of his conversation was dulled.'

' What words ? ' I asked, ' for thinking of other things I did not notice this.'

' Many times he said *caelos* and *caelorum orbes* and *eam doctrinam quae caelitus ad homines lapsa esset.*'

' What? Do you not think that these are correct ? '

' *Caelestia corpora* and *caelestes orbes* and *caelo lapsam doctrinam* I should have preferred.'

' You are not wrong indeed, but yet these words have authority. Servius cites from Cicero's Hortensius *Epicurei plures volunt caelos.* And these words are found in the second book of Lucretius, "Who can rule the universe? who can hold in his hand the strong reins of the deep and guide? who can turn his attention equally upon all the *caelos?*" Although the word *caelos* means worlds which they think to be innumerable, yet it is evident from this that the noun *caeli* among the Latins is both singular and plural. Now I remember that I was once before criticised about that word *caelitus* by some one who thought that no Latin word ought to be used which was not in Cicero. And so he laughed at me, not only when I cited Servius who explains *Si te digna manet divini gloria ruris* as meaning *if it is granted you from heaven (caelitus) to enjoy the glory of the country,* but also when I cited Lactantius, a much better imitator of Cicero, in whose fifth book of Institutions we find *There can be no doubt this teacher who is sent from heaven (caelitus) is perfect in knowledge as well as virtue.'*

' What do you mean? Do you think those men good enough authorities on Latinity?'

' I will tell you, Darius. For a long time I labored under the mistake that only those who were either contemporary or at least who lived but a little while before Cicero were worthy of being examples for one who wished to speak or write Latin. But later, after considering the whole question more carefully, it seemed to me that I was assuming too much to dare to pronounce about Seneca, Livy, Valerius, Celsus, Quintilian, Columella, both Plinies, Tacitus, Seutonius, Velleius, Q. Curtius, Lactantius, and other writers of this kind who, each in his own age, was considered most learned. No one of the old writers ever accused them of using bad Latin and we, after so long an interval, are certainly not good judges. Yes, many little words and many turns of speech are found in their books which are not in Cicero and his contemporaries. But when we have scarcely one-tenth of Cicero's writings, and what we have are mutilated and changed, hardly one-hundredth part of Sallust's, about the same of Varro's, and only one little selection (*De re rustica*) out of so many volumes of Cato; and when writings of so many philosophers, ancient orators, poets, historians, councillors have been lost, it is presumptuous for us, from these fragments which have come down to us of the Roman speech, to declare that what is not found in them was not in good usage among the ancients. How much more likely that, if the books were extant, many words which seem new and strange to us would be shòwn to be of frequent and good usage! But we dare to criticise them for using bad Latin though they had libraries full of every kind of books and most diligently studied them and were men of keenest discernment. Often we see it happen that many words which are for a long time censured as newly coined are afterwards discovered to have been used from remotest times by the best authors. What about the fact that there are many things in those very remnants of Cicero which are read only once? Therefore if a rat or a moth had eaten a bit of the page or mold and decay had ruined it or a spark from the lamp had fallen on some certain part of the book, to-day the words *pigrandi* and *contraversandi* and many others would be barbarisms. And that you may better understand that all this is based on a false standard, consider that many of these foolishly fastidious people find no meaning in anything not found in Cicero, and many of them when they go into public places stop their ears for fear of being offended by words that are not Ciceronian. These I have often tormented with great delight: I noticed that certain words used by Cicero were not included in the index of Nizzoli, which is the authority used by these people; so I took pains to sprinkle them in my speech when certain friends of mine afflicted with this disease came to listen to me. They, when they heard any one of these words, twisted their necks, shrugged their shoulders, wrinkled their brows, whispered to one another that such words racked their brains and pierced their ears. Nay even when the meeting was dismissed and they accompanied me home as was their custom, they complained that they had been treated badly. After fooling with them for some time, I made a bargain with them that if those very words were not in Cicero they might justly complain. What do you think? When I had convinced them this was true, the very words at once lost all harshness and were soft and sweet and pleasing to hear. Do you remember when the word *illustrissimus* was considered foreign? . . . and indeed no one was accustomed to use that word with greater sport than the man who they said was a Cicero himself. . . . When that man came to me when I was interpreting the books

of Aristotle and heard me say that there were innumerable things
in all parts of philosophy that could not be put in the strictest
Latin, he told me that he wondered that I should think that could
not be done which Perion had done so well.'

' You must mean the man who wrote *singulis quinque annis*
when he wished to say that a thing ought to be done every fifth
year.

' The very one,' I answer, ' and you see the eloquence of a
Cicero. But let me come back. Even if we grant that many
words have been coined since Cicero's time, why ought we reject
them? Why that phrase of Horace *ut folia in silva?* And this,
*It has been and always will be allowable to use a word bearing
the mark of present usage.* Did not Cicero coin many words
himself and did he not urge Cato and Varro and Brutus and
others to do the same? Or, perchance, that was a special privilege which belonged only to Cicero and his time and has been
denied to men since? Cicero coined *incomprehensibile.* Why
could not those who came after him coin other words in the same
fashion? Indeed, I think, if Cicero could have prolonged his life
to the time of Quintilian, the Plinies, and Tacitus, and had seen
the Roman tongue enriched by their work, he would have been
grateful to them and would have used those words gladly. To
listen to the madness of these people is interesting. They turn
away from Tacitus and Seutonius; they use words which those
writers would not with patience have heard in their kitchens. If
I am not mistaken, I can show you in the writings of some of
them who profess to be the leaders of this sect *speculationem, in-
gratitudinem, contrarietatem,* and very many others of this same
order. . .   This laborious and exquisite care has degenerated into stupidity; for what is more easy in practice than to turn
to Nizzoli for each individual word when you have begun to
write?'

' What do you say? Will you borrow from all the ancient
writers indiscriminately?'

' No, I will use judgment and will choose as far as possible
from Cicero, Caesar, Terence and others who were the best.
When I shall have formed my speech as far as possible after
their example, I shall take from others also the most beautiful,
and try to imitate each in what he especially has excelled. And I
should add to those whom I mentioned a little while ago Tertul-

lian, Arnobius, St. Jerome, St. Augustine, St. Ambrose, and what you will wonder at more, Apuleius, Cassiodorus, Martianus, and also Sidonius Apollinaris. I advise you, Darius, to do the same, and not to imitate the folly of those who are students of antiquity to the extent that even they reject words peculiar to the Christian religion and substitute for them others verging upon the sacrilegious; who say not *fidem* but *persuasionem*, not *sacramentum corporis Dominici* but *santificum crustulum*, not *excommunicare* but *diris devovere*, not *Angelos* but *genios*, not *baptizare* but *abluere;* who, I think if they were not afraid, even would say *Jovem optimum maximum* instead of Christ, for this is more Ciceronian. What insanity it is, when we read *porricere, impetrire, tripudium solistimum, pateras,* and *sympuvia,* to mark them as spoken wisely because they have been borrowed from the books of augury, while the words peculiar to the Christian religion and the ritual are condemned as not classic enough?'

Though I was prepared to continue the conversation, some friends entering interrupted."

Barring a few individual dissertations against Cicero and the Ciceronians scattered here and there along into the eighteenth century such as those of Schoppe, Taubmann, and Dornmeier, controversial writing on the question ceased with the contribution of Muretus; and fitting it is that the first and last word should come from Rome.

CHAPTER VII

THE INFLUENCE OF CICERONIANISM UPON EDUCATIONAL PRACTICE

At all times since the days of the Roman Republic, Cicero's works have had direct connection with the subject-matter and method of the schools. When Quintilian exalted him it was as a model of the perfect orator which embodied the highest aim of Roman education. During the Middle Ages he represented the liberal art of rhetoric. At the dawn of the Revival of Learning his writings were most eagerly sought and accepted as the model for all Latin composition whether in or out of school.

The names of the scholars and literary men discussed in the previous pages in connection with the history of Ciceronianism have been almost without exception great teachers as well as ardent cultivators of Ciceronian style. The chair of rhetoric in the universities of Italy during the Renaissance was especially sought by Ciceronians,—in the early days by the really humanistic Ciceronian and later by the sect of servile imitators.

Among the former may be mentioned a group of illustrious teachers,—Gasparino da Barzizza, Vittorino da Feltre, and Guarino da Verona.

Barzizza was a professor of eloquence at the Universities of Padua and Milan and devoted himself to the interpretation of Cicero with especial emphasis upon the *de Oratore* and Letters. His interpretation of imitation was that the spirit of the model should be copied, that grace and elegance should be attained with no emphasis upon the literal phraseology. For the purpose of aiding in the accomplishment of this end he arranged a series of exercises to be used as models by his students, called *Epistolae ad exercitationem accommodatae,* in which Sabbadini has estimated that he proved himself " a true disciple of Ciceronianism."[1] This book was used as a text in all the schools of Italy

---

[1] Storia del Ciceronianismo, 13-17.

and was the first book printed in France (1470).[2] Two other
text-books may be attributed to him, one on orthography and
one on grammar. Barzizza is not always ranked among the
great teachers of the Renaissance, but when we hear Guarino's
testimony that it was through him that Cicero was loved and
studied in all the schools of Italy,[3] and when we recognize that he
was the teacher of two other great Ciceronian teachers,—Vittorino and Guarino,—we realize that his influence was great. The
restoration of the complete manuscript of Quintilian's *Institutio
Oratoria* (1417) about the same time as the discovery of the
entire text of *de Oratore* (1422) accentuated the interest in
Cicero as a model. Barzizza devoted himself to the exposition
and emendation of both, and his disciples went forth from Padua
to incorporate their theories in the curricula and methods of
humanistic schools.

Vittorino established the famous school at Mantua (1423)
which is usually taken as an excellent type of the humanistic
schools of Italy. We have considerable information about its
organization. Woodward says that in it may be found an exposition of the precepts of Quintilian adapted to modern Italian
life.[4] We know that the basis of the curriculum was the Latin
and Greek classics, that the study of Cicero was much emphasized
and that he was used as the model for composition. Vittorino
lectured on the *de Oratore,* being excelled in his devotion and
adequate interpretation only by Barzizza, the greatest Ciceronian of all.[5] Professor Woodward believes that this school
with its spirit, curriculum and method is a landmark of critical
importance in the history of classical education.[6] While we may
not attribute this to the influence of Cicero alone, we can justly
claim that it is the spirit of the " rational Ciceronian "[7] of the
period and his attitude toward the classical heritage that furnished the conception of the type of school. The rational Ciceronian is to be distinguished from the servile imitator of a later
period by his aim to study the classics for content as well as for
style. Though Vittorino was the author of no text-books, there
issued from the school through his pupils two grammars of wide

[2] Sandys, Harvard Lectures, 153.
[3] Sabbadini, 13.
[4] Education during the Renaissance, 9
[5] Vittorino da Feltre, 13,
[6] Ibid, 24.
[7] Woodward, Education during the Renaissance, 24.

reputation: a small one, based on Vittorino's methods of teaching, compiled by Ognibene da Lonigo (1451); the other a larger
volume by Perotti (1468) which is called the first modern Latin
grammar.   There was also published by Giorgio da Trebisonda,
one of the teachers at the Mantuan school, " a recognized treatise
on rhetorical style."[8]

Guarino, though more learned in Greek than in Latin, was a
celebrated teacher.   He lectured at Florence, Venice, and Verona.
His longest period of service, however, was at Ferrara where he
was the first tutor of Lionello, the eldest son of Niccolò d'Este,
and afterward professor of rhetoric in the University.   The curriculum and method at Ferrara show a parallel to Vittorino's
school at Mantua.   They are described by Guarino's son, Battista, in *De ordine docendi et studendi* (1459), from which the
following extracts will show the influence of Cicero:

" Were we to follow Quintilian we should begin with Greek
first.   But this is impracticable since Greek is a dead language.
.   .   .   The epistles of Cicero will be taken in hand for the
purpose of declamation.   Committed to memory they serve as
one of the finest possible aids to purity, directness and facility
of style; yet I would not be understood to claim that the Letters
of Cicero alone offer a sufficient training in style.   For distinction of style is the fruit of a far wider field of study.   .   .   .
The first work to claim our attention in the more advanced grade
of the school is the Rhetoric of Cicero in which we find all the
points of oratory concisely but comprehensively set forth.   The
other rhetorical writings of Cicero will follow and the principles
therein laid down must be examined in the light of his own
speeches.   Indeed the student of eloquence must have Cicero
constantly in his hand.   Nor should the admirable Quintilian
be neglected in this same connection."[9]

An examination of the few other educational tracts of the
period will discover the same spirit of interest in Cicero as the
supreme stylist in composition and at the same time a generous
appreciation of all the great writers, even accepting their own
contemporaries.

Aeneas Sylvius in his *De liberorum educatione* (1450), written in the form of a letter to Ladislas, the young King of Bo-

---

[8] Woodward, Vittorino da Feltre, 56.
[9] Translation in Woodward's Vittorino da Feltre, 161 ff.

hemia, says: " In making our selection of individual authors, we must consider not poets only, but historians, philosophers, and orators. . . . As regards poets, amongst the Latins the foremost place belongs of perpetual right to Virgil. . . . Of orators with Cicero at their head, there is no small choice. Frank and straightforward in style he is always intelligible. To read his *de Officiis* is not merely a useful exercise but an absolutely necessary one. St. Ambrose wrote in imitation of it a work which may wisely be read to supplement his model, and so make Cicero's teaching good on the Christian side. Lactantius, Augustine, and Jerome has each a polished style, and Gregory may be profitably used. Of our own contemporaries, Leonardo Aretino, Guarino, Poggio, and Ambrogio exhibit a chaste diction which is valuable for study. . . . In rhetoric you will do wisely to betake yourself exclusively to Cicero, Quintilian and Aristotle."[10]

Leonardo Bruni, in a similar way, wrote his *De studiis et literis* (1472) for the benefit of Baptista, daughter of the Count of Urbino. He tells her that the foundations of all true learning must be laid in the sound and thorough knowledge of Latin, that the Christian writers, first among whom is Lactantius, may be followed. " But," he says, " of the classical authors Cicero will be your constant pleasure. Next to him rank Virgil, Livy, and Sallust and then the chief poets follow in their order. The usage of these authors will serve as your test of correctness in choice of vocabulary and of constructions."[11]

Coming to the Ciceronians of the second half of the fifteenth century among whom there was no longer universal agreement in regard to the definition of Latin scholarship and correct style, we may consider the influence of Poggio and Valla, of Politian and Cortesi upon the schools.

Poggio, an advocate of the strict literal imitation of the phraseology of Cicero, was not a schoolmaster but he belonged to that class of most influential scholars called Latin secretaries, represented by Aeneas Sylvius, Vergerio, Salutati, Bruni, and Bembo, who are not described in histories as having any political or educational influence, and yet who must have been the greatest authorities on style; for they

---

[10] Translation in Vittorino da Feltre, 136 ff.
[11] Ibid, 123 ff.

were chosen to office because of their surpassing Latinity and
their duty was to write the orations and letters of popes and
princes in the most elegant and acceptable Latin.

Valla, as opposed to Poggio, was trained by Vittorino at Mantua[12] and afterwards taught at Naples and later still at Rome,
where in 1454, he established a school, much to the disgust of
George of Trebizond,[13] with the avowed purpose of exalting
Quintilian over Cicero. It was the criticism by a pupil of Valla's
school at Rome upon the much boasted Ciceronian Latinity of
Poggio that brought on the bitter controversy between these two
men.[14] Just how influential Valla's schools were at Naples and
Rome or what were their specific curricula and methods we do
not know; but his critical treatment of Latin authors embodied
in the *Elegantiae Latinae linguae,* written during these years, was
most influential then and continued its influence into modern
times. This book passed through fifty-nine editions between
1471 and 1536 definitely displacing the inaccurate and incomplete
grammars of the Mediaeval Latinist from the new schools.[15]
Hallam says that a great part of the distinctions in Latin syntax,
inflection, and synonymy which our best grammars contain may
be traced to Valla's " Elegances of the Latin Language."[16]

Cortesi had practically no influence upon school-room practice personally, though his letter to Politian was used and cited
for many years to justify the theories of imitation advanced by
teachers of the strict Ciceronian sect. The influence of his *De
hominibus doctis* is estimated by Hallam to have been very great
in the history of literary criticism.[17]

Politian, on the other hand, was one of the most successful
educators of Florence. He was tutor to Lorenzo's children and
delivered public lectures in the capacity of professor of Greek
and Latin. From the letters quoted already[18] it is evident that
he did not exert his influence for strict, literal imitation but urged
rather the cultivation of a free and independent style based on
a wide reading of classical authors. He may be credited with
shaping to some degree the humanistic ideals of education car-

[12] Vittorino da Feltre, 86.
[13] Nisard, i., 222.
[14] Supra, pp. 10–14.
[15] Woodward, Vittorino da Feltre, 87.
[16] i, 150.
[17] Supra, p. 17.
[18] Supra, p. 14–19.

ried north from Italy; for such men as Linacre, Grocyn, and Reuchlin listened to his lectures at Florence.

Reviewing the work of this group of controversialists,—Poggio, Valla, Politian, and Cortesi,—it would seem that the rational Ciceronian still had control of the schools of Italy at the close of the fifteenth century, but that his position was being attacked and his supremacy questioned. Loss of this control, a little later, is well illustrated in the case of Padua. The University there, which had been the home of Barzizza and of that Humanism which sought the spirit of Cicero and not the letter merely, became by 1520 the seat of the strictest sect of literal imitators. Bembo, whose influence, though not that of a school-master, was recognized as most powerful with many directly connected with the schools of Italy and France, settled at Padua about 1517 and was the inspiration and guide of the servile sect. Villeneuve and Longueil lectured with great success on the new eloquence while the university was thronged with students from the north.

The chair of eloquence in other universities of Italy was soon held by Ciceronians of like views and enthusiasm, for example: Ricci at Ferrara (1545), Nizzoli at Parma (1547), and Muretus at Venice (1555). Of these, Ricci contributed to educational literature two works of some importance. The first was an *Apparatus Latinae locutionis* (Coloniae 1535) which is often mentioned among Ciceronian lexicons of that period. The second, *De imitatione tres libri* (Venice 1545), represents one of the type of books on method which were so common about that time especially in France and Germany. No ultra Ciceronian of all Italy exerted a wider or more lasting influence than Nizzoli through his *In M. T. Ciceronem observationes* (Brescia, 1535). It was the parent of a long line of lexicons enlarged and abridged that appeared at frequent intervals even into the nineteenth century.[19]

Giacomo Sadoleto, one of the most eminent Italian Ciceronians, in his capacity of bishop of Carpentras is said to have appointed Jacques Bording, one of Dolet's friends,[20] principal of the College of Carpentras, and also to have given Florentius Volusenus a position because the latter had charmed him with his Ciceronian style.[21] A contribution by Sadoleto to educational theory can be found in his *De liberis recte instituendis* (1530),

---

[19] Supra, 104.
[20] Christie, 67.
[21] Sandys, Classical Scholarship, ii, 247.

in which he states that Latin is to be the instrument of education and classical purity the goal, while Cicero is to be the supreme model for composition.

Passing to the consideration of the influence of the movement upon the schools of France, Germany, and England, notice will be taken: first, of those men who engaged in the controversies; second, of the text-books and theoretical writings of men actively engaged in school work; and third, of representative types of school organization.

Of the controversialists, Erasmus easily stands at the head so far as widespread and general influence is concerned, yet we shall find by examination of the school organizations that his plea for a living language did not ultimately win. His experience as a teacher was not great though he held the Lady Margaret professorship at Cambridge and supported himself by teaching at Paris for a time. The comprehensive treatment of the contributions of Erasmus to education recently made by Professor Woodward[22] precludes the necessity of reciting them here. Whatever he wrote was instantly popular. His *Colloquia* and *De copia rerum et verborum* were widely used as text-books in the schools. To the teacher who used these books Erasmus did not stand as the advocate of careless and mediaeval Latin but of a living classical tongue.

Peter Ramus exerted a direct and powerful influence upon educational ideals and methods in France. During the period of his service as professor in the University of Paris he waged a definite war against all slavery to set forms. It was his persistent criticism and open defiance of the old conception of logic and of the Ciceronians' interpretation of eloquence that broke down the strongholds of scholastic methods of teaching and introduced humanistic ones. Those interpretations of Cicero and Quintilian and the views embodied in the *Ciceronianus,* which occasioned the quarrels with Perion and Galland, were lectures, delivered at the university before crowds of interested and eager students, showing that logic could not be divorced from eloquence nor eloquence from life. The influence of Ramus was even greater in Germany than in France.

The participants in the controversies who directly opposed Erasmus and Ramus were forced to play a more or less losing

---

[22] Desiderius Erasmus concerning the aim and method of education, Cambridge, 1904.

game, as it would appear in examining their immediate influence upon the schools. J. C. Scaliger addressed his First Oration against Erasmus to the Colleges of Paris and had the disappointment of learning that it was ignored by them. The influence of Dolet as teacher was but nominal; while the tide of reform introduced by Ramus into the University of Paris was not stemmed by Perion, *docteur de Sorbonne,* nor by Galland, principal of the Collége de Boncour. The more definite influence of J. C. Scaliger and Dolet came later when the *De causis Latinae linguae* (1540) of the former and the *Commentarii Latinae linguae* (1536-8) of the latter came into general circulation.

Touching upon the text-books of the Renaissance the influence of the Ciceronians was very great in the two texts with which they were concerned,—dictionaries and rhetorics. Indeed, their influence was practically supreme beyond the province of the colloquies in teaching oral composition where the eclectics of the type of Erasmus furnished the books. As I have already said[23] the Observations of Nizzoli formed the basis of one of the most popular and widely used lexicons in all the schools of France and Germany. The Thesaurus of Robert Estienne, though not so exclusively Ciceronian, was the resulting product of enlargements of Perotti and Calepino. The third and distinctively Ciceronian Observations of Dolet, abridged and honored with an introduction by Sturm, was used in the schools. In 1564 Chutraeus writing of the text-books to be used says: " The Thesauri of Estienne, Ricci, and Dolet are celebrated, and these with the phrase-books of Nizzoli and Cardinal Adrian can be used."[24] In this same connection he quotes Ricci and Sturm as preferring the Theater of Camillo but says that it had not been published so far as he knew.

Under the discussion of rhetorics may be included a vast number of pamphlets and treatises on imitation as well as books with definite titles of rhetoric. Practically the whole trend and teaching of these writings perpetuates the Ciceronian ideal that Cicero is the best and only ultimate model and that composition can be learned only through imitation. It is usual to find in them chapters devoted to the two questions: ' What authors must be

---

[23] Supra, p. 104.
[24] De ratione discendi, etc.

imitated?' and 'How must this be accomplished?' Most of the treatises on rhetoric follow slavishly the ideas of Cicero and Quintilian.   These statements can be verified by an examination of such books as: the *De scribendi rescribendique epistolas ratione opusculum* of Pilorcius Rocchius; the *De ratione discendi et ordine studiorum in singulis artibus recte instituendi* of David Chutraeus; the *De imitatione oratoria libri tres,* the *De literarum ludis recte aperiendis liber,* the *Nobilitas litterata* and the *Classicae Epistolae* of Johann Sturm; the *Oratoriarum institutionum libri sex* and the *De imitatione oratoria* of Jan. Voss; and the " Schoolmaster " of Roger Ascham.

In the actual working organization of the schools the extent of the influence of the Ciceronians would be measured by the comparative attention given to the writings of Cicero in the curricula and by the use of their theories in the methods of teaching composition.   In the typical grammar schools of the Renaissance there was some diversity of opinion as to the value of spoken Latin.   Fitch states that the essential difference between Erasmus and Ascham and Sturm was that the two latter did not strive to make Latin a living tongue.   All the schools, however, had for their definite aim the writing of Latin,—to follow as soon as possible the acquirement of the rudiments of grammar,—and the majority followed the method outlined in the books of Sturm. In order to show the comparative attention given to Cicero's writings in the curricula I am appending an outline of two typical Renaissance grammar schools, that of the Collége de Guyenne at Bordeaux and of the Latin School at Strasburg.   The former is taken from Vinet's *Disciplina et ratio docendi* and the latter from Sturm's *De literarum ludis recte aperiendis liber.*

COLLÉGE DE GUYENNE

The aim of the school is stated to be the mastery of the Latin language.   The outline of subject-matter runs as follows:

10th Class

Alphabetum, Pater Noster, Ave Maria.   Libellus Puerulorum: a summary of inflections of regular nouns and verbs.   Writing.

9th Class

Reading and writing of French and Latin.   Disticha de Moribus of Cato.   Exempla partium orationis of Cordier (1540).

8th Class

Selected Letters of Cicero. Selected scenes from Terence. Colloquia of Cordier.

7th Class

Selected Letters of Cicero. Latin composition based on Cicero. Latin Grammar of Despautère.

6th Class

Cicero's Letters. Despautère's Grammar. **Latin Composition.**

5th Class

Cicero's Letters. An entire play of Terence. The epistles of Ovid.

4th Class

Orations of Cicero. Barzizza's Manual. De Copia of Erasmus. Tristia of Ovid. Despautère's Grammar. **Composition—prose** and verse. Greek begun.

3d Class—13–14 years

Cicero's Letters. Cicero's Orations. Manual of Rhetoric. Despautère's Grammar. Play of Terence. Fasti or Metamorphoses of Ovid. Greek continued. **Latin composition.**

2nd Class

Cicero's Oratorical Treatises illustrated by his Orations. Ancient history. Virgil, Ovid, Lucan. **Latin composition, prose** and verse. Greek continued. Mathematics.

1st Class

Precepts of oratory after Cicero and Quintilian. **Orations of Cicero in illustration as a model.** History from Livy, Justin, Seneca, Eutropius, P. Mela, or other authors. Virgil, Lucan, Persius; Juvenal, Horace, Ovid. **Latin composition.** Greek continued. Mathematics.

In the preface of his *Disciplina et ratio dicendi* (1583), Vinet says that he is issuing this manual of the method, inaugurated by André de Gouvéa and long and successfully used at the Collége de Guyenne, in order that it may be perpetuated and may serve as a guide for the future use of the teachers. This fixes the date of the actual use of the appended program of studies from 1534 until 1583. During this period it is evident that no other author has anything like the same position in the curriculum as Cicero. An examination of the list of professors for the same period will discover the names of Robert Britannus, Junius Rabirius, and Antonius Muretus, all ardent Ciceronians. No mention is made of the use of the Ciceronian lexicons, phrase-books and rhetorics in this tract, but we see listed Barzizza's Manual, and the *de Oratore* of Cicero, while the inference may be reasonably drawn that Cicero's writings themselves were used as the source for vocabulary and phrasing. Colloquia occupy a comparatively small amount of attention, while composition is continuous and persistent after the third year. It no doubt was exercised in the second year, for the 8th class is said to have copied lines from an author, then to have memorized them, paraphrased them into Latin and translated them into French; while the teacher questioned on grammar and construction.

LATIN SCHOOL AT STRASBURG

The aim of this school was the attainment of wisdom, eloquence and piety, where wisdom proves to be the content of classical literature. The outline of studies was as follows:

9th form

Reading and writing. Catechism. Latin grammar. **Letters of Cicero.**

8th form

Latin grammar   Eclogues of Virgil. **Letters of Cicero.** Conversation in Latin. Religious instruction.

7th form

Latin grammar. **De Amicitia and De Senectute of Cicero.** Poetry through selections from Virgil, Catullus, Tibullus and Horace. **Latin composition in prose** and verse. Religious training.

6th form

De Oratore of Cicero. Poetry through Virgil, etc. Caesar's Commentaries. **Latin composition.** Religious instruction.

5th form

Greek begun. **De Officiis of Cicero.** Georgics of Virgil. **Pro lege Manila or Pro Ligario of Cicero. Latin prose composition and rhetoric based on De Oratore** and Hermogenes. Religious training.

4th form

Greek and Latin equal. **Cicero** and Demosthenes; Virgil and Homer   **Rhetoric based on Cicero.** History — Sallust and

Plautus. Commentary on authors studied. Religious teaching in Greek and Latin.

3rd form

Dialectic—Aristotle. **Rhetoric—Cicero** and Hermogenes. Greek Orations. Commentary studied. History—Sallust, Caesar, Livy. Religious teaching.

2nd form

Dialectic—practice not theory. Dialogues of Plato and **Cicero. De Oratore of Cicero.** Religious teaching—Hebrew.

1st form

Practice in apt speaking. Aristotle. Arithmetic. Astrology. Demosthenes and Homer. **Oratorical books of Cicero.** Commentary and theory of style. Religious teaching—Hebrew.

Music throughout, once a week.

The Latin school at Strasburg stands as an exemplification of the life work and theory of Johann Sturm, " the German Cicero." At its organization (1538) Sturm published his *De literarum ludis recte aperiendis* as an illustration of his ideal and the basis of work. The program of studies differs but little from that of the Collége of Guyenne and is certainly much influenced by the prevalent preference for Cicero. In discussing the position of Cicero, Sturm says, " Quod vero nomen inter Graecos philosophos Plato, id inter Latinos oratores Cicero est consecutus, sapientissimus philosophus, oratorum omnium clarissimum lumen, et unicum omnium literatorum exemplum."[25] Small place is given to conversation in Latin and no mention of colloquia is found in the outline; yet from the various books written by Sturm we know that text-books in the form of colloquia were used and that spoken Latin was encouraged to some degree. The prevailing method, however, was the making of note-books in which were copied Ciceronian words and phrases and quotations to be memorized and used as a source book in composition. The original texts must have been largely used though Ciceronian phrase books were coming rapidly into vogue at this time. The actual practice at Strasburg must have varied considerably from Sturm's ideal as presented in the *De literarum ludis,* for he published in 1565 a series of Letters to his teachers reiterating his outline of studies on the basis that his method had not been understood, and admitting that the declamations and especially

---

[25] De literarum ludis, 36.

the argumentations of the pupils revealed emptiness of ideas and incapacity of using the Latin language in a correct and elegant manner.[26]

The influence of Sturm's theories was widespread. Roger Ascham in his " Schoolmaster " shows that Sturm is his leader and guide in educational theory. Many schools in Germany were directly modelled after Strasburg, among which may be mentioned Lavingen, Memmingen, Nêmes, Thomas Platter's schools at Bâle and Würtemberg, as well as a number of those controlled by the Jesuits.[27] The schools fostered or organized under the patronage of Melancthon were of the same type, as is shown by his reports and text-books.

In England Dean Colet's school of St. Paul's modified the curriculum so that it should contain no pagan authors but used the Ciceronian Church Fathers' books instead. Brinsley's *Ludus literarius* (1612) gives a picture of English grammar schools with aim, method and curriculum in the main identical with those of Strasburg and Bordeaux.

As a final conclusion of the present study the following deductions are drawn. At the close of the sixteenth century the Renaissance spirit in general had furnished to the schools as the aim of education the mastery of the Greek and Latin languages, but the cult of ultra Ciceronians had wielded so great influence that that aim, so far as Latin was concerned, had degenerated into the purely imitative treatment of the authors studied, among whom Cicero was given by far the greatest prominence. The dialectic of the Middle Ages had been largely supplanted by rhetoric and some effort had been made to connect this study with life, but on the whole the reign of form had been transferred from logic to rhetoric and was fighting for prestige there under the banner of New Learning.

---

[26] Engel, 108.
[27] Ibid, 30.

Part II
Translations of Controversial Writings

A Pamphlet on Imitation

By Gianfrancesco Pico

Addressed to Pietro Bembo

Gianfrancesco Pico to Pietro Bembo, greeting:—I was in doubt, Bembo, whether I ought to agree or disagree with you not only in your imitation of ancient writers but also in your opinions on imitation, for I find that the ancients themselves who are proposed as worthy of imitation not only differ from one another in regard to this but also have changed their minds from time to time, and the arguments were so nearly equal on both sides that it was difficult to decide which had the advantage. Indeed, such was my state until I thought it over more carefully, and then I decided that there should be some imitation but not continual, and that all good writers should be imitated, not some one exclusively nor wholly but just as each one thinks safe. And so many things seem to support this judgment that I think it will be easy to oppose you. Therefore I shall try by what argument I can if not to get judgment against you (for who would do this against a friend and such a friend as Bembo?), at least to make you feel perchance that the case is not all in your favor.

First of all, it is well established that imitators have been pointed out by Plato as men worthy of no title, and condemned to the inglorious name of "servile herd" by Horace. And all the authors which have stood out as most illustrious have sought fame from some other source than imitation and, by vying with their predecessors or leaning upon them only occasionally, have sought to surpass rather than follow. He who is always a hanger-on will never reach the top, though he may have natural aptitude and power.

You say that Homer imitated Orpheus to the extent that he boldly transferred the song which Orpheus intended for the poem on Ceres to the Iliad with only two words changed; yes, but universal praise was accorded him because he sang of Troy in a louder and grander strain. Imitation was harmful rather than helpful to Virgil; and almost the only criticism against him, a most celebrated poet and in regard to matters of poetic judgment the most celebrated of all, is that he imitated the ancient poets too extensively. I myself think him very free from this fault, for he did not imitate them slavishly; he has his own numbers, his own characteristics, his own peculiar arrangements; he is an emulator of the ancients rather than an imitator; and although he openly snatches here and there a standard, if you please, or tormenta from the ancients, to adorn his buildings, yet they are conspicuous and on the whole illustrious more by their own ornaments. Many believe that Cicero too zealously imitated Demosthenes and yet, though he imitated him in many ways, he retained his own outline and method of speaking. Livy had equal or even greater fame than Sallust, the most celebrated historian, yet he ran in a different course. Cornelius and Curtius were equally famous, yet they were very different. If you turn to Grecian history, what greater difference of style than between Herodotus and Xenophon? Yet they are both highly praised. If we come to Grecian philosophers, Aristotle is especially celebrated not only among the Greeks but also among the Latins who know Greek, and Plato has never been praised enough; yet the style of Aristotle and Plato is very different; and Xenophon is famous though neither like the Attic Muse so celebrated nor like Plato. Opportunity was not lacking to Aristotle of imitating him, especially since for twenty years he was very frequently busied at the threshold of his auditorium. Erudition nor judgment were lacking yet he preferred to walk in his own path rather than proceed in the broad way of others. Among the Latins, what difference, I ask, is there between Cicero and Varro? They do not imitate each other, in style or in order or method though both are most learned; for the most illustrious ancients never desired to imitate others in such a way as to bind themselves to the mechanics of the work as children in leading strings. They took from any source whatever and as much as seemed to strengthen or adorn their phrase and was recognized as appropriate to the theme. The same may be said of Celsus and Columella, illustrious, popular, elegant; in the one you will find remarkable nicety, in the other more frequent ornament; but in neither will you find much if any imitation. Each one followed his own genius and inclination.

Although a man may have the greatest power to imitate, which Aristotle has testified in his Problematics is due to the poetical nature of man, yet he discovers at the very beginning his own instinct and tendency and to break or turn that is to violate nature: so when there is in our minds an idea or root, as it were, by which we are encouraged to cultivate some gift, it is the reward of our labor to cherish this rather than to destroy it. Nature furnishes us with an idea of right speaking just as of other virtues, and fashions in our minds an image of this beauty which we, using as a standard, can tell what fits us and what does not; but no one has ever attained such perfection that it can be said in him exists a standard altogether beautiful, since nature distributes her gifts to one and all in such a way that the standard of beauty is established from the variety. Do you think that the wise painter was wrong when he decided that he could not find all the properties of beauty in one form? And so we need a standard of speaking in our minds with which we can measure our own and others' mistakes as well as virtues, whether it is an innate idea and perfect from the beginning or gained later by reading many authors. Using this individual standard Cicero did not always approve of Demosthenes, Asinius criticised the Patavinity of Livy; Brutus called Cicero weak, and others pronounced Asinius boastful, redundant, effeminate. For this reason I think Celsus and Fabius thought that no one should be imitated too scrupulously, and refrained from imitating Cicero though they praised him very highly.

Further, what is the reason that the teachers place so many different models before us unless it is that we may draw from them what pleases us?

Let him who does not agree tell me why those who praise Cicero so much have not imitated him in style of speaking? Could they not have done this easily? Celsus, Caecilius, Pliny, Fabius, and others in the age following Cicero, when Roman speech was still unmutilated and when they sucked Latin with their mother's milk? Were they ignorant of the value of imitation? We should not presume to say that they could not if they had wished.

Some one may say that we ought rather to imitate those who please us and I agree. Should Plato please, should Cicero, Platonic in thought and style, let us follow them. Though each one has his own cast of mind as of body so that it is not easy to find two persons altogether alike; yet there is more similarity among some than others and it would be easier for us to imitate those who please us; yet we must remember not to become apes who choose faults for imitation. There are those who desire to paint moles, scars, defects, with little or no idea of strength or grace. Not unlike these are the writers whose greatest care is to find some new word which perchance slipped out when Cicero was hurried or which has come into his books by the fault of time. . . .

Further, it is vain and foolish to apply imitation to every division of rhetoric. *Inventio* is not only more commendable but is more genuine and free and imitation here is hooted off the stage. Is there not a story somewhere that all those jests were condemned, even though sanctioned by Apollo and the Muses, which had sought favor through imitation and to him alone was given the palm by the critics who made an original jest although he delighted not so much the tastes of his table companions? *Dispositio* follows *inventio* with a view to order and correct arrangement, so that the intellectual body of your speech may not be deformed by members ill-suited. And you give it greater care if your own than if sought from others.   The more need of great strength here if we believe Pliny who firmly declares that the barbarians have great power of invention and expression, but that it is granted only to the learned to arrange correctly.   *Elocutio,* is it not a natural consequent of *inventio* when different phrasing is adapted to the themes?   Does it not accompany also *dispositio* where distributions are made so that the entire speech shows individuality?   *Memoria* and *pronunciatio* need not be mentioned, it seems to me, for neither is committed to writing. But as the second, though a gift of nature, may be improved by practice, the examples of the ancients will furnish no little help where reference can be made to their works.   You will be able to rival or surpass the *inventio* of some of them; you will be able to arrange better and to speak more ornately.

Our age does not seem to be lacking in creative power.   Nor has the divine Father been stingy in gifts of genius.   Would that they were as well nourished as our worldly interests and not fed on pulse and acorns, empty nothings and fables.   Some of these geniuses are so torn and distorted that they present the appearance of a ghost or empty shadow rather than a mind. Themes increase rather than decrease, for many things have happened in our own age and the one preceding which that learned antiquity did not know.   The ancients excelled in language, in both Latin and Greek.   In the case of us Italians, who speak Latin but learn Greek with great difficulty, a just critic of our age could prefer those who now speak moderately to those chiefs and leaders who perhaps, busied among the Goths, Vandals, and Huns, either use that early method of speaking forgotten for so many cycles or try to gain it by continual imitation.   There are some who wish to walk in the tracks of the ancients.   But if the tracks should be found to be larger than ours would our feet be firm in them or would we slip?   If they should be less than ours, would it be voted that the feet be kept out?   Further, a plain print which is perfect in every way is not to be found unless perchance in some of the shoes taken from the Roman ruins.   You see there are as many shoes of the ancients as there are feet and you cannot argue, Bembo, that, even if you should find in some remote treasure house antique sandals and should put them on, you could ever persuade the critics that they were really antique.

Jealousy will always create dissension in such a case, for the new will never be considered anything but imperfect.   This we have seen often illustrated in the case of works of art, which, though superior to those of ancient times, if circulated as new, are pronounced inferior, so completely does that empty shadow of a thousand years, as a pest, invade the judgments of men. If they are believed to be ancient, or if the critic is in doubt whether they are or not, there is no censure; but if it is found

that they have been recently wrought and the name of the workman is made known, then a thousand hissings of Aristarchus
will be heard, then not only a third Cato will fall from Heaven
but a Timon and a Momus will arise from the lower regions.
We have known a man, under the name of Cicero, to write letters
which received the greatest praise and admiration; and then again
the same man to sign his own name to the letters of Cicero with
just such words omitted as would betray the trick; and would
you believe, Bembo, that these same letters, which before under
an ancient title had never been praised enough, endured every
kind of censure for being a new composition? Therefore, he had
wasted his time before, seeking words, weighing the arrangement, choosing diversions, committing meters and observing out-
lines in order that they might seem like Cicero, for just the name
could gain this with little toil and trouble.

If what I said above concerning the relation of the divisions
of rhetoric be recalled, it will contribute to repressing a too great
desire for imitating, because the style of writing of even mediocre
authors, to say nothing of Cicero, cannot be imitated in every
particular; for when *inventio* which may be called the material
of speech, is not the same, then *dispositio* will not be the same.
Where will you find a single person, even if you arraign Aesop's
jack-daw adorned with borrowed feathers, who will be bold
enough to meditate upon appropriating material, arrangement,
and expression? But grant all things the same; thereupon re-
move the outline, vary the rhythm, take away the circumlocution;
you have destroyed the work but you have welded another from
these very same elements unaided, unmixed, and unchanged.
Thus arises a different style of writing because it adopts a different phraseology. For example, the orations of Cicero, *de Oratore, de Claris Oratoribus* and many others are flooded by a
great river or rather by an ocean of eloquence; but that vast river
barely irrigates the books on Rhetoric, *de Universitate,* and *de
Fato,* and it hardly comes in drops in the *Topica.* Cicero's style
changes too with age. It is quite different when he advises, en-
treats, interprets or inveighs. Likewise it differs to represent different mental and physical states, to say nothing of subjects which
are to be explained by the language itself.

Then you say that he alone must be imitated whom nature has
made the perfect exponent of eloquence; and by this you say
you can weave the very thread of Cicero, though he varies so
much, into every theme and treat it in Ciceronian style. This
might be true if it were not for two things. In the first place,
every one would not be like Cicero, for even if the words were
Cicero's, the arrangement would not be and it would be as if
some one had made a wall of Ciceronian stones and cemented
them rudely with foreign lime. In the second place, you seem to
insinuate that other authors are not legitimate products of nature.

If you think this, I will call to testify ancient and most approved masters of eloquence, even Cicero himself, who have set before themselves not one model only but many. ' Is it permitted me,' I ask, ' to admire and imitate the strength of Demosthenes in Demosthenes himself rather than in Cicero? to drink the wealth of Plato or the charm of Isocrates from the pure fount rather than from the sullied tributaries?' One point will please in one and another in another, so not without reason did the ancient rhetoricians think out various methods of saying the same thing which are wont to be called *chriae*. Different styles have been approved because of the diversity of judgments springing from the individuality of human temperament, now a full and august kind of speaking, now meager and thin, and now a mixture of both, or dry and barren or fertile and varied in hue. Whatever they are, they have been introduced by nature. One, by the bent of his nature, loves Laconic brevity; another, Asiatic fertility; another burns with the desire for the Attic golden mean; another is delighted with the Rhodian temperament. So many are the various delights of the mind that even about the numbers and feet of the ending of clauses much dissension arose among the ancients and also between Aristotle and Cicero. They dressed their minds with different garments just as we cover our bodies; and formerly as now, different material, figures and colors pleased different people. Very many in an emergency, unfortunately, would clothe themselves in a patch taken from the ample cloak of Cicero and the meager *subtegmen* of Pliny. They even accept the *trama* of Celsus and Columella. Others perhaps because they feel the cold try to roll out the *scrinium* of Carmenta to make a *peplum* fitted to them. Not content with this they approach those old rotten coffers of the Roman augurs and the brothers Marcii. And when they discover that Cato and Ennius have stores, they rush forth to despoil them. There are not lacking those who think the ass a beautiful animal and make a *lacerna* from his hair. But those who would think that my opinions are signs of a diseased mind may turn to the art of medicine and hear Hippocrates teach that medicine must be given according to the age, season, and habits.

Now by way summary: There are varying authors each approved in his own style, there are also varying tendencies of the human mind, and as a result ideas or standards of speaking differ even in the same mind. Rules are given after approved authors, especially Dionysius and Hermogenes. All that we turn over in our minds must be referred to one standard; the method must be considered; and a speech must be welded from all, yet like none and perfect. So far is it from my mind that any one should be exclusively and completely imitated that I should reject one who surpassed even the Lord Almighty if he were proposed, for we could not imitate his power, neither ought nor could we imitate his wisdom; still it is our task to cultivate that which he has willed to shine from his intellectual sun upon our minds for the purpose of manifesting his glory and of increasing in our hearts the love of divine goodness which is to be imitated by us as far as our human strength can accomplish, thereby increasing our virtue and ultimate happiness.

I have consumed, Bembo, six or seven hours speaking of imitation, more or less interrupted and without books, putting down rapidly whatever occurred to me. I pray indulgence if any mistakes have occurred. If there are any yawning gaps or faulty composition, if it is broken and rasping rather than smooth and flowing, I beg indulgence such as you granted recently to the song on the expelling of Venus and Cupid; for who could bring it to pass that in the face of these facts a just judge would not absolve me for reverting sometimes to poetic numbers, to milder studies, and to rhetoric as if returning home, weary from long toil with the rusty and barbarous language of theologians and philosophers? But in that rhythm and polished phrase brought from those early times, if you yourself have not gained the palm in our time you certainly are nearer or soon will be nearer first than third.

Rome, xiii. Calendas Octobris, 1512.

A Pamphlet on Imitation
By Pietro Bembo
Addressed to Gianfrancesco Pico

Bembo to Pico:—Rightly and lovingly you acted when you wished to have transmitted to me, by letter, your part in our recent conversation on imitation; for although your excellent distinction and my great affection made your words of weight, yet they will sink more deeply into my mind and will be more easily recalled if committed to writing. Then, ordinarily, what is committed to paper is fuller and richer than what men say in conversation, for style is added and the very delay of writing causes more thoughtful expression. And so that conversation of yours which pleased me so much when I listened was very much more charming when read. Since you challenge me most lovingly, I shall respond, not so much with the desire of opposing you, as of protecting myself; not so much for disproving your opinions as for giving you the reasons which impelled me to praise those who chose the one man to imitate, who they knew excelled others in that kind of writing in which they were employed.

But before I come to that, I beg you to tell me why you write in the beginning of your letter that all good writers should be imitated and later you criticise imitators in general. If you did this because you could approve of none, let me say in the first place that I do not claim that any art of imitating can be praised unreservedly or any one can be found among the hosts of imitators who has used that art perfectly. In the second place, if I grant you that no one has been correctly imitated (for I see that you think even Maro a poor imitator) why do you approve of that art in which though so many illustrious minds have exercised themselves, no one has attained reputation? And frankly, why would you not better have agreed with those who condemn all imitation? For it would have been fairer not to have enveighed against them whose art you approved or not to have approved of that art whose devotees you censured. For this, indeed, you could have accomplished most easily, such is your power and eloquence of writing, slapping them sharply and vehemently. If you had followed this plan and given yourself a freer field of disputing, I need not have had the trouble of responding to your letter. For I should have referred you to the letter of Paolo

8

Cortesi, beautiful, dignified, subtle, in which he broke the levity of his neighbor, Politian, a learned and clever but rather imprudent man, who, being unable to attain in any degree Ciceronian style, turned himself to condemning those who advocated it. And so Cortesi, very wisely and prudently opposing him, might have been able to satisfy you, if you had agreed with Politian.

But now, I do not see how you can declare that we must imitate not one but all good men, for if all those who are considered good in some one line of writing were equal in nobility of style and elegance, I perhaps might concede what you say; but when the method is found to be very different and one excels in one thing, another in another, why should we not give attention to the better and neglect the inferior? Or if, among those who are counted good, there is one so far superior that in him are found all the splendid things which appear individually in the others, why should we not imitate him, unless we wish to imitate the inferior and attain no distinction. Just as if one who has learned to paint like Apelles, whose art all the other painters have admired and granted first place without question, need turn also to the pictures of Polygnotus and Thymantis or as if one who would imitate the excellent and illustrious work of Lysippus need look also upon the rigid Calamis or even the more rigid Canachus. Yet those very artists, when they desired to fashion the portrait of Alexander, kept their mind and eyes intent upon him alone. Shall we who ought to place before us the most beautiful and perfect image, working diligently to reproduce this, give our care and attention to expressing the images of those which are not so beautiful? It seems to me, Pico, that it is a mistake. For we are not so fashioned by the immortal gods that when you furnish us what is first we rush after what is second, much less what is third. And so, as I said, I am very much surprised that you have not rather decided one of these two things: either that there should be no imitation at all; or, if there must be, that we should imitate not what is good but what is best and most perfect.

Now, what you write about ideas I am very loth to question, seeing that you are a most learned man and have great reputation. But how can you think that an idea of style is innately in your mind? As for me, I can only declare that I saw no form of style nor image of speaking in my mind till I had brought it about by thoughtfully reading the books of the ancients for many years and by long practice. Before I did this, I used to look into my mind and seek as from a mirror some shape from which I could fashion what I wished. But there was no image there. And when I tried to write, I was borne along at random by no law and no judgment. None of those things which you mention, no idea, no image guided me. Of course, I know that you express the opinion of the school of Plato who referred what was the best

in nature to divine ideas and images; and I agree that there exists
in God, the author and founder of the universe, not only a certain divine and altogether perfect image of justice, temperance,
and the other virtues, but also of correct writing. Xenophon,
Demosthenes and Plato, Crassus, Antonius, Julius, and, most of
all, Cicero, when they were composing and writing, directed their
minds and style to this as far as they could. And I think we
must try to do the same. But if those ideas are innate, as you
say, different in different individuals as they happen to be allotted
at birth; if we cannot direct our style away from these; why not
decide that we ought to imitate just the one only who is the best
and highest of all? If we cannot, why imitate all good writers?
It is spiteful not to place the best example before all who can
imitate it in any degree; and it is useless to say that all good
men should be imitated if nature has not given the power of turning from the innate idea. Thirdly and lastly, if those innate ideas
and images are such that in some minds they can be bent, and in
others they cannot, in either case your argument must fail; for
those who are denied the privilige of advancing at all ought not
to be invited to any kind of imitation and those who have un-
limited power ought to proceed only toward the best.

Those who have no native ability should neither attempt to
write nor to imitate. Those who have mediocre ability I am
not interested in; I do not care whether they write or not,
whether they wake or sleep. I am speaking of those who if they
take pains can accomplish something, whose genius, if it is cultivated, will bear rich and abundant fruits. Nor am I disturbed
because I know that there are very few who have been endowed
with such genius. It did not hinder Cicero from writing those
beautiful books of *de Oratore* because he had never read nor
heard of his ideal orator, nor did Plato refrain from writing the
laws of his Republic because they were not practical. Those who
present well some art do not work it out with the idea that all
can follow it but that whoever is able may have a perfect model.
Such a model the ordinary genius perchance may approach and
follow but never attain. So they leave out of consideration ordinary minds. Virgil's sailor pleases me when he advises Aeneas
to cast overboard everything unnecessary so that he may cross
into Italy more easily, whereupon the poet says: *Exigui numero
sed bello vivida virtus.* But still, I do not propose an imaginary
ideal as Plato and Cicero did when I place as model one who is
the best and most excellent of all, nor do I defend myself by citing
them. Yet one can teach the arts and disciplines by the method
of the *de Oratore* and the Republic so that he wishes imitators to
excel the image which they see or handle. All imitation deals
with example and must be sought from example. Otherwise,
how can there be any imitation? For that which we are discussing
is nothing but transferring the likeness of some one else's style

to your writings and using, if you please, the same organizing principle which he has used whom you have set before you as an example.

But I come back to your statement that all good writers must be imitated; and I ask if you wish the good to be imitated in such a way that we may express the whole method of any one of them we please, or do you hold it enough that we borrow from each what we consider best and thus construct one integral method? Tell me in which way you prefer this dogma of yours to be interpreted. But certainly not in the first way; for what is more absurd than to wish all their different ideas and forms of writing to be expressed in one style? As if you would think in one temple many examples of various temples could be represented. If in the second way your dogma is to be accepted, I answer that it is not imitation. This should rather be called making excerpts or, if you please, begging; for beggars gain the necessaries of life not from one but from many. Imitation includes the entire form of writing; it demands that you imitate the individual parts but it deals too with the whole structure and body of style. He who seeks the brevity of Sallust but fashions it in awkward structure and obsolete words does not imitate Sallust; and he who would express the moderation of Julius Caesar by using uncultured speech cannot be called the imitator of Caesar. It is necessary for an imitator to express all the features of the style which he wishes to imitate, as Cicero explained when he said that imitation was that by which we are driven on with careful reasoning so that we can be like another in speaking. Moreover, how can they who take from several individuals become like any? While they who take from all accomplish nothing.

If I grant your definition of the term, for I do not wish to seem egotistical, your method of imitating many is more easily talked of than accomplished. He who wishes to imitate several at the same time will gain nothing from any, for he allows his mind to be distracted. The person whose mind clings to no one can do nothing at all correctly, and he who follows first one then another is in trouble, for we are captured by novelty, most of us, and are so delighted with it that we condemn all things old. Add the diversity and dissimilarity of writers. Old precepts must be unlearned that we may adapt our minds and attention to new. A certain severity, if you please, attracts in one, and hilarity in another. When we learn to imitate the first and then turn to the second we are compelled to reject much that a little while before we sought with the greatest care and pains. And on this account we grow discouraged and careless, while we are tossed hither and yon by the variety of examples as if by waves.

Finally, your opinion that the individual virtues of each one must be imitated is to be considered. If you will think carefully, you will decide that there is no way to accomplish this; for what is best and most excellent in any author is moulded from all his parts, all his virtues, nay, all his vices if he has any. As the countenances of men show kindness, alertness or strength of mind, fertility of genius, majesty, comeliness; as individual traits are made up not only from the shape of the eyes and eyebrows but from the whole face; as, if any one wishes to paint some part of the face, he is compelled to express the whole: so in writing, the individual virtues of the model we can excel, only if we excel also the whole method of which they are the ornaments.

Do you think that you can imitate Caesar's wonderful purity of speech unless you use as much moderation as he used, which was more than can be found in others because he wrote of himself and therefore did not seem to be actuated by hatred or desire? and unless you show the same negligence of *elocutio* which he showed either from necessity, for he was so occupied with affairs that he could not give more care to writing, or which he assumed purposely that he might not be considered incompetent and that men might think he would have written better if he had had more leisure? Caesar's purity does not stand alone but seems to me to be made up of the other two qualities. If you do not imitate the two, that purity so much praised will never be yours. When you gain the purity you will wish also to acquire Ciceronian majesty which all laud to the skies, but you will not do this without throwing into confusion what you have already done, for as much as you add to the one you must take from the other. But if the candor of Caesar, the majesty of Cicero, the brevity of Sallust, the richness of Livy, the simplicity of Celsus, and the carefulness of Columella, if finally all the individual virtues of each one of these illustrious writers must be surpassed in your writings I fear you will pervert rather than imitate them. But if you escape the disappointment of your wish, certainly you will not escape the appearance of composing in a mediocre way. Then finally, if some God should show you, which I certainly cannot do, some new and plainly divine art by which you might imitate many, as you teach, even then you ought to hesitate to use that art; for how can it be brought about that you could coalesce into one style the speech of writers, one of whom is incoherent, another smooth, a third vigorous, a fourth ornate, a fifth negligent? How can your speech display these and six hundred other kinds and qualities of writing? For example, the ancient poets seem to have fashioned Proteus first as water, then as fire, and then as a beast, yet he never showed more than one form at a time, not only because they did not think this could be done but because they did not see how these things could be joined properly.

So much in answer to your letter up to this point or rather to that part of your letter to which I have thought it worth while to respond; for it was not necessary to answer it all, since you know from my writings and my opinions what my answer would be.

I come then to that part of your conversation where you say that I recommend Cicero as a model for prose and Virgil for poetry. To this opinion I was not brought instantly; but after much thought and through many steps I approached it, so that I did not seem to have pronounced it rashly. In the beginning, indeed, I thought that in style as in philosophy one ought not to be subjected to any laws, ought not to be bound to any one, but ought to follow what he liked. This theory indeed seems to have been akin to yours. I was led from this by the reasons I have stated, after many vain attempts at writing. When I gave this up, I brought myself to that point where I thought it better for each one to fashion his own method unsullied by others; and I was sure my idea would be universally praised. It pleased me and I experimented in it as far as I could, but all my thought, care, and study, all my labor was vexatious and void; for I invented nothing which could not easily have been drawn from the old writers; and when I tried to avoid that, it lacked the charm, the propriety, the majesty of those ages. In the disappointment of my labor this thought came that those who professed to imitate no one had accomplished little by their writing and that they lie despised along with their books. Therefore, when my last opinion was condemned, I decided to adopt another method which I will now speak of.

But I wish to describe the individual movements of my mind and changes of plans so that if my mistakes can be profitable to you in any degree, you may hear them. Now, since it has been arranged by nature that whenever men are busied with something great and arduous, their anxiety, labor, doubt, and difficulty is decreased, if they have an example of the work by others who have tried the same thing sometime before, I began to think the thing to be desired in those studies to which I had surrendered myself was to find one person to imitate. And so I was more active thereafter, whether because, as a traveler following a guide, I was proceeding with secure mind, or because we are incited to excellence and desire of fame by nothing more than the emulation of another. I decided then that I must choose a leader in poetic studies as in oratory.

When I was deliberating upon this matter, great hesitation came upon me whether I ought to follow at first mediocre models or those who were most eminent, whom I could cultivate in every study, to whose likeness I could most diligently compare myself. For, if I should take the highest I feared that the difficulty of the task would hinder me at first, or the greatness of the work discourage me; but if I surrendered myself to the mediocre I hoped that when I had profited as much from them as I wished, the transition to the best would be easier and safer. But I was troubled because I heard that style is fixed in the beginning as the scent of a vase; and also because my mind and thought much more freely interested itself in the best.   But fear or imbecility conquered, for I was drawn to the mediocre.   I surrendered myself to masters whose writings I did not so much praise as I accepted as stepping stones to the better.   Therefore, when I had set myself to them with all zeal till it seemed to me that I had gained a great part of that which I desired, I turned to those who were recognized as the best to follow them too and to lead my mind to drinking in and imbibing their methods.   When I had tried this again and again I found out that I had been deceived and deluded in my hope.   For I saw that not only the imitation of them had not been made easier by the imitation of others but that it had been made more difficult and the entrance had been cut off rather than opened up.   The work which I thought would be useful to me was a very great hindrance; for my mind, trained and accustomed by careful exercise to other methods of writing, retained for a long time the mode; and, inasmuch as that which had to be drawn from the best was very different from what I had thought, I was much less fitted to imitate them than I should have been if I had never devoted myself to the mediocre ones.   Wherefore, by my many labors I found out that I had accomplished one thing,—that it was not permitted me then even to begin to imitate the highest because I had infected my mind, as it were, with such blemishes that when they had settled, no face or image could be rightly painted there. In truth, it is not as easy as it is desirable often to blot out what one has introduced into one's mind by daily study.   But nothing is too difficult to be overcome, especially if we do our utmost; and so, after applying myself with the greatest diligence and after I had at length blotted from my memory those methods which had settled deep by the imitation of the mediocre, I turned all my study to the best and highest.

But if you ask me how far I have succeeded, I shall surely answer you nothing except that I am not sorry of my decision, especially when I read the writings of those who imitate either no one or all or some besides the best.   But it ought not to hinder you from taking up this method of writing, even if I seem not to have been successful.   I did not spend as much time on it as I might have, for I wrote some things in prose and verse in the vernacular, to which I gave more study because so many depraved and perverse things have been introduced into the language, that, the correct and proper use of writing being almost obsolete, it seemed shortly the language would lapse to the point where it would lie without honor, splendor, culture, or dignity unless some one sustained it.   Therefore it is not necessary for you to take an example from my writings, thinking that as much as I have accomplished in imitating and emulating the best in the Latin language others can accomplish and no more; but think rather that, since I have accomplished something, however little, they who decide to try nothing else will accomplish whatever they wish.

You have my method, by what perplexing thinking, by what meanderings I came at length to that opinion which I wish you could approve. From now on I shall rest more freely, because, all other ways having been tried diligently before, this received me after being tossed about long in error. They who enter this at first and who never allow themselves to be turned from it will more quickly accomplish the race than those who have slipped so often and will come to the goal without any hindrance whatever goal their genius or industry has set. Chance seems to play no small part in life, turning the mind from the course begun. Yet all ought to strive to bring it about that those who delight in oratory or poetry hold fast to the imitation of Cicero and Virgil only. For if they have not all the ornaments of genius, all the virtues of style, I should say we ought nevertheless to follow them because with them as leaders we proceed more nearly to perfection than with any others. And, since there is no brilliancy of style, no remarkable native ability, no praise, no virtue at all which may not be found in both these in a far more perfect degree than in others we should have to work more constantly and more diligently if we choose others as models lest we seem not to have been prudent in choosing or timid in following. For no one certainly hesitates about Virgil. All declare that in him, of all the Latin poets, are found the most admirable virtues and the highest individuality and dignity.

Cicero is considered sometimes rather verbose, especially when he is talking of his own deeds or his consulate: yet it is agreed that not only he is the most eloquent but that eloquence was conceived and brought to life by him. His lengthy speech may be excused often by his position or by his dignity or malice of enemies or some condition of the republic, or it may be remembered that those things which seem superfluous in reading could have been considered necessary in public delivery; yet I do not strive especially to defend him, for if it is a fault it is not of style but of temperament or of judgment if things were said by him which should have been passed by in silence. In truth his style retains always that remarkable and superior native quality, the same splendor and majesty. And for this reason it seems that he ought not to be accused so much if at all, because he often spoke when it would have been more fitting to have kept silent; but rather he ought to be praised because his style was so inimitable when he did speak. Suppose that these same people do say he was inconsistent or weaker than his dignity warranted, will we have to refrain from imitating him for this reason? And yet if I believed this, his character might perchance be criticised by me; still the method of speech and style need not be condemned, which can be perfect in a life not perfect. Even if this should be judged a fault of *oratio,* I do not extend my imitation to faults, moles on the face, ulcers and scars. Those who do this are deservedly ridiculed by Horace in the passage to which you refer.

I limit the method so that if any one is superior, industrious, or fortunate enough to surpass his master, he ought to do it. Indeed, I quite approve of Phidias who excelled Eladus in sculpturing, Polycletus who surpassed his master in painting, and Apelles who left his teacher far behind. And it seems very desirable to me that each one should hope to be the most eloquent of all men; and although this may seem a rash hope, there is nothing in nature to prohibit it. Just as Cicero stood out among the Latins because he, only, excelled all good teachers of writing before him, so it will be possible for another sometime to excel all the rest and even Cicero himself. But this can happen most easily by imitating with the greatest care the person whom we especially wish to excel; for it is absurd to believe that we can discover a better way than that which Cicero not so much discovered as followed.

After we have imitated any one a long time, then we may try to surpass him; but all our desire, all our labor, all our thought must be centered upon equalling him, for it is not so arduous to surpass the one whom you equal as to equal whom you imitate. Wherefore in all this theory, Pico, this can be the law: first, to place the best before us for imitating; second, to imitate in such a way that we strive to attain; and finally to try to surpass. So let us have in our minds these two remarkable instruments, emulation and hope. But though emulation has always been joined with imitation, our hope cannot as properly follow imitation as the success of it. And the imitation of Cicero will be fitting for all who wish to write on any theme in prose, for the same style can be suited to innumerable themes. Nor ought those be listened to who think the history of Pliny could not be written in Ciceronian style as well as it was by Pliny in his own way, though the work would necessarily have assumed infinite proportions if Cicero had added his exuberance of speech. But if the magnitude of these books had grown, they would have been much more pleasing to us, for they would have drawn, in proportion, more dignity and beauty from Cicero's genius and workmanship.

We cannot say the same thing of Virgil, that he is a suitable model for all who wish to write verse; for the Virgilian structure, rhythm, or even method will not especially fit elegiac and lyric verse nor tragedies and comedies. But he who would devote himself to writing heroic verse must learn, imbibe, and express Virgil as far as possible.

This imitation of Virgil, Cicero, and other excellent writers, I do not wish to be considered in such light that nothing is to be taken except the style and method; for who can fashion any legitimate work who borrows nothing, who takes nothing from any one to introduce into and scatter along in his writings? who does not take thoughts, figures, and brilliant sayings, descriptions of places and times? who does not take some examples of war or peace or storms or loves or other things from those whom he has read much and long, not only in Latin but in Greek and also in the vernacular? This borrowing is legitimate, but let it be done sparingly and wisely. We can borrow because great and illustrious men have done it, but not too much; for it is more distinguished to invent than to borrow. That borrowing may be approved which causes the result to shine more splendidly than the original so that we adorn as well as invent. I do not approve of Atilius who is said to have made a poor translation of the most elegantly written Electra of Sophocles; but of our Maro who, taking many things from the Georgics of Hesiod, transferred them and by doing so made them all the better. Indeed, so many things of this kind fill all the books of Virgil that it appears that he sought not so much to draw from himself as to excel, that much more glory might appear in victory than in invention. I wished to speak of this because some not only include in the one word, imitation, that which pertains to style but the things which I mention and which are of another kind. They indeed seem not to have read carefully the passage of Cicero which I recalled above where he gives a definition of imitation; for if, indeed, that is imitation by which we are impelled so that we can be like others in writing; and if there is included not only method of style, but material, arrangement and other things outside of style; why may I not borrow all of Virgil's Aeneid, merely changing the names of Aeneas, Ascanius, Dido, and Lavinia? Therefore, if they do not wish to be inconsistent, let them see the difference between borrowing and imitating, and when they say that Virgil imitated the method of the heroic verse of Catullus, then if only they will declare that he not only borrowed many things from him but also from other Latin and Greek poets and orators and philosophers too, they will tell the truth. Indeed you, sometimes in your letter, seem to have felt that imitation and borrowing were the same thing. If this is so, indeed I rejoice that, by changing the interpretation of one word, the controversy between us is practically finished, for then I shall have said almost the same things you say,—that all good men ought to be imitated.

And what could be more pleasing to me, both on account of our friendship and your reputation for learning, than the knowledge that I do not differ essentially from you, a man of greatest genius, renowned for integrity, temperate in prosperity, strong in adversity and a great and respected man in every walk of life, a man whose books are read and thumbed so much that he can easily surpass me in reputation as well as excel me in writings? But if this is not the case, still I rejoice that no differences and controversies between us can be so great or so serious that my respect for you and your love for me would suffer; especially since you are writing a book on love, and I am sure that you who teach others will have learned yourself that truth first must be loved.

Yet I am not one who thinks that you cannot prove me mistaken, especially since you find reason to criticise the Aristotelian books in many places and almost all the philosophy of the ancients. For it can happen that we each may think the other entirely wrong. Nor do I presume that by this letter I may convert you and others to my way of thinking; for what more foolish than to think that I by one letter could persuade a person to imitate either Virgil or Cicero when these men themselves have not done so by the divine majesty of their numerous great writings? Yet it is a characteristic of the human mind, not to be despised I think, to wish to inform as many as possible of his opinions upon important subjects under debate, so that either he can correct himself by their censure or strengthen his belief by their approbation. I beg you again and again to believe that this has been my only desire.

Rome, Calends of January, 1513.

Ciceronianus

OR

A Dialogue on the Best Style of Speaking

Bulephorus: Whom do I see walking yonder in the most retired part of the porch? If I am not mistaken it is my old friend and fellow student, Nosoponus.

Hypologus: Is this that Nosoponus who was once the most charming of all jolly companions, delightfully ruddy and stout, bubbling over with Loves and Graces?

Bu.—The very one.

Hyp.—Whence this new shape? More like to ghost he seems than man. Has he some disease?

Bu.—Yes, a very serious one.

Hyp.—What I pray? Not dropsy?

Bu.—The ailment is deeper than the skin.

Hyp.—It isn't that new kind of leprosy which people to-day flatter by the name of mange?

Bu.—The infection is indeed deeper than that.

Hyp.—It isn't the spitting malady?

Bu.—The trouble is more deeply seated than in the lungs.

Hyp.—It isn't jaundice?

Bu.—It is something deeper than the liver.

Hyp.—Perhaps a fever ravaging the veins and heart?

Bu.—It is a fever, and yet not a fever, something burning deeper, advancing from the inmost recesses of the mind. But cease vainly divining. It is a new kind of disease.

Hyp.—Has it then not yet a name?

Bu.—Among the Romans, not yet. The Greeks call it Zeloduléan.

Hyp.—Has it come on recently? Or is it a trouble χρόνιον.[1]

Bu.—For more than seven years the unfortunate man has been suffering. But we are observed. He seems to be turning his

---

[1] Of long standing.

steps hither. You will find out better from him what the trouble is. I shall act the part of Davus; do you help the conversation along and take a part in the play.

Hyp.—Indeed I would do it gladly, if I knew what you desired.

Bu.—I desire very much to relieve my dear old friend of so serious a malady.

Hyp.—What. Are you skilled in medicine?

Bu.—You know that there is a kind of madness that does not take away the whole mind, but affects one part only in such an extraordinary degree that the victims believe they wear bull's horns on their heads or are burdened with long noses or carry on scrawny necks great earthen heads sure to be broken if they move ever so little, or think themselves dead and shudder at the approach of the living.

Hyp.—Yes, I know.

Bu.—There is no better way to heal them than to pretend that you have the same trouble.

Hyp.—I have heard frequently of that cure.

Bu.—It shall be tried in this case.

Hyp.—Not only a spectator of this play, but a willing helper will I be, for I am particularly well disposed toward the man.

Bu.—Then compose your countenance and play your part so that nothing may suggest to him that there has been an agreement.

Hyp.—It shall be done.

Bu.—I bid Nosoponus a very hearty good-day.

Hyp.—And Hypologus salutes Nosoponus.

Nosoponus: Indeed I wish you both the same in turn. And may your wish for me be realized!

Bu.—It could not fail, if giving were as easy as wishing. But, pray, what is the matter; for your thinness forebodes some ill or other? There is clearly some trouble with your liver.

No.—With my heart, my dear sir.

Hyp.—Heaven forbid! I hope it is not incurable.

Bu.—Is there no help from doctors?

No.—In human remedies there is no hope. Help must come from above.

Bu.—A dreadful disease! But succor from what god, pray, must you have?

No.—It is the goddess who is called by the Greeks, πειθώ.[1]

Bu.—I know, the goddess which moves men's souls.

No.—I am desperately in love with her and am doomed to die unless I win her.

Bu.—No wonder you pine away, Nosoponus. I know what a powerful thing Love is and what it is to be νυμφόληπτον.[2] How long have you been in love?

No.—The years are almost ten since I began to roll this stone with no avail. But I am determined to die in the attempt or gain at length the object of my love.

Bu.—You tell of a love as enduring as it is unhappy, since in so many years it neither has been able to fade nor to win its object.

Hyp.—Perhaps the possession of his nymph pains him more than the lack of her.

No.—On the contrary, I am pining away for want of her.

Bu.—How is it possible? When you alone of all up to the present time have so excelled in eloquence that many say of you what formerly was said of Pericles, "Persuasion sits upon your lips?"

No.—In a word, all eloquence except Ciceronian is distasteful to me. This is that nymph for love of whom I am pining away.

Bu.—Now I know your trouble. You are seeking to gain that splendid and longed for name, Ciceronian.

No.—So much that I consider life bitter unless I attain it.

Bu.—Henceforth I cease to wonder; for you have directed your mind to the attainment of a most beautiful thing, but the common saying is only too true, δύσκολα τὰ καλά.[3] I am in my heart looking with favor upon your wishes myself, if some god will turn propitiously to me.

No.—What do you mean?

Bu.—I will tell you, if you can suffer a rival.

No.—What do you mean?

Bu.—Love of the same nymph distracts me.

No.—What! You possessed with the same desire?

Bu.—Completely, and the flames increase daily.

---

[1] Persuasion.
[2] The captive of a nymph.
[3] " The beautiful is hard to attain."

No.—Indeed in that role you are dearer to me, Bulephorus; for though I have always esteemed you highly, now also I shall begin to love you, since our minds unite in a common wish.

Bu.—You would, perhaps, be loath to be cured of this disease if some one should promise help from herbs, gems, or charms.

No.—It would be killing, not curing. Either I must die or attain. There is no middle ground.

Bu.—How easily I divined your mood from my own.

No.—I will hide nothing then from you, initiated, as it were, into the same mysteries.

Bu.—Be assured, you can speak with safety, Nosoponus.

No.—Not only the splendor of a most beautiful name torments me but also the insolent impertinence of those Italians, who, though they approve of no language at all except Ciceronian and think it the greatest disgrace for one not to be a Ciceronian, nevertheless declare that the honor of this name has never fallen to any on this side the Alps except to Christophe de Longueil, recently deceased, of whom (that I may not seem to grude him due praise) I would make bold to declare what Quintilian wrote of Calvus, "Early death did him an injury."

Hyp.—The too early death of De Longueil did less injury to him than to letters. For what could he not have recovered in literature if to such genius and industry the gods had added a fair space of life?

Bu.—But what hinders that which has been given to one, by the consent of the Muses, to belong to others?

No.—He died while engaged in this most noble work, fortunate, I think; for what is more beautiful, more glorious, more magnificent than for a Cisalpine to be called a Ciceronian by the vote of the Italians?

Bu.—I think he is to be congratulated upon his good fortune in dying at the right time, before any shadow darkened his glory either because of growing zeal for Greek letters or a cloud arising from the Christian authors from whom perhaps he would not have kept himself absolutely if he had lived longer.

Hyp.—I agree with you that he was fortunate to die while engaged in this most noble task; but I hope that we shall survive, not perish in our work.

No.—I second your wish! Upon my life, I prefer this honor to being canonized.

Bu.—Who pray would not rather be celebrated in the eyes of posterity as a Ciceronian than as a saint? But since this kind of love knows no jealousy, I beg you in the name of our common hopes and fears to share with me at least your plans—how you seek to win your mistress. Perhaps we shall both gain her more quickly if we help each other.

No.—The Muses know not envy, much less the Graces, companions of the Muses. To the comrade of one's aims nothing must be denied. All possessions of friends should be common.

Bu.—You will make me perfectly happy.

Hyp.—Will you receive me too into your alliance? For I have long been driven by the same frenzy.

No.—We will. Now I shall reveal the mysteries to those consecrated, as it were, to the same god. For seven whole years I have touched nothing except Ciceronian books, refraining from others as religiously as the Carthusians refrain from flesh.

Bu.—Why so?

No.—Lest somewhere some foreign phrase should creep in and, as it were, dull the splendor of Ciceronian speech. Also I have enclosed in their cases and removed from sight all other books lest I should sin inadvertently; and hereafter there is no place in my library for any one except Cicero.

Bu.—How neglectful I have been! Never with such care have I cherished Cicero.

No.—Not only in the chapel and library but also in every doorway have I a picture of him beautifully painted, and I wear one engraved on a gem so that he may ever be in my thoughts. No other vision comes to me in sleep except that of Cicero.

Bu.—I do not wonder.

Hyp.—Among the apostles in my calendar I have given a place to Cicero.

Bu.—Quite right. For they used to call him the god of eloquence.

No.—I have been so diligent too in reading and rereading his writings that I have learned by heart almost all of them.

Bu.—What industry!

No.—Now I am girded for imitation.

Bu.—How much time have you allotted for this?

No.—As much as for the reading.

Bu.—It is too little for such an arduous task. Would that there might fall to my lot, even at the age of seventy, the glory of so illustrious a name!

No.—But hold, I am not content with this. There is not a word in all the books of that divine man which I have not set in order in an alphabetical lexicon.

Bu.—A huge volume it must be.

No.—Two strong carriers well saddled could scarcely carry it on their backs.

Bu.—Whew! I have seen them at Paris who could carry an elephant.

No.—And there is a second volume even bigger than this in which I have arranged alphabetically the phrases peculiar to Cicero.

Bu.—Now, at last, I am ashamed of my laziness.

No.—There is a third.

Bu.—Whew! A third too?

No.—It had to be. In this I have gathered all the metrical feet with which Cicero ever begins or ends his periods and their subdivisions, the rhythms which he uses in between and the cadences which he chooses for each kind of sentence, so that no little point could escape.

Bu.—But how can it be that the first volume is so much greater than the whole of Cicero?

No.—Listen and you will understand. You perhaps think that I am content to note the mere words.

Bu.—I thought so. Is there more?

No.—On the contrary, that is a mere beginning.

Bu.—How?

No.—See how far you miss the mark. The same word is not always used in the same way: for example, the verb *refero* has one force when Cicero says *referre gratiam;* another, when he says *Liberi parentes et forma corporis et moribus referunt;* another, when he says *Refero me ad intermissa studia;* again another, when he says *Si quid erit, quod mea referat scire;* finally another, when he says *Non ignota referam.* Likewise *orare Lentulum* is one thing; *orare causam* is another. Again, *contendit* at one time means *he strives with another;* at another time it means *he earnestly seeks something from some one;* at another time, *he strives with great zeal to accomplish something;* and at another time, *he puts together two things and compares them.*

Hyp.—Wonderful! This is drawing up a veritable λεξικοὺς ἐλέγχους.[1]

Bu.—Now, at last, I appreciate both your industry and my laziness.

No.—I do not note individual words unrelated but give the context. And I am not satisfied to have noted one or two passages as some are; but as often as the word is found in Cicero, however similar the form, I note the page, the side of the page, and number of the line, affixing a mark which indicates whether the word is in the middle of the line, at the beginning, or at the end. In this way you see one word takes up several pages.

Bu.—Ye Gods! What may not such care accomplish!

No.—Just a second, Bulephorus. You have heard nothing yet.

Bu.—What else can there be?

No.—What advantage to know a word if you stumble on its forms, derivatives, compounds?

Bu.—I do not know exactly what you mean.

No.—I will explain. What more trite or common than the verbs: *amo, lego, scribo?*

Bu.—No question about these, is there?

No.—Or than these nouns: *amor, lectio, scriptor?*

Bu.—Nothing.

No.—But believe me it is both necessary and needful for one who seeks the dignity of the title, Ciceronian, to be so exact that he will not use these very common words without weighing their meaning—unless, perchance, you think it safe to trust to the Grammarians, who inflect verbs through all moods, persons, genders, and tenses, and nouns, pronouns, and participles through all cases and numbers, though we have no right to use any of them not used by Cicero. It is not great to speak like a Grammarian, but it is divine to speak like Cicero.

Bu.—Explain, I pray, more fully.

No.—*Amo, amas, amat* (for this may be cited as an example), I find in Cicero; but *amamus* and *amatis* perhaps I do not find.

---

[1] Inventory of words.

Likewise I find *amabo,* I do not find *amabatis.* Again *amaveras* I find, *amaras* I do not; in contrast, *amasti* I find, *amavisti* I do not. And what if you should find *legeram, legeras, legerat,* and should not find *legeratis?* If you should find *scripseram* and not *scripseratis?* In the same way you may form conclusions about the inflections of all verbs. About the inflections of the cases, the method is the same. *Amor, amoris, amorem, amori,* I am sure of in Cicero; *O amor, hos amores, horum amorum, his amoribus, O amores,* I do not find. Likewise *lectio, lectionis, lectioni, lectionem,* I find; *lectiones, lectionibus, lectionum, has lectiones,* and *O lectiones,* I do not. So *scriptorem* and *scriptores,* I find; *scriptoribus* and *scriptorum* as a substantive noun I do not find. These things of course must seem ridiculous, if you are bold enough to use *stultitias* and *stultitiarum, vigilantias* and *vigilantiarum, speciebus* and *specierum, fractuum, ornatuum, cultuum, vultuum, ambitibus,* and *ambituum,* and innumerable others of this sort. From these few examples you can judge concerning all which are inflected in the same way.

Hyp.—[1]*Intenui labor.*

Bu.—[2]*At tenuis non gloria.*

No.—I too will join in the refrain,[3] *Si quem numina laeva sinunt, auditque vocatus Apollo.* Now about derivatives—*lego* I should dare to use, *legor* I should not; *nasutus* I should, *nasutior* and *nasutissimus* never; *ornatus* and *ornatissumus, laudatus* and *laudatissimus* I use without hesitation, *ornatior* and *laudatior* I scruple to use unless I find them. Nor would I dare to say *scriptorculus* and *lectiuncula* just because I find in Cicero *scriptor* and *lectio.*

Bu.—I see an immense forest.

No.—Now learn about compounds. *Amo, adamo, redamo* I may say but not *deamo.* *Perspicio* I may use but not *dispicio.* *Scribo, describo, subscribo, rescribo, inscribo* I may say; *transcribo* I may not unless I have found it in Cicero's works.

Bu.—Do not tire yourself by citing in detail. We understand perfectly, Nosoponus.

No.—The smallest volume of all contains these.

Bu.—A camel's pack.

---

[1] Vergil G. IV. 6. Slight is the subject,—
[2] But not slight the praise.
[3] If heaven assist and Apollo hear my lays.

Hyp.—And indeed a full one.

Bu.—How comes it that you make no mistakes in such a wilderness?

No.—In the first place I do not rely upon the Grammarians or other authors however well approved, or precepts, or rules, or analogies, which deceive most people. In the Elenchus I take note of all inflections of root words, derivatives, compounds. Those that occur in Cicero I mark with a red mark; those that do not, with a black. So it is not possible to make a mistake.

Bu.—What if a word is found in Terence or in an equally approved author? Will it be marked with a black mark?

No.—There is no exception. A Ciceronian he will not be in whose books there is found a single little word which he cannot show in the writing of Cicero: and a man's whole vocabulary I deem spurious just like a counterfeit coin if there is in it even a single word which has not the stamp of the Ciceronian die; for to him alone, as the prince of eloquence, it has been given by the gods above to stamp the coin of Roman speech.

Bu.—The law is more severe than those of Draco, if a whole volume is condemned, however choice and eloquent it otherwise is, on account of one little word unlike Cicero's.

Hyp.—But it is fair. Do you not see that on account of one little counterfeit piece of money great wealth is confiscated, and on account of one wart, however small, the whole form of a maiden, otherwise beautiful, is robbed of charm?

Bu.—I grant it.

No.—If now from what I have said you draw a conclusion as to the whole, you will see well enough the bulk of this volume—how much larger it is than the volume in which I have gathered the formulas of speech, tropes, figures, gnomes, epiphonemas, witticisms, and all like sweet morsels of speech; or than the third volume which contains all the rhythms and feet in which Cicero begins, develops, and ends his periods. For there is no passage in all Cicero which I have not reduced to definite feet.

Bu.—This load would surely need an elephant carrier.

Hyp.—You mean a wagon.

No.—But I am not misrepresenting at all.

Bu.—Truly your seven years have not been ill spent. Now that you are finely equipped with dictionaries, ·tell us, as συμμύσταις·[1] how you are accustomed to turn this noble collection of yours to the needs of speaking and writing.

No.—I shall keep no secrets from you. And I shall speak of writing first, as it has been said truly that the pen is the best teacher of eloquence.

In the first place, I never gird myself to writing, except at dead of night when profound quiet and deep silence reign over all, or if you prefer Vergil's lines:

> [2]Placidum quun carpunt fessa soporem
> Corpora per terras, sylvaeque et saeva quierunt
> Aequora, cum medio volvuntur sidera lapsu,
> Quum tacet omnis ager, pecudes pictaeque volucres.

Or again, when there is such tranquillity that if Pythagoras were alive he could hear clearly the harmony of the celestial spheres. For at such a time the gods and goddesses delight to join in converse with pure souls.

Hyp.—At that time of night the uninitiated are afraid of meeting ghosts.

No.—But the Muses have given us power to scorn ill-omened ghosts and the carping crowd.

Bu.—Yes, but there are nights so quiet that the winds amuse themselves with falling houses and piteous ship-wrecks.

No.—I know, but I choose the perfectly tranquil nights. Ovid has aptly said: [3]*Est deus in nobis, agitante calescimus illo.* If, as I was saying, the soul of man has anything divine it comes out in this most profound silence.

Bu.—I have noticed that the seclusion of which you speak is seized upon by the most able men whenever they attempt anything worthy of immortality.

No.—I have a library in the most inmost part of my house with thick walls, double doors and windows, and all the cracks stopped carefully with pitch and plaster so that by day scarcely a ray of light can break through or a sound unless it is unusually loud such as that of women's quarrels or of workmen's hammers.

---

[1] Friends and brothers.

[2] When wearied bodies through the lands are snatching peaceful sleep: when forest and fierce seas are calm; when in the middle of their course the stars are rolled; when all the earth is silent; silent all the herds and winged things of varied hue. Vergil — Aeneid IV. 522-5.

[3] There is a divinity in us, and when he stirs our souls we glow. Ovid F. 6, 5.

Bu.—Thundering of human voices and noises of workshops certainly prevent concentration.

No.—Not even in an adjoining room do I allow a bed lest talking in sleep or snoring break in upon the privacy of my thought.

Hyp.—Frequently the shrew-mice disturb me at night when I fain would write.

No.—In my house there is not even a fly.

Bu.—You are indeed wise and fortunate as well, Nosoponus, if you can shut out also the anxieties of the mind; for, if they accompany us into our retreat, what shall we have accomplished by our seclusion?

No.—You are right, Bulephorus. I know that those turmoils are often more troublesome than the hammers of neighboring workmen.

Bu.—What about love, hate, envy, hope, fear, jealousy? Do they never trouble you?

No.—To answer briefly, always bear this in mind, Bulephorus, that those who are bound by love, jealousy, ambition, avarice, and like diseases vainly seek this honor for which we are candidates. Such a divine thing requires a heart not only free from all vice but also from all anxiety, just as do those more occult sciences—Magic, Astrology, and Alchemy. Though these lighter cares yield readily to keen and serious attention, yet I drive them away if there are any such, before I enter that sanctuary, for there I have accustomed my mind to close study. I have decided too that it is most important to remain unwed; not because I ignore the sanctity of marriage, but because a wife, children, and relatives can but bring with them much cause for anxiety.

Bu.—You are wise, Nosoponus; for if I should prepare to work on Cicero to that extent at night my wife would burst open the door, would tear the books, and would burn the pages that are absorbed in Cicero. And what is even more intolerable, while I was working on Cicero, she would find another lover.

No.—Since I know that some have had this experience, I have taken warning and have guarded myself in time. For the same reason I have not wished to undertake any public duty or ecclesiastical office, lest some anxiety should come to my mind.

Bu.—Yet these offices are sought by others most eagerly.

No.—Indeed I do not envy them. As for me, better than a consulate or rule of the pope is it to be and to be considered a Ciceronian.

Hy.—He loves truly who can love but one.

No.—In the second place, if I am preparing for anything of this kind I forego dinner, having also breakfasted lightly, lest something of crass matter should invade the seat of etherial mind or lest some cloud exhaled from the stomach should weigh down and [1]*affigat humo divinae particulam aurae.*

Bu.—Thus I believe Hesiod was affected when he wrote.

Hyp.—But [2]*Eunius ipse pater numquam nisi potus ad arma prosiliit dicenda.*

No.—And therefore he wrote songs redolent of wine.

Bu.—And [3]*satur, quum Horatius dicit Ohe.*

No.—We are not concerned with poetic frenzy. To be a Ciceronian is a sober task.

Hyp.—My brain deserts me when I fast.

No.—It is not absolutely fasting. I take ten small raisins, the kind they call currants. This is neither food nor drink and yet it is both.

Bu.—I know. They dissolve slowly and aid the brain and memory.

No.—And three coriander seeds coated with sugar.

Bu.—Excellent. To counteract the currants .

No.—And I do not choose nights indiscriminately for this work.

Bu.—No? You have excepted those on which the winds rage. Possibly you avoid winter nights on account of the cold.

No.—A glowing hearth readily dispels that discomfort.

Hyp.—But sometimes smoke and the crackling of fuel is distracting.

No.—I use wood so dry that it emits no smoke in burning.

Bu.—Well, what nights do you choose?

No.—Favorable seasons for this work are few indeed, therefore I choose auspicious nights.

---

[1] Chain to earth that particle of essence divine.   Horace Sat. 2. 2. 79.
[2] Horace Epistle 1. 19. 8
   Father Ennius ne'er caught up his lyre
   To sing of fights, till wine had lent him fire.—Martin.
[3] He is filled when Horace says Ohe!   Juvenal Sat. VII, 62.

Bu.—By what means, pray?

No.—By astrology.

Bu.—Since you are so completely engrossed in Cicero how have you leisure to learn astrology?

No.—I bought the book of an expert in this art. I act upon his advice.

Hyp.—I hear that many have been deceived by such books, because the author has reckoned wrong.

No.—I did not buy until I had examined it carefully.

Bu.—This is what writing means! Then I no longer marvel, Hypologus, that our works are crude and unpolished. But tell me, according to this rule, which is of first importance, attention to subject or to language.

No.—Both.

Bu.—You have given me a puzzle, not an answer.

No.—But I will explain the puzzle. In general, attention to subject matter is prior to thought of words; in particular, it is secondary.

Bu.—It is not quite clear what you mean.

No.—I will make it clear with an illustration. Imagine that I have decided to write to Titius asking him to see, as soon as possible, that the books are returned which I loaned, if he wishes our friendship to continue, for something has happened that I am in great need of them. If he does this, there is nothing in my possession which he may not consider his own; if not, I shall break the bond of old friendship. Here no doubt the first thought is of the facts, but in a general way.

Bu.—I see.

No.—Then follows the question of the words. I read as many letters of Cicero as possible; I consult all my lists; I select some words strikingly Ciceronian, some tropes, and phrases, and rhythms. Finally, when furnished sufficiently with this kind of material, I examine what figures of speech I can use and where I can use them. Then I return to the question of sentences. For this now is a work of art to find meanings for these verbal embellishments.

Hyp.—Just as an illustrious workman prepares an exquisite dress, necklace, rings, and gems; and afterward fashions a waxen image upon which he may fit these adornments, or rather, which he may mould to the adornments.

Bu.—Why not? But come Nosoponus, is the whole night given to one letter?

No.—Why do you say *one?* I deem myself very fortunate if a winter night shall have finished a single sentence.

Bu.—Do you write such long letters upon so trivial a subject?

No.—Not at all. Very short ones, not more than a half dozen sentences.

Bu.—And it takes six nights to finish it?

No.—As if it were enough to write just once. Ten times must you reshape what you have written, ten times test it by your dictionary lest by chance some little counterfeit word may have escaped you. Then there is still the examination of tropes and phrases and, lastly, of rhythms and style.

Bu.—No wonder it is a task to finish your work.

No.—Not even is this enough, my dear sir; for, since the finished work is your greatest possible anxiety, it must be laid aside for several days so that after an interval, when the love of invention has grown cold, you may cull, as it were, the barbarisms which are your own. Here then a severe censorship is exercised. This is a severe, and, as the Greeks say ἀδέκαζον[1]· judgment, when he who writes ceases to be a parent and becomes an Areopagite. Here it often happens that you turn your pen and erase everything.

Bu.—It is true that in this way your books show the result of great care but in the meantime the other type of writer enjoys some books which you have not.

No.—This inconvenience I should prefer to submit to rather than to send forth anything which is not Ciceronian. Each one is led by his own judgment. I prefer quality to quantity.

Bu.—We have your theory of writing. What preparation do you make for speaking?

No.—The first precaution is, not to converse in Latin if I can help it.

Bu.—Not in Latin? Yet they say that by practice we learn to speak well. It is a new plan to learn to speak by keeping silent.

No.—By speaking we come to speak readily but never to speak Ciceronian Latin. Those who prepare themselves for equestrian contest keep the blooded horses from the course

---

[1] Unbribed.

that they may come to race with unimpaired strength. The hunter keeps back the high-bred dog till the game is seen. French or Dutch is good enough for babbling about trifles. In common and profane conversations I' do not contaminate the sacred tongue. But, if I am compelled to speak in Latin, I speak briefly and carefully. And for this purpose I have some set phrases.

Bu.—What phrases do you mean?

No.—For example, when you must greet or return the greeting of a learned friend whom you chance to meet; or you must compliment one who has complimented you; or must congratulate one who has returned from a long trip abroad or recovered from a serious illness; or must thank someone who has done you a favor; or congratulate one who has recently married; or condole with one whose wife has died,—for these and like occasions I have provided myself with phrases selected and arranged from Cicero. I have learned them so that I may use them, as it were, *ex tempore*. Then if an occasion arises that the conversation must be extended further, by much reading I wash away the taint. And I am not unaware how great a wrong I am committing through this very conversation which is being held with you, how great a loss I am sustaining in the matter of my ambition. Indeed a month's reading will hardly make amends.

Bu.—Suppose you have time for meditation?

No.—Then I learn carefully what has been worked out in this way; and, in order that I may remember better, I repeat them to myself so that when occasion arises I may pronounce them as if from the written word.

Bu.—What if some exigency should demand an extemporaneous speech?

No.—How can that happen to one who has no public life? But if I should have occasion I am not better than Demosthenes, who would never get up unless he had prepared himself however much he was called by the shouts of the people. And I could not think that I need be ashamed of what is praised in the chief orator among the Greeks or that I should be sorry for the censure if any one should say τὸν λύχνον ἀπόζειν·[1]

---

[1] That my language was bookish.

Bu.—I admire your purpose and your determination more than I can tell. Indeed, I should feel envy if in this kind of enterprise or among such fast friends and companions such misfortune could befall. But inasmuch as what we seek is arduous and the way is not only long and difficult but doubtful, even if the danger were peculiarly your own, nevertheless I should think it due to our long and intimate friendship that I advise my friend unreservedly: lest he undertake so many cares and spend many wakeful hours with loss of health and property to no purpose; lest he continue to do this when once he has begun; and lest, as too frequently we see happen in human affairs, instead of a treasure long and diligently sought he find only charcoal at last. And since we all are led by the same desire and are held by the love of the same nymph (for even Hypologus is of the same mind) it will be an act of kindness on your part to listen to our advice and, if you have anything better, to suggest it freely to your friends.

No.—A very reasonable thing, Bulephorus. Therefore I shall neither listen to you unwillingly nor if I can give any advice shall I make the contribution grudgingly.

Bu.—In the first place this is agreed between us, I think, that he who seeks a reputation for writing or speaking, having learned and mastered carefully the rules of his art, must choose from the many noted writers a master whom he will imitate and whom he will set himself to reproduce.

No.—Yes.

Bu.—But there is no one at least among the Romans who excels in more points of eloquence than Cicero of whom with perfect right it has been said, as was said of Apelles, "In him alone was fused whatever was extraordinary or singular in other painters."

No.—Who can deny this?

Bu.—You will pardon me if I draw my conclusions rather crassly and roughly, for I am unversed in logic.

No.—Anything goes among friends. And yet in general he reasons acutely enough for me who reasons truly.

Bu.—Well, what then do you think of Zeuxis of Heraclea?

No.—What else than what is worthy of the most excellent draughtsman?

Bu.—And this, for you think him to have great talent and wisdom?

No.—How could so great skill be without wisdom?

Bu.—You answer well. What idea then occurred to him when about to paint the picture of Helen for the inhabitants of Crotona —a picture in which he determined to put all the power of his art and to bring forth a perfect and lifelike example of womanly beauty (for in this kind of work he is said to have excelled others) in which no portion of charm would be missing? He did not use as a model the most beautiful woman, but from all who offered themselves to him he chose several who were more excellent than the rest in order that he might select from each what was most comely, and thus at last he completed that wonderful monument of his art.

No.—His work was most carefully done.

Bu.—Consider then whether we are following the right plan when we think we must seek our model of eloquence from Cicero alone, however excellent he may be.

No.—If Zeuxis had found a virgin of such beauty as Cicero, perhaps he would have been content with one single model.

Bu.—Yet in what way could he have reached this very decision, if he had not carefully examined many?

No.—Believe me. I am firm.

Bu.—You think then that there is no virtue worthy of imitation in other orators not found in the highest degree in Cicero?

No.—Yes.

Bu.—And that there is no blemish in him which is not greater in others?

No.—Exactly so.

Bu.—In this connection I will not cite [1]Marcus Brutus, who disagreed entirely with Cicero; for, although the main contention of the defense and the propositions of the division are the pillars, as it were, of the case and the chief part of the argument in *Pro Milone,* which we all so admire, Brutus disapproved of the first and second points employed by Cicero, and handled the same case in a different way. I will not cite [2]Pomponius Atticus, whose finger nails and red pencil Cicero says he feared. I will not cite Cato who called Cicero ridiculous when he thought

---

[1]Quintilian Inst. Or. III. c. 6. & XII. c. 1.
[2]Ep. Ad Atticum XV, 14, & XVI, 11.

himself most witty. Thus far I have mentioned men who are of importance and friends of Cicero. If I add Gallus, Lartius, Licinius, Cestius, Calvus, Asinius, Caelius, Seneca too, and many others, who not only have not felt deeply enough the genius of Cicero but have even condemned his kind of oratory— some calling him dry, jejune, sapless, bloodless, disjointed, weak and unmanly; others, bombastic, Asiatic, and redundant—you will say that these are judgments either of enemies or of jealous persons who, exiled by proscription of the triumvirate, have sought if not to destroy, at least to dull his fame.

No.—You divine rightly. For I certainly should have given this very answer and I think it would have been perfectly fair.

Bu.—Although these judgments may be attributed to hate and envy, you will surely acknowledge that with all scholars wit is a part of the rhetorical art.

No.—If not, why should orators lay so much stress upon it?

Bu.—No one denies that Cicero indulged much in joking. Some say too much, even out of season and almost bordering upon scurrility. Certainly a great majority of scholars hold that in this he lacked moderation just as Demosthenes lacked ability; nor does [1]Quintilian exonerate him when he puts the blame on Tiro, who allowed the number of Cicero's *bon mots* to become far too large and who showed more zeal in collecting than wisdom in selecting them. In fact, this criticism of Tiro falls back upon his patron. But, however this may be, did any one ever in point of wit give the first rank to Cicero? Wit was the peculiar gift of the Spartans and after them of the natives of Attica. It was so exclusively theirs, that, when the pastoral poem and comedy was most highly praised for its grace and wit, the Romans did not even aspire to it. There is, therefore, some oratorical excellence which is more rightly sought from others than from Cicero.

No.—We are speaking of the Romans.

Bu.—Well, do we dare to compare the jokes of Cicero with those of Caius Caesar or of Octavius Caesar?

No.—Hardly would I dare what no scholar has dared.

Bu.—Well then, if the theme should demand mirth, it would not be right for me to borrow from the wit of Octavius?

No.—Not if you wish to be a Ciceronian.

---

[1]Inst. Orator. VI, c. 3.

Bu.—Again, may I ask whether you class moral reflections among ornaments of speech?

No.—Gems they are and shining lights. Far be it from me to exclude them from art.

Bu.—My next question. Do you think Cicero excelled all others in these reflections?

No.—I know that [1]Seneca ranked Publius [2]Mimographus first in this; but it does not follow that Seneca's estimate is true, for he is extravagant and indulges in certain foibles.

Hy.—You mean to say that the judgment of Quintilian and of Aulus Gellius could be disregarded because they both seemed jealous of Seneca; one on account of rivalry, the other on account of likeness in talent and diction?

Bu.—Yes, but this same Gellius, even granting him unfair, acknowledges that among Seneca's reflections there were some which could not be surpassed,—and one could not expect all to be equally good when the whole work is made up of them. Truly from Seneca's reflections you can find something to imitate more easily than from others where maxims are neither frequent nor striking. But tell me, does a subject sometimes demand brevity?

No.—Perhaps.

Bu.—Will you seek the best example of this from Sallust or Brutus or Cicero?

No.—Cicero has not striven after brevity.

Bu.—In Demosthenes forcefulness is praised, that is, something vigorous and natural. From which of the two shall we seek this most properly?

No.—We are speaking of the Romans.

Bu.—But these are common points of all languages. Again, sometimes the subject demands austerity. Shall we seek this more rightly from Cicero or Brutus and Pollio?

Hyp.—If I may answer for my friend here, from the latter who are distinguished for this characteristic.

Bu.—When the case is involved, when it must be set forth in divisions, shall we go to Cicero or to Hortensius and his school?

---

[1]Epis. VIII & Cap. IX ad Marciam & Cap. XI. de Tranquill.
[2]Writer of mimes.

No.—Why shall we go to one of whom there is nothing left but a memory?

Bu.—But for the sake of the argument let us imagine that his works are extant.

No.—There is no need of imagining. Let us deal with the known and the true.

Bu.—Everyone will acknowledge that trustworthiness in an orator is the chief thing. A reputation for honesty and serious-mindedness gains this, while a suspicion of artfulness and lack of moderation lessens it. While Cicero may be considered a good man—a thing which Fabius, though a strong partisan of his, hardly dares to allow; yet we must admit that he makes a greater display of his skill, boasts more, and inveighs more freely against others than Cato, Brutus, or Caelius to whom Quintilian ascribes conscientiousness. Do we not then more properly seek an example of these things from Aristides, Phocion, Cato, or Brutus than from Cicero?

No.—One would think you had come to this conclusion by studying how to disparage Cicero.

Bu.—By no means. If you will wait the end of my speech, you will see that I am pleading Cicero's case along with our own. For Cicero I am pleading that we may not obscure his glory by imitating him badly as unskilled painters are wont to dishonor those whose portraits they have made quite different from the originals; for ourselves, that we may not misplace our affection and fall upon something as ridiculous and unfortunate as is said to have happened to Ixion who embraced an unsubstantial cloud instead of his beloved Juno, or to Paris who for stolen Helen waged war ten years, all the while embracing a counterfeit image of Helen, while she herself, no doubt, had been carried far away to Egypt by the cunning gods. For what is more unfortunate for us or more ridiculous if nothing results from all our toil except a false and empty shadow of Cicero?

No.—God forbid!

Bu.—Such is my prayer and I am doing all I can to prevent it.

No.—It is helpful in our imitation of Cicero to hold the highest possible opinion of him.

Bu.—It is a new standard of truth, however, if we think of Cicero better than he thinks of himself. Grant that it may be attributed to his modesty if he speak disparagingly of himself.

Yet did any one of the ancients ever so admire Cicero that he thought all ornaments of speech ought to be sought from him alone?

No.—Perhaps not, but today very many think so.

Bu.—I care not at all for your *very many*. I do not believe that any one person is all wise. Has nature yet favored any mortal even in a given field so that he alone excels all others in each particular division; that he has left nothing to be desired; or that he has accomplished so much that he could not be excelled by others? How much more incredible is this in oratory which involves practically all fields of study, which demands many things that cannot be reduced to rules! Let us imagine Cicero alive today and also some such one as [1]Trachallus. Would you prefer to seek modulation from Cicero or from Trachallus? I think from the one who was master of all in this particular. Would you prefer to seek a pattern of propriety and modesty from Crassus, if he were alive, or from Cicero? In general, would you not take from each that in which each excelled?

Hyp.—Who, except the indiscriminating or envious, would not choose the better?

Bu.—Therefore the example of Zeuxis commands my approval, and of Quintilian who taught that not just one model must be chosen nor yet all nor any at random but some few choice ones, among whom he gave Cicero first but not sole rank; for he wished him to be foremost among the masters but not alone.

No.—If we give ear to the counsels of Quintilian we shall share his experience.

Bu.—What pray?

No.—That we shall fall short of the Ciceronian standard. We aim higher than that.

Bu.—Will he fail to be Ciceronian who has something more than what he has gotten from Cicero?

No.—So they say.

Bu.—Even if what he gets from someone else is better or is not in Cicero?

No.—Why not?

---

[1] See Quintilian X, 1, 119.

Bu.—In passing I would have you consider, most excellent Nosoponus, what proportion of Cicero's books have perished, among which is that divine work, *De Republica,* a fragment of which by some fate or other preserved torments our souls with a constant desire for the other volumes and allows us to judge the lion, as they say, by the claws—not to mention, for the moment, the many volumes of letters, the many orations stolen by the waste of time, the three volumes in which Cicero's freedman Tiro is said to have gathered his jokes and clever sayings, and the utter loss of his other writings   How then can you be a perfect Ciceronian who have not read so many of his works? Add that Cicero has not handled all subjects.   If, therefore, we are compelled to speak on themes which he has not touched, where, pray, shall we seek a store of phrases?   Shall we go forth into the Elysian fields to ask him in what words he would have described such things?

No.—Those themes only will I handle which can be expressed in the words of Cicero.

Bu.—Well, do you not think that Cicero is the most excellent of orators?

No.—By far.

Bu.—And Apelles?   Is he not the best of painters?

No.—People say so and I believe it.

Bu.—Would you call him an Apellean who could paint pictures only from studies which Apelles had painted before, and who also had not seen all the pictures which had been painted by the hand of Apelles?

Hyp.—Who would say this except perchance that painter of Horace's jest, who being hired to paint a shipwreck painted a cypress and asked his patron, who expressed indignation, whether he wished to be painted clinging to the cypress?

Bu.—What else is Ciceronianism except something exactly like this?

No.—It is nothing else.

Bu.—Does he seem like Cicero who can speak only on a limited number of subjects?

No.—Go on.

Bu.—He would be considered in my mind unworthy of the title even of orator.   If Cicero was able to speak most excellently upon any subject you please, he to me would be a Ciceronian who could discourse skillfully upon any theme whatever; just as he would be an Apellean who could portray with his brush the forms of gods and men and of living things.

No.—For my part I deem it a greater accomplishment to write three letters in Ciceronian style than a hundred volumes in any other as polished as you please.

Bu.—But if this idea is definitely fixed in our minds, I fear not only we shall not become Ciceronians, but we shall even seem strangers to Cicero. Tell me, I pray, truly, do you think that Cicero must be imitated in every point or in part?

No.—In every point as far as he goes and wholly.

Bu.—How can we imitate him completely when he has not expressed himself completely? Furthermore, how mutilated he is and scarcely half extant in that field in which he has accomplished most! And in the very works which are extant he has not always satisfied himself. For he, as it were, condemned *De Inventione* and substituted *De Oratore.* And he calls the oration in behalf of Dejotarus a poor work. And again, in those books which he merely wrote and did not even revise Cicero himself was not a Ciceronian,—for example, *De Legibus* and many others. How then can we take him for our only example who is mutilated and abridged and sometimes uncorrected and unnatural? Unless perchance you are going to approve of one who, by imitating the unfinished canvasses of Apelles or the rough statues of Lysippus, would hope to become a second Apelles or Lysippus. If Apelles himself, who they say was a man of frank and independent mind, of free and splendid genius, should see this, would he not exclaim. "What are you doing Κακόξηλε·[1] This is not Apelles." If one had before him as a model an illustrious statue of Lysippus whose mouth and chin was rust-eaten or unfinished, would he, unwilling to take the pattern of this part from some other workman, think it better to imitate a disfigured and imperfect face than to give up the model to which he had devoted himself and supply what was lacking from the statue of another workman?

No.—"As we can," the adage runs, "since we may not as we will."

Bu.—That adage would be better quoted by those, Nosoponus, who make good from other writers the deficiencies of Cicero;

[1] Miserable imitator.

for they, though they would prefer to follow him alone either because it is easier or because no one speaks more happily than he, borrow from others when necessary. How can we gainsay the fact that Cicero's works, as we have them, are not only so mutilated but also so distorted that if he should come to life, I venture he would not recognize his own writings nor could he restore those which have been corrupted by the boldness, carelessness and ignorance of copyists and pseudo-scholars (mostly Teutons according to Politian, but while I am unwilling to defend them, yet at the same time I think just as many blunders have been made by certain bold Italian sciolists), not to mention for the moment, the forgeries and works claiming Cicero as author under false title. Of this class are the four books on rhetoric dedicated to Herennius, the work of a man by no means learned and a stammerer in comparison with Cicero. And there are among Cicero's orations some which do not seem to have been written by him, but by some scholar for the sake of practice in oratory. There has been added recently an oration, *Pro M. Valerio,* which is actually full of solecisms and utterly unlike Cicero. Some read the declamation of Porcius Latro against Catiline as a speech of Cicero's. Then if we with devoted minds dedicate ourselves to Cicero alone, intending to express whatever we find without regard to choice, shall we not find ourselves in the greatest danger, after long and earnest exertion, of appropriating and imitating only Gothic words and Teuton solecisms instead of Ciceronian flowerets?

No.—May the Muses avert that ill!

Bu.—I fear that this may happen to us often while the Muses sleep, Nosoponus. For more than once have we seen this sport. How often have they who thought themselves Ciceronians laughed at a fragment culled from Cicero with the title of some German added and called it a barbarian's work! Or, when something composed only the day before was brought out with the name of Cicero attached and pretence made that an original had been found in a very old library, how they have worshipped! How they have adored the divine and inimitable phrasing of Cicero! What about the fact too that scholars admit there are inexcusable blunders in Cicero's writings, such as have been made by learned men in all times, when, absorbed in their subject, they remember rather the preceding thought than the words and thus it happens that the close of the period does not agree with the beginning? As, for example, in *Diutius commorans Athenis, quoniam venti negabant solvendi facultatem, erat animus ad te scribere,* the writer first thought *volebam* or *statueram,* then afterward *in animo erat* was more pleasing; and, though the words made the same sense, yet they fitted poorly with those which preceded. Further, Aulus Gellius cites a passage from the second book of Cicero's *De Gloria,* in which plainly there is a mistake, assigning some verses from Homer's Iliad to Ajax when there they are spoken by Hector. Shall we try to imitate this too? We must if we imitate him in every point. Once more, there is a tradition that Cicero has said some things which scholars have thought ought not to be imitated; for example, *in potestatem esse,* instead of *in potestate esse.* It is of course possible that a slip of the pen or some other mishap in writing made that *tem* for *te* in the original or that the lazy scribe introduced it in the later manuscripts. Again, in the edict of Marc Antony Cicero condemns as a barbarism, unheard of by the Romans, the word [1]*piissimus* from *pius,* though this word is found in the most approved authors. He likewise criticised as a solecism Antony's use of the phrase [2]*facere contumeliam* just as we say *facere injuriam,* although in Terence—the best representative, if I mistake not, of polished Latinity—Thais speaks thus: *Nam si ego digna hac contumelia sim maxime, at tu indignus qui faceres tamen,* where, I think, *contumeliam* is understood to be repeated. Likewise he refrained from using the words [3]*novissime* and *novissimus,* on the ground that they were poor Latin, though Cato and Sallust did not hesitate to employ them. Aulus Gellius bears witness of Cicero's dislike of this word and many others which were often used by good Latin authors both before and after him. And he is said to have written *ss* whenever a long vowel preceded, as in *caussa, visse, remissi* for *causa, vise, remisi.* Shall we then, following Cicero exactly, refrain from those things which pleased scholars but did not please Cicero or follow those which no scholar would imitate or could excuse?

Hyp.—It is, to be sure, a characteristic of lovers to kiss the blemishes of those they love.

[1]Philipp. XIII, c. 19.
[2]Philipp. III, c. 9.
[3]Aulus Gellius X, c. 21.

Bu.—If he is to be copied exactly, shall we write verses after his example, without the aid of Apollo and the Muses?

No.—I make exception of verse.

Bu.—You surely make exception of a good part of his stock when you except verse. What hinders our making use of this exception at least where he is excelled by others, as in this whole field he is inferior to many, not to say all? How many quotations does he use from Homer, Sophocles, Euripides, poorly translated, in iambic verse, contrary to the practice of the Greeks, and with a freedom which Latin writers of comedy have permitted themselves. If you should wish to do something of the same sort would you fear to make a better and more literal translation, lest you be too unlike Cicero? And does he not mar his prose by mingling with it verses of his own translation that fail to harmonize with the rest of the language? Furthermore, since he constantly inserts in his books verses from Ennius, Naevius, Pacuvius, and Lucilius which smack of that uncouth and uncultured antiquity, will it be a point of honor with you to quote like verses, or rather I should say unlike verses, from Vergil, Horace, Ovid, Lucan, or Persius, whose works have as much less crudeness as they have more elegance and erudition? Do you fear in this to seem unlike Cicero?

No.—Of course we shall vary a little from the model we are trying to reproduce.

Bu.—But why is it necessary to imitate exactly and always, when often it is better to rival and sometimes easier to surpass?

No.—I think that even the Muses themselves will never speak better than Cicero.

Hyp.—Perhaps they could if they tried very hard, writing at night, supperless, near a small lamp.

Bu.—Do not get excited, I beg of you, Nosoponus; for I stipulated, once for all, the right to say with impunity what I pleased. When one is as devoted and pledged to Cicero as we are now, is there not danger that one, blind with love, will mistake faults for virtues, or knowingly will portray even his very faults?

No.—Ἡράκλεις![1] Faults in Cicero!

Bu.—Yes, unless perchance a solecism is a fault in others and not in Cicero; for, as we have said, scholars have pointed out

[1]Hercules!

solecisms in his books. Or unless a slip of memory is not a fault, which too has been pointed out by scholars. Or unless it is not a fault to annoy one's client with immoderate mention of one's own praises, which Asconius Pedianus declares was done in *Pro Milone;* and which was almost always a source of annoyance in Cicero because of his desire, as Seneca most aptly says, of [1]*non sine causa, sed sine fine glorians.* And I do not know in which he was the more intemperate—in boasting of himself or in censuring others. With whatever zeal we may defend these characteristics, we shall not be able to deny that at least in this respect a better model can be found.

No.—Let us leave off talking of personal characteristics and revert to the discussion of strength and beauty of speech.

Bu.—I should gladly do so if the rhetoricians did not declare that one cannot be a good orator who is not also a good man. But reverting, does it not seem to you to be faulty composition for a word following another to begin with the same syllables with which the preceding ended, as it were, carrying back a mocking echo; for example, if you should say, *ne mihi dona donata, ne voces referas feras, ne per imperitos scribas scribas Basso?*

No.—I grant that the collocation is foolish and absurd.

Bu.—But such is quoted from our beloved Cicero: [2]*O fortunatam natam me Consule Roman.*

No.—I have already once made exception of his poetry.

Bu.—In my way of thinking, when once you except this you except the whole of Cicero. But you have not yet escaped. Quintilian quotes for you from Cicero's prose as perfect a collocation, *Res mihi invisae visae sunt Brute*—or if you prefer to pronounce after the fashion of Cicero, *invissae sunt*—not to do injustice to the two molossi in the close of the sentence.

No.—That was in a familiar letter.

Bu.—I do not object to it. I only ask if you think it ought to be imitated. Certainly you will acknowledge that some better phrasing could be made.

No.—Perhaps.

Bu.—Do I recall something in this connection about the clashing of vowels which renders speech open and disagreeable? Has

---

[1]Boasting not without reason but without end. De brevitate vitae, Cap. V.
[2]Quintilian IX, c. 4. Inst. Orator.

not this too been marked by scholars in Cicero? He was indifferent, you say. I do not deny it, but let us acknowledge
that there is something in other writers different or better. And
let me inquire, what writer have you known so alert and so
fortunate that he has never been caught napping at any point?

No.—Why not? They are men.

Bu.—Among men then you number Cicero?

No.—Sometimes.

Bu.—Do you then consider it better to imitate Cicero napping
than Sallust or Brutus or Caesar awake?

Hyp.—Who would not prefer to copy one awake?

Bu.—Did not Vergil imitate Homer, though he corrected many
of his faults? Did he not imitate Hesiod so that he sometimes
excelled him? Did not Horace imitate the Greek lyric poets,
culling from each one what was most beatuiful and thus surpassing them all? [1]*"Ego,"* he says, *"apis Matinae More
modoque Grata carpentis thyma per laborem Plurimum, circa
nemus, uvidique Tiburis ripas, operosa parvus Carmina fingo."*
And did he not imitate Lucilius, consciously omitting certain
things and designedly taking from others what was more worthy
of imitation? Need I mention others? Did Cicero himself draw
his marvelous fluency from any one model, or rather did he not
by sifting equally together Greek and Latin philosophers, historians, rhetoricians, comic, tragic, and lyric poets, weave and
finish that divine style of his? If it behooves us to imitate Cicero
in every point, why shall we not imitate this example too?

Hyp.—Bulephorus is speaking sense, Nosoponus.

Bu.—What of this? Did not Cicero himself teach that the
height of art was to conceal art? [2]*" Friget enim, et fide caret, ac
velut insidiosa timetur oratis, quae significationem artis dedit.
Quis enim ab eo non metuat, qui fucum et vim parat animis
nostris?"* And so if we should want to imitate Cicero successfully,
the fact that we are imitating must carefully be hidden. But he
who never departs from Cicero's lines, who follows him in words,
figures, rhythms, imitating things unworthy of imitation, as the
pupils of Plato imitated their teacher by contracting their
shoulders, as the disciples of Aristotle copied a sort of stutter-

---

[1] "I", he says, "as a Matine bee culling the liquid from the pleasing thyme wearily mid
groves and on the banks of the tawny Tiber, a tiny minstrel, fashion toilsome lays."

[2] For speech is unconvincing and untrustworthy, and shunned as dangerous, which
makes a show of art. Who would not shrink from one who tries to deceive?

ing which he is reputed to have had—will he ever, for the very reason that he shows plainly his desire to imitate, have the credit of speaking his mind or gain any reputation? He may be as fortunate as writers of centos who please perhaps for a little while and only the idlers, but who do not teach or move or persuade. This is his highest praise, "He understands Vergil well, he has fashioned a mosaic with such care."

No.—The more manifest the imitation, the more I shall be regarded a Ciceronian. This is my greatest wish.

Bu.—You are right, if we are seeking eloquence for display, not for use. But there is a very great difference between an actor and an orator. The one needs only to please, the other desires also to profit, provided he is a good man; and if he is not good, he cannot claim the name of orator. Already I have shown, I think, that some things in Cicero ought not to be imitated, that some are wanting, and that some are not as good as can be found in more successful authors. But let us grant that there is no kind of embellishment in which he does not either rival or surpass others: to be sure in some authors one beauty, in others another stands out more prominently on account of its rare occurrence, while in Cicero these are lost in the wealth of ornamentation, just as you will find more easily a certain star which you seek, if the stars are far apart than if the whole sky is studded, or as the individual gems on a garment will impress you less, if you see an entire garment covered with gems.

No.—He who absolutely absorbs all of Cicero can give forth nothing but Cicero.

Bu.—We come back to the same point. I will acknowledge him eloquent who copies Cicero successfully; but he must copy him as a whole and his very faults too. I will put up with that suggestion of emptiness, that stroking of the chin with the left hand, the long and thin neck, the continual straining of the voice, the unbecoming and unmanly nervousness as he begins to speak, the excessive number of jokes, and everything else which in Cicero is displeasing to himself or to others, provided only he copy those other traits too by which he concealed these or compensated for them.

No.—I hope that I may attain this before I die.

Bu.—That is just what I am trying to do, Nosoponus. You see how much he covers in how few words who speaks of Cicero in his entirety. But O Muses! how little of Cicero do those apes bring us, who show us only the surface, or rather the veneer of Cicero by a few words, phrases, tropes, and endings of periods, collected here and there. In this way, formerly, certain ones tried to reproduce the Attic style of oratory; but it mattered not that they were dry, jejune, cold, and always, as the saying is, held their hand under their mantles; they could never in any degree attain either the simplicity, the saneness, or the grace of the writers of the Attic school. With perfect justice [1]Quintilian ridicules those who wished to be considered Cicero's own brothers because they ended a period several times with the words, *esse videatur*—a phrase repeatedly used by Cicero whenever the period was rather elaborately developed, especially in the opening sentences of his early works. And a good many now are very proud and count themselves, as they say, second Ciceros, if the first word of the oration is *quamquam* or *etsi* or *animadverti* or *quum* or *si,* because Cicero begins his *De Officiis* with *Quamquam te Marce fili,* and takes full nine lines for the first sentence; his *Pro lege Manilia* with *Quamquam mihi semper;* that much praised speech, *Pro Milone,* with *Et si vereor, judices;* the twelfth Philippic with *Etsi minime decere videtur;* and also the *Pro C. Rabirio* with *Etsi Quirites;* and several letters in the same way. Probably these persons attribute to Cicero the work dedicated to Herennius because the book begins with *Etsi.* The fifth book of *De Finibus* begins *Quum audivissem Antiochum, Brute.* The *Tusculanae Quaestiones* begin *Quum defensionum laboribus;* and the fourth book of the same work, *Quum multis in locis nostrorum hominum ingenia.* *Pro L. Flacco* begins *Quum in maximis periculis.* Likewise *Pro Domo suo ad Pontifices* begins *Quum multa divinitus.* Again *Pro Plancio, quum propter egregiam.* The first book of *De Natura Deorum, Quum multae res in Philosophia;* and the *Scipionis Somnium, Quum Multae res in Africa.* *Pro Rabirio, Animadverti, judices.* Again *Ad Brutus de Paradoxis Stoicorum, Animadverti, Brute.* *Pro L. Cornelio Balbo* begins *Si auctoritas patronorum; Pro Publio Sestio, Si quis antea judices; Pro Caecinna, Si quantum in agro; Pro Archia Poeta, Si quid est in me ingenii; In Vatinium*

---

[1]Inst. Orator. X, c. 2.

Testem, Si tua tantummodo Vatini; " To the Knights when he was on the point of going into exile," *Si quando inimicorum;* " To the Senate, after his return," *Si P. C. vestris; Pro Marco Caelio, Si quis judices; De Provinciis Consularibus, Si quis vestrum, P. C.* What could be more ridiculous and more unlike Cicero than to confine the introduction of a speech to such words as these! If any one should ask Cicero why he began with these words, he would, I think, make the same reply that in the Blessed Isles Homer made to Lucian's query as to why he began the Iliad with the word μῆνιν (for this question had troubled Grammarians for many ages). [1]" Because," said Homer, " that word at the moment happened to occur to me " Of like effrontery are those who think themselves ultra Ciceronians because at different times they prop themselves on these phrases: *etiam atque etiam* used for *vehementer; majorum in modum* for *valde; indentidem* for *subinde; quum* and *tum* whenever there are things of unequal weight to join, *tum* and *tum* when equal; *tuorum in me meritorum. Quid quaeris* for *in summa* or *breviter;* and *Non solum peto, verum etiam oro contendoque. Ante hac dilexisse tantum, nunc etiam amare mihi videor. Valetudinem tuam cura, et me, ut facis, ama. Non ille quidem vir malus, sed parum diligens,* in which last phrase Cicero seemed so to delight that you may find it repeatedly on the same page. Likewise when by the pronoun *illud* he indicates not what precedes but what soon follows. And if perchance in his letters Cicero has said occasionally, *cogitabam in Tusculanum,* then he considers himself a Ciceronian who repeatedly says, *Romam cogitabam,* instead of what he means, *in animo habebam* or *statueram proficisci Romam.*

Cicero does not date his letters by the year, only by the day of the month. Then a person will not be a Ciceronian, will he, if he dates the year from the birth of Christ, which is often necessary and always useful? These same persons do not permit one, as a courtesy, to put the name of the one to whom he writes before his own; for example, *Carolo Caesari Codrus Urceus salutum.* And they consider it as great a fault if one adds to a proper name any word of dignity or honor, as " Velius greets Ferdinand the Great, King of Pannonia and Bohemia." They cannot pardon Pliny the Younger because he uses the word *suum* in addressing a letter to a friend, simply because no example of

---

[1]Verae Historiae II.

4

this kind is extant in Cicero. They refuse the title to one who follows the model which some scholars have borrowed from *The Duties of Princes* and have recently begun to adopt; viz, to place at the beginning the main point of the letter which they are preparing to answer, because this has never been done by Cicero. I have known some to be criticised as guilty of a solecism because instead of S. D. in the salutation they placed S. P. D., that is, *salutem plurimam dicit,* which was said not to be in Cicero. And some think that even this little thing is Ciceronian, to put the salutation on the back of the letter instead of the front because the carrier is thus told without omitting the courtesy of salutation which letter he is to deliver to each person. Such a little thing causes us to lose the palm of glory? Indeed far from a Ciceronian is he who uses in the salutation this formula, *Hilarius Bertulphus, Levino Panagatho totius hominis salutem, aut salutem perpetuam;* and farther the one who begins his letter *Gratia, pax, et misericordia a Deo Patre, et Domino Jesu Christo* or instead of *cura ut recte valeas,* closes it with *Sospitet te Dominus Jesus* or *Incolumen te servet Dominus totius salutis auctor.* What peals of laughter, what jeers would the Ciceronians raise at this! And what offence? Are they not Latin words, beautiful, well-sounding, even splendid? If you should consider the sense, how much more there is in them than in *Salutem dicit* and *bene vale?* A master shows this courtesy to a slave, an enemy to an enemy. But who would regard *dicit illi salutem* and *jubet illum salvere* as good Latin if it were not Classic usage? This, at the beginning of the letter. Now, at the close, we say *vale* even to those whom we wish ill. How much more significance in the phrases used by Christians, provided we are true Christians! *Gratia* implies the voluntary giving up of wrongs done; *pax,* quiet and joy of conscience because God is gracious; *misercordia,* varying gifts of body and mind with which the kindness of the mysterious Spirit enriches his own, and when we wish to express our hope more clearly that these may be lasting we add *A 'Deo Patre et Domino nostro Jesu Christo.* When you hear Father you lay aside servile fear, admitted into the love of the Son; when you hear Lord, you grow strong against the strength of Satan. Nor will he desert you, because he has purchased you so dearly and he alone is more powerful than all the cohorts of Satan. What sweeter than these words to one who feels that these blessings are already his! What more useful than this admonition to one who has not yet entered into this love! And so while in choice of words we are not surpassed, but rather surpass; in sense we far excel. There remains to be considered the element of beauty and fitness which is most desirable. And how much more these modern phrases suit the Christian than the *salutem dicit* and *cura ut valeas* of the Romans!

But you say, "Away with these childish imaginations, for Cicero did not use such phrases." What wonder he did not when he did not know them! How many thousands of things there are in our every day conversation of which Cicero did not even dream? But if he were alive he would use the same phrases. Are we not indifferent imitators if we copy Cicero by the observance of such trivial things as rhythms, tropes, phrases, which pleased Cicero or fell frequently from his lips and neglect so many excellent qualities? Perhaps these things do not interest you, Nosoponus, but, inasmuch as we happened to be talking of imitators of Cicero, it did not seem amiss to speak of them. Such people ought to be equally distasteful to us and to Cicero: because we who are trying to be Ciceronians are drawn by them into jest and gossip and are rated by their stupidity; while Cicero, as we have said before, is dishonored by such imitators just as a good teacher is dishonored by bad pupils or a reputable man by unprincipled children or a beautiful woman by a poor artist. Quintilian understood this when he [1]complained that Seneca was being dishonored by the immoderate zeal of those who imitated merely his faults, causing people who had not read Seneca to judge of him by their writings. Just as none boast more of their teachers and ancestors than the poor pupils and wayward sons, grasping at a reputation from any source since they cannot win it through their own good qualities; so none exult more immoderately in the name of Cicero than those who are most unlike him. I have known physicians markedly unskilled in the art they professed, in order to increase their income, to boast that they were pupils of some celebrated doctor whom they had scarcely seen; and, when asked why contrary to medical practice they gave this or that to a patient, would answer roughly, "Are you more learned than so and so? He is my authority." And yet they imitate practically nothing except

---

[1]Inst. Orator. X, c. 1.

what ought to be avoided; as for instance, too great sternness and peevishness in answering questioners or too much severity in exacting pay. What feelings do you think that illustrious physician would have toward such pupils?

Hyp.—No doubt he would be very bitter, unless he had absolutely no regard for his reputation.

Bu.—What feelings would the real and genuine pupils of the same doctor have?

Hyp.—Just as bitter, because they would suffer the same reputation as this boastful imposter had established. But if you will permit me to interrupt, I will give you an illustration of this.

Bu.—Certainly.

Hyp.—Some one happens to see Erasmus writing with a reed pen to which is fastened a piece of wood; he begins at once to fasten a stick to his pen and thinks he is writing in the style of Erasmus. But go on.

Bu.—What you say is well said and to the point. But I will resume. Do we not hear fathers scolding their ill-mannered sons, "You disgrace me in the eyes of my fellow-citizens; you have dimmed the images of your ancestors; I am ashamed of such children; if you go on I shall disown you?" Do we not in like manner sometimes hear a man, angry at his brother, declaring that his reputation is injured by the brother's wicked ways? Cicero no doubt feels the same toward his ridiculous apes, and so ought we who desire to be considered γνήσια τέκνα.[1]

No.—In a matter so splendid to be even a shadow is worth while.

Bu.—It may be something worth while for those who are satisfied to be called shadows of Cicero, but I have no desire to be called a shadow even of Apollo. I should prefer to be a living Crassus than a shadow of Cicero. But to return, suppose we assume that some one does copy Cicero exactly in words, figures, rhythms (which thing itself I doubt if many can do), how much will he have of Cicero? Suppose he is as good in imitating Cicero as was Zeuxis in portraying the feminine form. Zeuxis reproduced the form, the coloring, the age and—a sign of the highest workmanship—something of the mood; that is, of grief, joy, anger, fear, intentness, sleep. He who has shown these, has he not reached the limit of what art can do? As far

---

[1] His true sons.

as was possible he put a living life into a mute statue. Nothing more could be asked of a painter. You recognize the form of the one who has been painted, you see the age and the mood, perhaps even the condition of health, and besides, as we have read, the physiognomist recognizes the disposition, the habits, and the length of life. And yet how far it falls short of a living being? What can be seen on the surface is represented; but since a human being consists of soul and body, how little there is in this of even one half of him and that the worse? Where is the brain, the flesh, the veins, the muscles and bones, the intestines, the blood, the breath and the phlegm, life, movement, sense, voice and speech, and what belong to man peculiarly— mind, talent, memory, judgment? Just as these, the chief essentials of man, cannot be portrayed by the painter; so we cannot affect the highest virtues of the orator but must get them from ourselves. Indeed nothing else is required of a painter except that he portray what his art professes; but of us something quite different is required if we wish fully to represent Cicero. If our representation is devoid of life, of action, of mood, of muscles and bones what could be more indifferent? Still it will be much more ridiculous, if, by great effort we make the reader recognize that we have read Cicero because of swellings, of warts, of scars, or some deformity of limb in our representation.

Hyp.—A certain painter of this kind was but recently a source of amusement to us. He had engaged to paint our friend, Murius, and since he could not paint the true form of the man, he looked about if he had anything noteworthy on his body or clothes. He began in the summer and had already for the most part finished the picture, had painted a ring which he was wearing, a purse and girdle, and had carefully copied the felt cap on his head. Then he noticed that on the finger of his left hand there was a scar; this he represented with studied care. Then on the right wrist he found a large swelling and painted that. On the left eyebrow he put some hairs in different directions. On the cheek too he put a scar, the mark of a wound. Time went on and he had many sittings. If, when he came, he saw that the beard had been shaved, he painted a new chin; again if he saw that the beard had grown out he changed the chin, because that pleased him more. Between times a slight fever seized Murius which, as is usual, left a sore on his lip; the painter portrayed this. At length winter came, another cap was put on; he changed the picture. Winter clothing of furs was put on, he painted a new dress. Cold changed the complexion and as usual shrunk the skin, he changed the entire skin. A rheum broke out which affected the left eye and made the nose somewhat larger and very much redder, he painted a new eye and a new nose. If ever he saw him uncombed, he ruffled up the hair. If perchance Murius was sleeping while he painted, he represented him sleeping. If he had taken medicine which caused relaxation, he changed the face. If he could have painted the true and native form of the man, he would not have taken refuge in these incidental things. And so if we imitate Cicero in this way, may not Horace deservedly cry out against us:

[1]*O imitatores servum pecus, ut mihi saepe*
  Risum, saepe jocum vestri movere tumultus?

But suppose we have represented Cicero as successfully as the consummate painter can represent his model, where is the mind of Cicero, where the originality so abounding and happy, where the power of arrangement, where the thinking out of propositions, where the wisdom in handling arguments, where the power of persuasion, the felicity, the memory so fruitful and ready, the versatility, where in short that soul breathing even now in his writings, that genius, manifesting such peculiar, subtle power? If these are lacking, how indifferent will be our imitation!

No.—You argue cleverly, Bulephorus, but to what end except to keep young men from copying Cicero?

Bu.—Heaven forbid, Nosoponus! My aim is rather this, that, spurning the foolish harangue of certain apes, we may imitate Cicero, as far as may be, both exactly and successfully.

No.—In this certainly we agree.

Bu.—Unless this be done skillfully, we shall strive diligently but not very successfully and shall become most unlike Cicero. For be assured that there is nothing more dangerous than to

---

[1] Hor. Epis. I, 19. 19. O imitators, servile band, how often have your efforts moved me to laughter and to mirth.

aim at being the image of Cicero.   Misfortune came to the giants in their striving to reach the seat of Jove.   Destruction came through challenging the Gods.   It is a work full of dangerous chance, to reproduce that divine and superhuman tongue.   Another Cicero may possibly be born, but none can be made.

No.—What are you driving at?

Bu.—Because while his virtues are the highest, they are yet nearest to vices.   Furthermore imitation must fail which desires to follow only, not to surpass.   The more zealously you aim at the reproduction, the nearer you are to this vice.

No.—I do not quite understand what you mean.

Bu.—I will make you understand.   Do not the doctors declare that the best health of body is the most dangerous because it is nearest to bad health?

No.—I have heard so.   What next?

Bu.—Is not absolute monarchy very near to tyranny?

No.—They say so.

Bu.—And yet nothing is better than absolute monarchy without tyranny.   Again, is not great generosity a neighbor to prodigality?   And does not unusual rigor border on barbarity?

No.—Yes.

Bu.—And wit and humour, do they not approach the neighborhood of coarseness and levity?

No.—Do not mention other instances.   Take it for granted I agree to all.

Bu.—First hear this quotation from Horace:

[1]*Brevis esse labore,*
Obscurus fio; sectantem lenia, nervi,
Deficiunt, animique; professus grandia turget.

Thus those who aim at the Attic style become dry instead of clever and charming; at the Rhodian, diffuse; at the Asiatic, bombastic.   Brevity is praised in the work of Sallust.   Would there not be danger of becoming unduly concise and abrupt, if one should try to imitate this with painful precision?

No.—Perhaps.

---

[1] Horace Ars Poetica, 25–27
I prove obscure in trying to be terse;
Attempts at ease emasculate my verse;
Who aims at grandeur into bombast falls.—*Conington·*

Bu.—Adequacy and conciseness of language and argument are exemplified in Demosthenes.

No.—According to Quintilian, yes.

Bu.—If any one should set himself anxiously to work to imitate this, to be a Demosthenean, he would be in danger of saying too little. Isocrates is praised for structure and rhythm. He who strives greatly for this may weary his reader by too much precision of periods and may forfeit confidence by the ostentation of his art. Seneca is praised for fluency. The heedless and enthusiastic imitator runs a risk of becoming redundant and extravagant instead of fluent. If you should anxiously imitate the dignity of Brutus you would probably become austere and repellant; if the charm of Sallust, you might become foolish and trivial instead of pleasing. I have known people to prate weak and inane verses when trying to express that wonderful facility of Ovid. But not to weary you with long illustration, I will speak in general. In some a sublety of argument is prominent. One who is strongly attracted to this runs the risk of becoming either cold or obscure. In others we marvel at the happy disregard of art. One who strives to achieve this will probably fall into a common style of speaking, or rather of prating. In another there is prominent the closest observance of rules. He who strives to follow him may fall into a kind of stage style of speaking. Barrenness is nigh to Attic frugality; loquacity to fluency. In swaying the feelings frenzy is close to sublimity just as pomposity follows close to grandeur and recklessness to confident assertion.

No.—I grant all you say.

Bu.—But there are some of these characteristics which are so prominent in authors that they might be considered faults if they were not offset by allied virtues: for example, in Seneca an abruptness and a profusion of aphorisms are offset by the moral purity of his precepts, the splendor of his themes, the charm of his language; in Isocrates the faults of composition are offset by clearness and weight of thought.

No.—All you have said is true, but I do not yet see what you are driving at.

Bu.—At just this. Inasmuch as there are in the single person of Cicero so many of these qualities, an exact and slavish imitation of him seems dangerous to me, for we cannot imitate the virtues which either adorn or conceal them.

No.—What, pray, do you mean by this?

Bu.—His diction is so fluent that he might be criticised at times as loose and free; so exuberant that he could be called redundant; so rhetorical that he seems a declaimer, at the expense of fidelity seeking the glory of the workman, rather than an orator; so free in censure that he could be held malicious; so immoderate in jesting that as consul he seemed ridiculous to Cato; so flattering that he seems humble; so orderly that by rather severe critics he might be called weak and unmanly. And though we acknowledge that in Cicero these are not faults on account of that remarkably happy nature to which everything he does is becoming, that they are even virtues; yet they are found in him in such a form that before a prejudiced judge they would surely be reckoned as faults. Still he balanced every fault by so many excellent virtues that whoever tries to find fault with anything in Cicero's style is by common consent considered a bold slanderer. We do not hope to imitate these virtues; and if we believe Quintilian, they are inimitable and cannot be gained from example or precept but only from native genius. If native genius is lacking, what sort of imitation will there be of those qualities which we have mentioned? Therefore, we conclude that imitation of no one is more dangerous than of Cicero, not only because he is the greatest orator and most talented (for which reason Horace advises against the imitation of Pindar, citing the fate of Icarus), but also because there are many things in him so perfect that they are very nigh to faults. Hence the danger of failure.

No.—But we agreed that the especially splendid qualities were most fit for imitation; for though we fall short somewhat of our ideal, yet we gain the reputation of correct speech.

Bu.—It is one thing to reproduce the same effects, but another thing to give like effects; one thing to have a rule, but another to be a slave to it and follow nothing else. In short, he fails to reproduce his model who does not reproduce also the qualities which bar criticism. And Quintilian points out that these in Cicero are almost inimitable even by those who are fortunate enough to be geniuses.

No.—I do not admit to the contest any except the most extra-ordinary and divine geniuses. Add unremitting zeal to this native ability and there will be hope of imitating Cicero successfully.

Bu.—Perhaps, but so few that they are not worth considering. You know there are some clever people that distinguish between imitation and emulation. They say that imitation looks toward likeness, but emulation looks toward superiority. And so if you put before you Cicero, entire and alone, with the view not only of copying him but of excelling him, you must not merely over-take him but you must outstrip him; otherwise if you wish to add to his fullness of expression, you will become redundant; if to his freedom you will become pert; if to his jests you will become scurrilous; if to his style you will become a poet instead of an orator. Therefore, if you should desire to equal Cicero, you would run the risk of speaking worse because you cannot attain, though doubtless you have attained other things, the divine virtues of this man with which he offsets those things which are either faults or very nigh to faults; and if you try to surpass him also, even if you equal him in those things for which you have native ability, yet whatever you add will be faulty, since it seems truly to have been declared that nothing can be added to Cicero's eloquence, as in the case of Demosthenes nothing can be subtracted. You see, Nosoponus, the risk.

No.—The risk does not at all frighten me provided at last I may attain the name, Ciceronian.

Bu.—If you scorn all I've said, there is another cause for anxiety, which disturbs me more, if it will not bore you to listen.

No.—It is your privilege.

Bu.—Do you think the man deserves to be called eloquent who does not speak appropriately?

No.—Not at all, inasmuch as this is the first requisite of an orator.

Bu.—Whence is true propriety? Is it not partly from the sub-ject, partly from the character of the speaker and the listener, partly from place, time, and other circumstances?

No.—Certainly.

Bu.—Furthermore do you not expect a Ciceronian to be an illustrious orator?

No.—Why not?

Bu.—Then one will not be a Ciceronian if he discourses in the theater on the paradoxes of the Stoics and on the subtilities of Chrysippus; or if he indulges in witticisms in the presence of the Areopagites when a man is on trial for his life; or if he speaks of cooking in words and figures of the tragic poets.

No.—He will be as ridiculous an orator as if in tragic dress he danced in the Atellan farce; or put a yellow robe on a cat, as the saying goes; or purple upon the ape; or adorned Bacchus or Sardanapalus with the skin of a lion and the club of Hercules. For the deed merits no praise, however magnificent in itself, if it is out of place.

Bu.—Exactly so. Therefore, Cicero, who in his own age had no rival, would not have excelled if he had spoken in like fashion in the age of Cato the Censor, of Scipio, or of Ennius.

No.—Ears accustomed to harsher sounds would not have suffered, to be sure, that ornamental and rhythmical kind of diction. For their speech corresponded to the manners of their times.

Bu.—Then you say that style is the dress of the ideas?

No.—Yes, unless you like better to call it the picture.

Bu.—Well, a dress which is becoming to a boy is not becoming to an old man; one suitable for a woman is not suitable for a man; what is meet for a wedding is not meet for a funeral; nor would fashions of a hundred years ago be approved of today.

No.—No, they would be received with general hissings and laughter. Look at the dress of the court ladies and nobles in pictures painted perhaps sixty years ago. If anyone should appear anywhere in public now in this dress, boys and knaves would throw rotten apples at him.

Bu.—You speak the truth, indeed. For who now would endure respectable women to wear horns, pyramids, very tall cones standing out on their heads, foreheads and temples bald, hair skilfully plucked almost to the middle of the head; and men to wear bulging caps with great tails hanging down, borders of clothing notched, swelling humps on the shoulders, hair shaved the width of two fingers above the ears, garments far too short to extend to the knees scarcely covering the loins, high topped boots with silver chains bound round from knee to heel. Nor at that time would have been less curious the dress which is now considered respectable.

No.—We agree about dress.

Bu.—Will you not grant that Apelles, who was counted the best painter of his age would be said to paint badly, if he should return now and should paint the Germans as he formerly painted the Greeks, and kings as he formerly painted Alexander?

No.—Badly because inappropriately.

Bu.—If one should paint God the Father in such a dress as Apelles painted Jove or Christ as he painted Apollo, would you accept the picture?

No.—Not at all.

Bu.—What if some one should today portray the Virgin Mother as Apelles portrayed Diana, or the Holy Virgin as he painted Venus Anadyomene celebrated in all literature, or Saint Thekla as he painted Lais, would you say that he was like Apelles?

No.—I suppose not.

Bu.—And if anyone should adorn our temples with statues like those with which Lysippus adorned the temples of the Gods, would you say that he was like Lysippus?

No.—I should not.

Bu.—Why not?

No.—Because the statues would not fit the subjects. I should say the same if any one should paint an ass in the guise of a gazelle or a hawk with the figure of a cuckoo, even if he should expend in other respects the greatest care and skill on the picture.

Hyp.—Nor should I call him a clever painter who would make a deformed man beautiful.

Bu.—What if he should in some other way show great artistic power?

Hyp.—I should not say that the picture was void of art but that it was untrue. For he could have painted it otherwise if he had wished but he preferred either to flatter his model or to make sport of him. Come now, do you think him an honest workman?

No.—He certainly has not shown that he is.

Bu.—Then do you think him a good man?

No.—Neither a good workman, nor a good man, since, indeed, it is the height of art to represent things as they are.

Bu.—To do this, there is no especial need of Ciceronian eloquence; for our rhetoricians grant to eloquence the license to lie, to exalt the lowly, to cast down the haughty (which surely is a kind of legerdemain) to steal by strategy into the minds of the listener, and finally by appealing to the emotions—which is a kind of sorcery—to force conviction.

No.—True, when the listener deserves to be deceived.

Bu.—But let us omit these more irrelevant things. It is enough for my purpose that you do not approve of the inappropriate dress, that you condemn the flattering picture.

No.—But what end have these Socratic importations (εἰσαγωγαί) of yours in view?

Bu.—I was plainly coming to this point, namely, that we agree in thinking that Cicero speaks best of all.

No.—We do.

Bu.—And that this most noble name of Ciceronian is not deserved unless one can speak as Cicero does.

No.—Precisely.

Bu.—And that he does not even speak well whose language is inappropriate.

No.—We agree in that too.

Bu.—Further, that we speak fittingly only when our speech is consistent with the persons and conditions of present day life.

No.—Of course.

Bu.—Well then, do the present conditions agree with those of the time when Cicero lived and spoke, considering our absolutely different religion, government, laws, customs, occupations, the very face of the men?

No.—No, not at all.

Bu.—What effrontery then would he have who should insist that we speak, on all occasions, as Cicero did? Let him bring back to us first that Rome which was; let him give us the Senate and the senate house, the Conscript Fathers, the Knights, the people in tribes and centuries; let him give back the college of augurs and soothsayers, the chief priests, the flamens and vestals, the aediles, praetors, tribunes of the people, consuls, dictators, Caesars, the assemblies, laws, decrees of the senate, plebiscites, statues, triumphs, ovations. thanksgivings, shrines, sanctuaries, feasts of the gods, sacred rites, gods and goddesses, the Capitol, and sacred fire; let him give back the provinces, the colonies, the municipal town, and the allies of the city which was mistress of the world. Then, since on every hand the entire

scene of things is changed, who can today speak fittingly unless
he is unlike Cicero? Therefore, it seems to me that our argument brings us to a different conclusion. You say that no one
can speak with propriety unless he copy Cicero; but the fact
itself convinces us that no one can speak well unless he wisely
withdraw from the example of Cicero. Wherever I turn I see
things changed, I stand on another stage, I see another theater,
yes, another world. What shall I do? I, a Christian, must
speak to Christians about the Christian religion. In order that
I may speak fittingly, shall I imagine that I am living in the
age of Cicero and speaking in a crowded senate in the presence
of the senators on the Tarpeian Rock? And shall I borrow
words, figures, rhythms from the orations which Cicero delivered
in the Senate? I must address a promiscuous crowd in which
there are young women, wives, and widows; I must speak of
fasting, of repentance, of the fruits of prayer, the utility of alms,
the sanctity of marriage, the contempt of changing things, the
study of the Divine Word. How will the eloquence of Cicero
help me here to whom the themes as well as the vocabulary
were unknown? Will not an orator be cold who sews, as it
were, patches taken from Cicero upon his garments?

I shall not repeat rumors but what I have heard with my own
ears, seen with my eyes. There flourished when I was in Rome
Petrus Phaedrus, most celebrated in eloquence, and Camillus,
younger but greater in power of expression, save that Phaedrus
had already gained the height of this distinction. But neither
of these, if I am not mistaken, was a Roman by birth. Now an
invitation was extended to any one who would speak of the
death of Christ on the holy day which they call the day of
preparation, in the presence of the Pope. Some days before I
was invited by some learned men to listen to this oration. "Be
sure to be there," they said, "now at last you will hear how
Roman speech sounds on Roman lips." I went eagerly, I stood
next to the platform, not to lose anything. Julius II was present
in person, a thing which very rarely happened, on account, I
think, of his health. A crowded assembly of cardinals and
bishops was there and many scholars who were then living in
Rome, besides the common throng. I shall not mention the
name of the speaker, lest I should seem to cast reflection on a
respectable and learned man. He thought as you do now,

Nosoponus, and was no doubt a candidate for Ciceronianism. The introduction and peroration, longer almost than the real sermon, were occupied in proclaiming the praises of Julius II, whom he called Jupiter Optimus Maximus holding and brandishing in his powerful right hand the three-cleft and fatal thunderbolt and causing by a mere nod whatever he wished. All that had been done in France, Germany, Spain, Portugal, Africa, and Greece, he declared, had been done by the will of Julius alone. So spoke at Rome a Roman in Roman tongue and Roman style. But what had this characterization to do with Julius, the high priest of the Christian religion, vice-gerent of Christ, successor of Peter and Paul? What with cardinals and bishops performing the duties of the other apostles? Could any theme be more sacred, more real, more wonderful, more sublime, better fitted to move the feelings than the one which he had undertaken to present. Could not any man, furnished with any kind of eloquence on this subject, move even men of stone to tears? This was the plan of the discourse:—first to depict the death of Christ as sad, then, with a turn of words, to describe it as glorious and triumphant intending of course to exhibit to us an example of Ciceronian δεινώσεως[1] 'by which he could sway the minds of the listeners in any way he wished.

Hy.—Well, did he succeed?

Bu.—To be honest, I wanted to laugh when he gave expression to that tragic feeling which rhetoricians call πάθη·[2] I did not see a single man in that whole assembly a whit sadder when he enlarged with all the strength of eloquence upon the undeserved punishments of the innocent Christ. Nor again any one a bit more joyful when he was wholly absorbed in portraying to us that death triumphant, praiseworthy, and glorious. He called to mind the Decii and Quintus Curtius who had sacrificed themselves for the safety of the Republic; Cecrops, Menoetius, Iphigenia, and several others to whom the safety and dignity of their fatherland had been dearer than life itself; he deplored too very dolefully that, while gratitude had been shown by public decrees to brave men who had aided the Republic at their own risk—to some by a golden statue erected in the forum, to others by divine honors decreed—Christ in return for his

---

[1] Effectiveness.
[2] Pathos.

benefactions at the hands of the ungrateful Jews had borne the cross, enduring hardships and the deepest disgrace. And thus he deplored the death of that good and innocent man who merited the best from his race as he would have deplored the death of Socrates or Phocion, who, though they had committed no crime, were compelled through the ingratitude of their fellow-citizens to drink the hemlock; or of Epaminondas who on account of his brilliant campaigns was compelled to plead for his life before his people; or of Scipio who after so many services to the Republic went out to exile; or of Aristides whom the people of Athens ordered to go into exile offended because he was called just on account of his great integrity of character. I ask what could be more unconvincing or more inappropriate than this? And yet in strength he emulated Cicero. But no mention of the secret plan of the omnipotent Father to redeem the human race from the tyrany of the devil by the unparallelled death of his only son nor of the mysteries—what it is to die with Christ, to be buried with him, with him to rise again. The suffering of the innocent Christ was deplored; the ingratitude of the Jews held up to scorn; but no mention of the ill-will and ingratitude of those of us who, though thus redeemed, thus enriched by so many blessings, and called forth to such happiness through un-heard of kindness, in return, so far as in us lies, crucify him by returning to the tyranny of Satan, becoming slaves to avarice, luxury, ambition, given more to this world than ever were the heathens, to whom God had not yet opened up this celestial philosophy. When he was struggling to transport us with joy, I wished rather to weep upon hearing the triumphs of Scipio, of Paulus Aemilius, of Caius Caesar and of the deified Emperors compared with the triumph of the cross. If he had wished to glorify Christ, he ought to have emulated the apostle Paul rather than Cicero, who exults, is lifted up with pride, conquers, triumphs, looks from above with disdain upon all things earthly whenever he touches upon the preaching of the Cross. But why make a long story? In so Roman a fashion spoke that Roman that I heard nothing about the death of Christ. And yet, he was a most ambitious candidate for Ciceronian eloquence and seemed to the Ciceronians to have spoken wonderfully, though he said almost nothing on the subject which he seemed neither to know nor to care for, nothing to the point, and moved no one's feelings. He merited only this praise that he had spoken like a Roman and had reproduced something of Cicero. The speech could have been approved as a specimen of talent and genius, if it had been delivered by a school boy; but what good was it for such a day, before such auditors, and on such a theme, I pray?

No.—You will not tell the name of the speaker?

Bu.—I prefer not, for I have not intended to cast aspersion upon the name of any but to show an error to be avoided which deceives not a few today under the shadow of a splendid name. This mistaken idea is of interest to us, Nosoponus; the name of the man of whom I have told the story matters not at all. Moreover, this misapprehension also concerns the glory of Cicero, whom I see you favor beyond measure, whom all the learned men of the world justly favor; for these apes not only exert a harmful influence upon youth but also dishonor Cicero by the help of whose name they glorify themselves though they are anything but Ciceronians. Just as men dishonor St. Benedict by boasting themselves Benedictines when in dress, in title, and in life they approach nearer Sardanapalus than St. Benedict; and St. Francis—that man incapable of ill-will—when they boast of his name though they represent in their characters more nearly the Pharisees; and St. Augustine when they say that they are Augustinians though they are far removed from the doctrine as well as the piety of so great a man; and possibly Christ when they have nothing of him except the title: so men cast a blot on the fame of Cicero who have nothing on their tongues except Cicero and Ciceronians, when none are farther from the eloquence of Cicero than they. Wonderful how they criticise the crudeness of St. Thomas Aquinas, of Duns Scotus, of Durandus, and such men! And yet in all fairness these men, though they boast themselves neither eloquent nor Ciceronians, are more Ciceronian than those who demand to be considered not only Ciceronians but even Ciceros.

No.—Strange things you tell.

Bu.—Truth is not strange. Do you not acknowledge that he who has great versatility is very like Cicero?

No.—Yes.

5

Bu.—Two things are conducive to good speaking: that you know your subject thoroughly, and that the heart and feelings furnish words.

No.—That indeed Horace and Quintilian teach, and it is very true regardless of authority; therefore I shall not attempt to deny it.

Bu.—Whence then will he get the name of Ciceronian who speaks of things which he neither knows thoroughly nor pursues heartily and, I might say, which he clearly neglects and hates?

Hyp.—This is indeed a hard question. For how could a painter, however clever a workmen, paint the figure of a man whom he had never looked at carefully and perhaps had never even seen? And too, you can scarcely make workmen of this class express the thing skillfully, unless they are delighted with the subject.

Bu.—This then must be the particular care of the Ciceronians that they know the mysteries of the Christian religion and read the sacred books with as much zeal as Cicero read those of the philosophers, poets, augurs, historians, and jurists. It was because of his thorough knowledge of these things that Cicero was Cicero. If we do not touch the laws, prophets, histories, commentators of our religion; if we spurn and shrink from them, how pray shall we be Ciceronians? Another point, you must speak before Christians on a secular subject—the electing of a magistrate, marriage, concluding a treaty, or undertaking war. Of these things shall we Christians speak in the same way as heathen Cicero spoke to the heathen? Are not all our actions gauged by the rules of Christ from which if our speech departs we shall be neither good orators nor good men?

Further, if the Ciceronian utters no word except from his dictionary, what will he do when the changes of time have brought new words, for he will not find those in the books of Cicero nor in his own word list? If, whatever is not found in his books is discarded, in spite of the fact that so many of his works have been lost, see how many words we shall shun as barbarisms which have been handed down by Cicero, and how many which he would have used if he had needed to speak on subjects of this kind! Never in Cicero did we see *Jesus Christ,* the *Word of God, Holy Ghost, Trinity, gospel, evangelist, Moses, prophet, pentateuch, psalms, bishop, archbishop, deacon, sub-deacon, acolyte, exorcist, church, faith, hope and love, The Trinity, heresy, symbol, the seven sacraments of the church, baptism, baptizer, confirmation, eucharist, extreme unction, repentance, sacramental confession, contrition, absolution, excommunication, church burial, mass,* and other innumerable things in which consist the whole life of Christians. These are always coming up. No matter of what one tries to speak, they thrust themselves upon one. What shall we do? Whither shall our painfully precise Ciceronian turn? Shall he use *Jupiter Optimus Maximus* for the *Father of our Lord?* For the *Son,* shall he say *Apollo* or *Aesculapius?* For the *Queen of Virgins,* shall he say *Diana?* For *heathen, public enemy?* For the *church* shall he say *sacred assembly* or the *state* or the *republic?* for *heresy, faction?* for *schism, sedition?* for *Christian faith, Christian persuasion?* for *excommunication, proscription?* for *to excommunicate,* to *devote to the Furies* or what will be more satisfactory to some *to forbid water and fire?* for *apostles, embassadors* or *couriers?* for the *Roman Pontiff, Flamen of Jove?* for *an assembly of cardinals, conscript fathers,* for a *generous synod,* the *Senate* and *People of the Christian Republic?* for *bishops, defenders of the provinces?* for the *elections of the bishops,* the *comitia?* for the *synod's ordinances,* the *decree of the senate?* for the *Pope,* the *chief prefect of the state?* for *Christ the head of the Church,* the *highest guardian of the Republic?* for the *devil, sychophant?* for *prophet, soothsayer* or *diviner?* for *prophecies, oracles of the gods?* for *baptism, dipping a victim?* for *mass,* a *sacrifice?* for *consecration of the Lord's body, consecrated bread?* for the *eucharist,* the *sanctifying of bread?* for the *priest,* a *sacrificing priest* or a *master of the sacrifices?* for a *deacon,* a *minister* or *priest of the curia?* for the *grace of God, munificence of the Divine Will?* for *absolution, manumission?* You see how few of the innumerable throng of like words I have mentioned. How will the candidate for Ciceronianism act in such a case? Will he keep silent or will he change to words acceptable to Christians?

No.—What else?

Bu.—Let us then imagine an example. This thought, *Jesus Christ, the Word, and Son of the Eternal Father, according to the prophets came into the world and was made man; of his own will he suffered death and redeemed his church; turned the wrath of the offended father from us; reconciled us to Him so*

*that, justified by the grace of faith and freed from tyranny, we
are brought into the church and, persevering in the communion
of the church, after this life we reach the kingdom of heaven,*
a Ciceronian would express thus: *The interpreter and son of most
excellent and mighty Jove, preserver and king, in accordance with
the response of the soothsayer, flew down from Olympus to earth
and, assuming the shape of man, sacrificed himself voluntarily to
the shades below for the safety of the Republic and thus freed
the state; he extinguished the lightning of most excellent and
mighty Jove which flashed about our heads, restored us to his
favor so that we, rendered innocent by the wealth of persuasion
and freed from the mastery of a deceiver, are admitted into the
state; and if we persevere in the fellowship of the Republic we
shall gain the highest happiness, when the fates shall have called
us from this life, into the society of the Gods.*

No.—You are surely jesting, Bulephorus.

Bu.—I call to witness our beloved Goddess πειθώ[1] that I am
treating a serious subject. Suppose occasion arises for a discussion of the most difficult questions in our dogmas, how much
of illumination will the discussion have if it proceed by the help
of such petty figures? What else but smoke shall I add to the
darkness of the subject matter? How often will the reader
come to a standstill at difficulties? But suppose up to this point
I ape Cicero, what will I do when the theme demands the testimony of the divine scriptures? When something must be cited
from the teachings of the decalogue, shall I simply add "Read
the law?" When there shall be need to pronounce an ordinance
of the synod, shall I add, "Read the decree of the Senate?"
When something must be related from the prophets or apostles,
will it be enough to say, "Read the testimony?" These are
Cicero's regular phrases. And so I shall evade the subjects lest
I contaminate Ciceronian diction with words that are not
Ciceronian?

No.—How now? Do you advise us to use the phrases of
Thomas Aquinas and Duns Scotus?

Bu.—If propriety is an essential, it is better in speaking of
sacred things than to copy Cicero. And yet there is a certain
happy mean between the Scotists and the extreme Ciceronians.

---

[1] Persuasion.

It does not necessarily follow that all Latin is bad which is not found in Cicero: for, as it has been said often already, his works are not all extant; he did not treat of all subjects of his own time; nor did he know or discuss subjects peculiar to our time. Finally, in propriety and elegance of language Marcus Varro equals Cicero and Caius Caesar surpasses him, for Cicero was not the author and parent of the Roman speech. He was a very great orator and a pleader in civil cases of the first rank, but in some other things he was of the second rank—an indifferent poet, rather a poor translator from the Greek, of uncertain promise in other fields. If I should have to speak of matrimony, a state which is quite different from what it was formerly and a subject upon which Cicero has left us nothing, should I hesitate to choose thoughts and language from Aristotle, Xenophon, Plutarch, the Bible, Tertullian, St. Jerome or St. Augustine for fear of seeming not much of a Ciceronian? And if there is need of teaching on a rural theme, shall I have no right to take what I please from Vergil, Cato, Varro, Columella?

If newly coined words are considered barbarisms, every word was once a barbarism. How many new words will you find in Cicero himself? Especially in those books in which he treats of rhetoric and of philosophy? Who before Cicero heard of *beatitas* or *beatitudo?* What does *finis bonorum* mean to the Latins, though in Cicero it signifies the highest good, or that in which one expresses the highest happiness? How does *visum,* and *visio, species, praepositum,* and *rejectum* sound to us? How would *occupatio, contentio, superlatio, complexio, traductio, frequentatio, licentia, gradatio, status,* and *constitutio, judicatio, continens, firmamentum, demonstrativum genus, inductio, propositum, aggressio, insinuatio, acclamatio* sound to Latin ears? Or innumerable other words, unheard of, before by the Latins, which he either dared to coin or to use in such a new sense that the Roman people did not recognize them? He did not hesitate to do this, in spite of protestation, when he translated the doctrines of Grecian philosophers; he also naturalized in Latin several foreign words in order to explain the content of the rules of the rhetoricians by specific words formed for this special purpose; yet we think it a crime, if in handling new themes we use a few new words? There is no art to which we do not grant the right of using its own vocabulary: the grammarians may say, *supine* and *gerund;* the mathematicians may say *sesquialteral* and *superbipartient;* the farmers and mechanics have vocabularies adapted to their arts. Shall we then confound heaven and earth, if we explain the mysteries of our religion in language peculiar to it? Since the Christian religion first came to us from Palestine, Asia Minor, and Greece, some Hebraic and many Greek words were carried in along with these ideas themselves; for example, *osanna, amen, ecclesia, Apostolus, Episcopus, catholicus, orthodoxus, hereticus, schisma, charisma, dogma, Chrisma, Christus, baptizo, Paracletus, Evangelium, evangelizare, Evangelista, proselitus, catechumenus, Exorcismus, Eucharistia, symbolum, anathema.* The first priests of the Christian religion in order to disseminate their sublime doctrine used ὁμούσιος which we translate *consubstantialis* and *fides, gratia, Mediator,* and others which either were entirely new to the Latins or used in a different sense. Then is being called Ciceronian of so much consequence that we are absolutely silent about things of which we above all others ought to speak? Shall we abstain from words of the Apostles and from those brought into currency by our fathers which are even now in good repute and contrive others in their place? No, indeed. The Greeks introduced *honey, pepper, mustard* into their language, the Romans did the same. Shall we shrink from those words which have come to us along with that divine religion through Christ, the apostles, and the Holy Fathers, and take refuge in Cicero, intending thereafter to borrow words from him, εν τῇ φακῇ μύρον[1] as the Greeks say? If any one should dispute with us seriously, he would very quickly say that the majesty of the Christian religion is marred by the words, figures, and rhythms of Cicero. But I do not agree, for elegance and terseness of speech pleases me always. You may say that he does not speak Ciceronian who, a Christian among Christians, speaks on a Christian theme as Cicero, a heathen among heathens, spoke on a heathen theme; but I say that if Cicero were alive now and endowed with such genius as he was then, with such skill of speaking, with such knowledge of our times as he had of his own, if he were inflamed with such zeal toward the Christian state as he showed for the Roman City and the majesty of the Roman name, he would speak today as a Christian among Chris-

---

[1] Perfume on pulse.

tians. He who can do this may step forth and we shall gladly dub him a Ciceronian if he longs for the name. Cicero, if he were alive today would not consider *God the Father* less elegant than *Jupiter Optimus Maximus,* or *Jesus Christ* less pleasing to the ear than *Romulus* or *Scipio Africanus* or *Quintus Curtius* or *Marcus Decius;* nor less splendid would he think the name of the Catholic Church than that of the Conscript Fathers, the Knights, the Senate of the Roman people. He would say with us *faith in Christ,* he would call those out of Christ *infidels,* he would say *The Holy Comforter, The Holy Trinity.* I offer proofs for my statements. Did the desire of elegance hinder him from using the set phrase rather than rhetorical Latin in the *Philippics* when he was reciting the formula of the senate's decree? Does he not use in *Topics* legal terms very different from the language of the rhetoricans? Would he have spurned words peculiar to our religion?

No.—Your proofs seem convincing.

Bu.—Furthermore, does not the beauty of language in great measure depend upon figures and allusions? Where does Cicero get these? Is it not from Homer, Euripides, Sophocles, Ennius, Lucilius, Accius, Pecuvius, Naevius, from the philosophers and the historians?

No.—I grant that without these ornaments, speech is mean and common. With them it becomes admirable.

Bu.—What if we should borrow as he did from Vergil, Horace, Ovid, Seneca, Lucan, Martial, would we be unlike Cicero to that extent?

No.—That is granted, perhaps reluctantly; for the antiquity of those whose words he quotes has a sort of majesty in Cicero.

Bu.—How comes it then that we think the whole oration defiled if from the most ancient prophets, from Moses, the psalms, the Gospels and apostolic letters we seek the adornments which Cicero sought as a heathen from the heathens? Is it admirable to borrow from Socrates, but blameworthy to borrow from the proverbs of Solomon? Does Solomon compare unfavorably with Socrates in our estimation? Will the oration be made brilliant by a word from Pindar or Horace and defiled by an appropriate one from the sacred psalms? Are weight and dignity added to an oration by introducing a thought from Plato and the charm destroyed by a thought of Christ from the

Gospels? Whence these absurdities? Do we admire the wisdom of Plato more than the wisdom of Christ? Are the books revealed by the Holy Spirit mean in comparison to the writings of Homer, Euripides, or Ennius? But let us make no mention of the Holy Spirit in this connection lest we seem sacrilegious. History, if you take away fidelity deserves not the name of history. Compare, if you will, the story teller, Herodotus, with Moses; compare the story of the creation of the world beginning from Egypt with the stories of Diodorus; compare the books of Judges and Kings with Livy who often contradicts himself, to say nothing of his untrustworthiness; compare Plato with Christ; the εἰρωνείας[1] of Socrates with the divine oracles of Christ; the psalms so spiritual with the eulogies of Pindar; the songs of Solomon with the ditties of Theocritus. Whether you look at the authors or the subjects, there is no resemblance. Divine wisdom has an eloquence of its own and no wonder if somewhat different from that of Demosthenes or Cicero; for one dress becomes the wife of a king, another the mistress of a braggart soldier.

I was going to ask, if any one should begin to compare words, figures, rhythms:—Does *Thessalian vale* sound sweeter to us than *Mount Zion?* Or has *granted by the immortal Gods* more of majesty than *granted by God the Father?* Or is *Socrates, son of Sophroniscus*, more pleasing to our ears than *Lord Jesus, son of God?* Is *Hannibal, the commander of the Carthaginians*, a sweeter sound then *Paul, teacher of the Gentiles?* If you compare the characters; Hannibal strove for the destruction of the Roman people while Paul introduced a religion of salvation. If you compare the words, I ask what is the difference?

Hyp.—If we are willing to acknowledge the truth, there is no difference, save that a deep-rooted fancy has taught us that the words of the one are polished and splendid, of the other ugly and crude.

Bu.—You have hit the nail on the head. But to what is this fancy due?

Hyp.—I do not know.

Bu.—To the facts in the case?

Hyp.—I think not.

Bu.—Do you wish me to speak what is truer than truth?

[1] Irony.

Hyp.—You have my permission.

Bu.—I am waiting for our friend's permission here.

No.—Enjoy the right of our bargain.

Bu.—But I fear what I am about to say will not seem very Ciceronian.

No.—That does not matter at all.

Bu.—It is due to paganism, Nosoponus. It is paganism which influences our ears and minds. We are Christians only in name. The body is baptized in sacred water but the mind is unwashed; the forehead is signed with the cross, the mind curses the cross; we profess Jesus with our mouths, we wear Jupiter Optimus Maximus and Romulus in our hearts. Otherwise, if we were truly what we are called, what name pray under the sun ought to be more pleasing to our thoughts or our ears than the name of Jesus, through whom we are rescued from so great evil; by whose gracious kindness we are called to such dignity and invited to eternal happiness; at the mention of whose name evil spirits—more than deadly enemies of the human race —tremble and angels bow their heads and knees; whose name is so efficacious that demons flee at the invocation of him, incurable diseases yield and the dead come to life; so kind and friendly that the bitterest calamities are solaced if you sincerely speak the name of Jesus? Are we then persuaded that by this name the luster of oratory is dulled, while Hannibal and Camillus are its true lights? Let us absolutely uproot and cast forth from the mind this paganism. A truly Christian heart let us bring to the reading and we shall see a brilliant star added to our style whenever the name of Jesus Christ is spoken and an exquisite gem when the name of the Virgin Mother, of Peter, or of Paul is used. Added beauty too, we shall see when from the inner sanctuary of the divine writings, from the cruses and ointment boxes of the Holy Ghost, a thought is thrown in appropriately and sincerely; and thus much more dignity will be found in the diction than if there had been added ten thousand phrases from the writings of Ennius and Accius.

Hyp.—Certainly theologians are kept in this way from bringing the charge of heresy.

Bu.—Granted that Cicero's language is full of figures, ours is as full; while in majesty of themes and in trustworthiness we are far superior to him. Only about words does our pagan fancy trick us, does the lukewarm Christian feeling deceive; because those things which are most beautiful by their own nature are distasteful to us; because we do not love—would that we did not hate. For, according to Theocritis, to Love beautiful are even those things which are not beautiful, just as to Hate there is nothing that is not deformed. I come to allusions which if you destroy, you know yourself how you destroy the beauty of speech. Why does one please us very much more, if when pointing out some person in very unsuitable surroundings, he should say "Wild pulse among kitchen vegetables" than if he should say "Saul among the soothsayers" or if, pointing out something said or done at the wrong time, he should say "Perfume on lentils" rather than "A gold ring in a hog's nose," or if, pointing out that not fortune but good conscience is to be trusted, he should say "Hope must be placed in the protection of the sacred anchor" rather than "We must lean upon the solid rock," or if, wishing to act the part of a good man on the stage and to devote himself to the comforts of others rather than to self-aggrandizement, one should say "Nothing is less becoming to a Christian than to play the role of an Aspendian harper" rather than alluding to the word of Paul, "We must look rather to what is lawful than to what is convenient?" If I should try to exhaust such illustrations, it would take a whole volume. I am content to have given a few. How we gape, how we stand stupified if we find an image or even the fragment of an image of the ancient divinities, while we look askance at the images of Christ and the saints! How we marvel at an epigram or epitaph found in some decaying rock or other:—"To the departed spirit of my most beloved wife, Lucia, deprived of life before her time, Marcellus has set up this stone. O unfortunate me! Why do I live!" Notwithstanding we find very often in passages of this kind, not only foolish and pagan sentiments, but also extraordinary solecisms; yet we cherish them, venerating and almost adoring antiquity, while we deride the relics of the apostles. If any one should quote from the Twelve Tables, who would not consider him worthy of the most sacred place? And yet do any of us venerate and cherish the laws inscribed by the finger of God? How we treasure the image of Hercules or Mercury or Fortune or Victory or Alexander the Great or any of the Caesars stamped upon a coin; but smile at them as superstitious who have among their cherished possessions wood of the cross, images of the Trinity and of the Saints!

If ever you have visited the libraries of the Ciceronians at Rome, recall, I pray, whether you saw an image of the crucifix or of the sacred Trinity or of the apostles. You will find them all full of monuments of heathenism. Among the pictures, "Jupiter Slipping into the Lap of Danae through the Impluvium" attracts our attention rather than "Gabriel Announcing the Immaculate Conception to the Holy Virgin;" "Ganymede Stolen by the Eagle" delights us rather than "Christ Ascending into Heaven." Our eyes linger on the portrayal of bacchanalian feasts and festivals of Terminus full of disgrace and obscenity rather than on "The Raising of Lazarus" or "The Baptism of Christ by John." These are mysteries hidden under the veil of the Ciceronian name. Under the show of a beautiful name, I assure you, snares are held out to simple minded and credulous youths. We do not dare to profess paganism. We plead as an excuse Ciceronianism. But how much better it would be to be silent!

No.—I was waiting to see how you would advance our cause. But by slipping away into some other channel you have weakened my purpose and frustrated my plans.

Bu.—I said before and I repeat, I am not drawing your mind away from your noble ambitions but I am lifting it to the best. Nor have I mentioned these things because I think that you share my feelings about them, but because I am striving with all my might that we may attain true Ciceronian eloquence; that we may not aim at it diligently with absolutely incorrect ideas and achieve nothing else than that while we desire very much to be considered Ciceronians we become anything but Ciceronians tested by your own premises; viz, that it is a characteristic of Cicero to speak with absolute perfection, that he does not speak even well who speaks inappropriately, and that any diction is cold and dead which does not come from the heart.

No.—How then shall we ever become true Ciceronians? For I shall not be loth to follow your plan if it is better than mine.

Bu.—There is not much else that I could wish for myself or that I could teach you. I can wish for talent and natural ability, I cannot furnish it. Minds of men have individual bent, and this has such power that if they are adapted to one style of speaking by nature they may strive in vain for another. θεομαχία[1] yields victory to none as the Greeks say.

No.—I know that [2]Quintilian insistently urges the same thing.

Bu.—This then is my first advice, that no one devote himself to copying Cicero whose bent of mind is very unlike Cicero's; for if he does he will come out a monstrosity who has lost his own native beauty and has not gained another's. Therefore especial care must be taken to find out the field you are fitted for by nature; and this is desirable also because if there is any faith to be put in Astrology no one can be successful in that with which his horoscope is at variance. One who is destined for letters will never be fortunate in war, and he who is born for war will never succeed in letters. He who is born for wedlock will never be a good monk. He who is naturally a farmer will never have success at court and *vice versa*.

No.—But there is nothing which persistent labor cannot over-come. By human skill we see stone turned into water, lead into silver, brass into gold; through cultivation plants lay aside their wild character. What hinders the genius of man also from being transformed by training and practice?

Bu.—Training improves the pliable nature, wins over the slightly rebellious, and corrects the perverted one; but you will trouble yourself to no purpose, Nosoponus, about a nature an-tagonistic and set for a different course. A horse learns to be driven around the race course, he learns a pacing gate; but it would be of no use to lead the oxen to the ring, to call the dog to the plough, or the gazelle to the race-course. Water is perhaps turned into air, air into fire—if fire is ever an elementary substance; but earth is never turned into fire, nor fire into water.

No.—But what hinders us from adapting the language of Cicero to every subject?

Bu.—I acknowledge that there are certain general principles that can be applied to any theme, such as purity, clearness, elegance of expression, order, and such things, but this does not satisfy those apes of Cicero. They demand the absolute reproduction of words—the very thing, which, granting that it could be done somehow or other, in certain allied subjects,

---

[1] A battle with the Gods.
[2] Inst. Orat. X, c. 2.

would be impossible in wholly different subjects. You will acknowledge, I think, that Vergil holds first place among Latin poets just as Cicero among Latin orators.

No.—Yes.

Bu.—Well, if you are preparing to write lyric verse, will you place before you Horace or Vergil?

No.—Horace is the greatest in his class.

Bu.—What if satire?

No.—Horace, with much more reason.

Bu.—What if you are contemplating comedy.

No.—I will go to Terence for a model.

Bu.—To be sure, on account of the great difference of theme.

No.—But the language of Cicero has some peculiar, indefinable adaptability.

Bu.—Exactly the same I could say, "indefinable." Immoderate love for Cicero deceives many, because to adapt the language of Cicero to an entirely different theme is to come out unlike him. But here let me say, it is not necessary to aim at likeness if one may be equal or at least approximate though unlike. What more unlike than the emerald and the gold-bronze! And yet they are equally precious and pleasing. The rose is different from the lily, of different odor; and yet the one equals the other. Have you not often seen two girls of different feature, but both of such beauty that their excellence would make it hard to choose between them? That is not necessarily best which is most like Cicero: for, as I was going to say, no animal in all its members approaches nearer to the figure of man than the ape, and so like is it that if nature had added a voice it could seem a man; again nothing is more unlike man than a peacock or a swan—and yet, I think, you would prefer to be a swan or a peacock rather than an ape.

Hyp.—I should prefer to be a camel or gazelle to being the most beautiful of apes.

Bu.—Tell me, Nosoponus, would you prefer the voice of a nightingale or a cuckoo?

No.—Of a nightingale.

Bu.—And yet the cuckoo approaches nearer to the voice of man. Would you prefer to sing with the larks or to croak with the crows?

No.—To sing with the larks.

Bu.—And yet the voice of the crow is more like that of man. Would you prefer to bray with the asses or to whinny with the horses?

No.—To whinny with the horses, if the fates drove to either.

Bu.—And yet the ass tries, as it were, to speak in human fashion.

No.—But I think that my ability does not differ so much as that from Cicero's. And what is lacking by nature, practice will perfect. But finish your advice to me.

Bu.—You do well to call me back to the path, for my talk was about to slip away in another direction. It is of the greatest importance that we really accomplish our desire of expressing Cicero completely, though he is complete neither in words nor in phrases nor in rhythms; nor indeed are hardly half his works extant as has been explained sufficiently before.

No.—Where then is he complete?

Bu.—Nowhere except in himself. But if you wish to express Cicero exactly, you cannot express yourself. If you do not express yourself, your speech will be a false mirror and will be as absurd as if, by smearing your face with colors, you pretend to be Petronius instead of Nosoponus.

No.—You speak in riddles.

Bu.—I will use more homely phrase. They play the fool who distort themselves to copy Cicero exactly; for it would not be possible, if it were desirable; and it would not be desirable, if it were possible. But he can be expressed exactly in this way: if we strive in our imitation to express not his exact virtues, but as great ones, or it may be greater. Thus it can happen that he is most a Ciceronian who is most unlike Cicero, that is, who speaks best and most pointedly, though in a different way; and this is not surprising for the environment is now entirely different. To illustrate—if one should wish to paint an old man whom Apelles had painted in youth he would be different from Apelles in this very thing, if he should paint him in the same way, though the model were now quite changed.

Hyp.—A riddle worthy of the Sphinx, that someone is unlike in that very thing in which he is like.

Bu.—Would not this happen if any one should sing at a funeral as Hermogenes sang at a marriage, or should plead a case before the Areopagites with such gestures as Roscius made while dancing in the theatre? But we may be like Cicero.

No.—How?

Bu.—Did he devote himself to the imitation of one person? No, he strove to copy what was especially appropriate in every one. Demosthenes was his first but not his only model; nor did he take him as model in order to copy him exactly, but to cull the suitable; not to be content to follow, but to choose and wisely shun some traits and improve upon others and to imitate those which he approved of in such a way as to surpass if possible. Besides, the sanctuary of his heart he filled to over-flowing with the authors of all the branches of knowledge old and new. He learned by heart the families of the state, the rites, customs, laws, edicts, plebiscites. Not only he busied himself industriously at the shrines of the philosophers, but also betook himself frequently into the retreats of the Muses, learning pronunciation from one, gesture from another. He who does exactly these things will come out very different from Cicero; he who does like or equal things will earn the name, Ciceronian.

No.—Speak somewhat more clearly.

Bu.—He who busies himself with the same zeal in the field of the Christian religion as Cicero did in that of secular things; who drinks in the psalms and prophets with that feeling which Cicero drank in the books of the poets; who desires to find out the decrees of the apostles, the rites of the church, the rise, progress, and decline of the Christian Republic with such vigilance as Cicero labored to learn thoroughly the rights and laws of the provinces, towns, and allies of the Roman City; and who adapts what has been compiled from all these studies to present themes,—that one can claim with some right the name, Ciceronian.

No.—I do not see the point of all your talk unless it is that we speak in Christian style, not Ciceronian.

Bu.—What! He is not a Ciceronian to you who speaks inaptly and is ignorant of the subject about which he is talking!

No.—By no means.

Bu.—But this is the tendency of those who now desire to be called Ciceronians. We are inquiring into this so that we may

not fall into the same error.   There is no reason why one should
not speak in a style at once Christian and Ciceronian, provided
you acknowledge him a Ciceronian who speaks clearly, fluently,
forcibly, and appropriately, in harmony with the nature of the
theme, the condition of the times, and the characters.   Now
some have thought the faculty of speaking well was not due to
training but to judgment, and Cicero himself in his *Partitiones*
nicely defines eloquence as "wisdom speaking fluently."   There
can be no doubt that he sought this kind of eloquence.   Ye
Gods! how far away from this ideal are those who wish to
speak, in Ciceronian style, on widely varying themes which they
neither know nor care for.   That everything which is not in
harmony with Cicero seems sordid and faulty is a dangerous
and deceitful dream of our minds, to be relegated far from us,
if we wish to enjoy that distinction among Christians which
Cicero enjoyed among his contemporaries.   [1]*Scribendi recte
sapere est et principium et fons,* says that most clever of critics.
What pray is the fount then of Ciceronian eloquence?—A mind
richly instructed in general knowledge with especial care on those
subjects about which you have determined to write, a mind prepared by the rules of rhetoric, by much practice in speaking and
writing and by daily meditation, and what is the essential point
of the whole matter, a heart loving those things for which it
pleads, hating those things which it condemns.   Joined to all this
must be a natural insight, discrimination, and wisdom which
cannot be embodied in precepts.   How, pray tell me, do these
things come to those who read nothing by day or night but
Cicero?

No.—But it has been said, and not without shrewdness, that
they who work long in the sun take color, and those who sit
long in a perfumed dwelling carry the odor of the place with
them when they leave.

Bu.—This comparison pleases me very much indeed.   They
take with them only the coloring of the skin and a whiff quickly
vanishing.   Those who are content with such glory may sit as
much as they please amid the ointment boxes and the rose
gardens of Cicero, may bask in his sunshine.   I should prefer,
to put the good spices into my stomach, to inject them into my

---

[1] Wisdom is the font and source of good writing.   Horace, Ars Poet. 309.

veins so that not only I might sprinkle my neighbors with the delicate perfume, but that I myself might feel the glow and might become so animated that upon occasion a word might come forth which would seem the issue of a sane and well-fed mind. For out of the inmost veins, not out of the skin, is born the style which holds the listener, moves him, and carries him where you will. I do not say these things because I think that out of the books of Cicero is gathered a common and pitiable store, but because Cicero alone is not enough to furnish richness of speech on every theme.

What conclusion then, except that we may learn from Cicero himself how to imitate Cicero? Let us imitate him as he imitated others. If he settled down to the reading of one author, if he devoted himself to the copying of one, if he cared more for words than for ideas, if he did not write except in bed at night, if he worried himself a whole month over one letter, if he thought something eloquent which was irrelevant, let us do the same thing that we may be Ciceronians. But if Cicero did not do these things, which we must grant, let us, after his example, fill our hearts with a store of general knowledge; let us care first for thoughts, then for words; let us adapt the words to the subjects, not subjects to words; and while speaking let us never move our eyes from that which is seemly. Thus, in short, will the oration be alive only when it is born in the heart and does not float on the lips. The precepts of art let us not ignore, for they contribute most to the invention, disposition, and handling of arguments; and let us avoid those things which either are superfluous or hinder the case; but, when a serious case is to be handled let wisdom hold first place. And in fictitious cases which are handled for the sake of practice, it is best for the arguments to seem as true as possible. Cicero has written that the soul of Laelius breathed forth in his writings; but it is stupid for you to try to write with the taste of another and to take pains that the soul of Cicero may breathe forth from your writings. That must be digested which you devour in your varied daily reading, must be made your own by meditation rather than memorized or put into a book, so that your mind crammed with every kind of food may give birth to a style which smells not of any flower, shrub, or grass but of your own native talent and feeling; so that he who reads may not recognize fragments culled

6

from Cicero but the reflection of a well-stored mind. Cicero
had read all his predecessors and weighed carefully what was
worthy of sanction or censure in each; yet you would not
recognize any one of them in particular in Cicero but the force
of a mind animated by the thoughts of them all.

If Cicero's method is not convincing, let us consider an
example from nature. Do bees gather the material for their
honeycomb from one shrub? Do they not rather fly about
all kinds of flowers, shrubs, bushes, with wonderful zeal, frequently seeking from afar what they may store in their hive?
Nor is what they bring straightway honey. They fashion a
liquid with their organs, and after it is made their own, they
give that forth in which you do not recognize the taste or the
odor of flower or shrub but a product mingled in due proportion from them all. Nor do the she-goats feed upon one kind
of foliage that they may give milk like only to these; but they
feed on every kind of leaf and give forth not the juice of herbs
but milk transformed from them.

No.—Yet it makes a difference where the bee gathers the
liquid, or upon what leaf the she-goat feeds. If, indeed, yew-
tree honey is made from the yew-tree, will not likewise the taste
of the milk from the she-goat savor of oak leaves and willows?

Bu.—Well, take artists. Do those who seek fame in plastic
or graphic art devote themselves to the imitation of only one
master or do they take what they please from each for the perfection of art, so imitating that they may possibly surpass?
What about the architect? Does he, when preparing to build
some great house, take all the details from a single building?
Not at all, he selects from many what he finds to his taste, else
no great praise would he gain when the spectator recognizes
this or that building reproduced. And yet to be a slave to the
copy in art is more tolerable than in oratory. What is the
reason then that we have devoted ourselves so religiously to
Cicero alone? They sin twice who not only set themselves to
just one copy but also, being ignorant of rhetorical rules, read
no one except ·Cicero and nothing outside to teach them how
to appreciate him. For what profits it to have your eyes fixed
on Cicero if you have not skillful eyes? What would it profit
me who am ignorant of the art of drawing, if I should look
whole days at the pictures of Apelles and Zeuxis? But when

you have learned the rules of rhetoric and when some skilled artist has pointed out to you in several of those orations in which Cicero has reached the height of his art the essential elements of his style:—propositions happily devised—their order, division, treatment, enrichment, perfecting seeds of the entire oration in the introduction; the conjunction of the individual parts; his wisdom and judgment which can be appreciated but not learned by rule; when likewise you have seen clearly the discrimination of the orator—what he has included and where, what he has omitted and why, what he has deferred and to what point of the speech; furthermore, in what way he handles the emotions; and lastly, the splendor, range, and ornamentation of his discourse,—then at length you will see wonderful things in Cicero which your busy imitator never sees. For he does not imitate art who does not understand it and no one understands save the artist. A skillfully wrought piece of work fills with some satisfaction even those who are ignorant of art but how little there is which your imitator sees!

No.—From whom do you seek art more properly than from Cicero?

Bu.—I acknowledge it. No one has bequeathed it to us more happily, no one had practiced it more perfectly; and yet Quintilian has taught it with greater care and also in greater detail, because he not only gives rules but also illustrates first principles, development, method, execution, preparation, adding many things which Cicero either has omitted or has but incidentally touched, such as, the way of exciting the feelings, the kinds and use of aphorisms, the methods of amplifying, the formulation of propositions, their division and arrangement, the transposition and uniting of the essential points, the proper way of reading, imitating, writing. But while we ought not to be ignorant of rules, yet we ought not to be pedantic about them, or to be slaves to them, for the anxious observation of rules causes us to speak worse, whereas the business of art is to make us speak better. That skilled teacher has contributed much more than rules. Not only some of the Greeks, but also some of the Romans have tried the same but have not succeeded so well. We must be careful then, Nosoponus, not to think, as some of your friends do, that we may become Ciceronians with no knowledge of rhetoric, simply by constantly reading Cicero. For if they get anything of Cicero, they get only a kind of outer skin, shadow, and breath.

No.—I do not deny, Bulephorus, that there are many such, and their method has never pleased me.

Bu.—There is no personal reference to you. It applies to Hypologus and myself. With this understanding, let us consider, my dear friend, whether, in the first place, it would be proper for us; in the second, whether it would be worth the while to buy with such vigils the honor of the name, Ciceronian?

No.—There is nothing more honorable; and what is honorable cannot be improper.

Bu.—To discuss the propriety: You will acknowledge I think, that Cicero's language would not have pleased the age of Cato, the Censor; certainly it was more ornate and more luxuriant than was agreeable to that age, frugal in life and in speech. Aye, even when Cicero lived, there were men who breathed forth that early severity—Cato of Utica, for example, and Brutus, and Asinius Pollio—who vainly sought in Cicero's eloquence something more severe, less theatrical, more masculine, in spite of the fact that at that time eloquence flourished so mightily in the popular assembly, in the senate, in the courts, that the judges both expected and demanded an ornate and attractive style from the lawyers. If Cicero's style was lacking in manly vigor, do you think it appropriate for Christians, whose every plan looks rather to living virtuously than to speaking ornately and elegantly, from whose lives all paint and theatrical effects ought to be far removed?

But suppose that it is appropriate, what reward for all your toil? The aim of all this work is to persuade. But how much more powerful in persuasion was Phocion than Demosthenes, Aristides than Themistocles, how much more effective Cato than Cicero, who sometimes injured the prisoner by his defence, or aided him by his accusation? I will not linger here over those very magnificently delivered speeches. It is more beautiful to be a Phidias than a keeper of the chest or a cook, though their work is more useful to the Republic than the statues of Phidias. The skill of painters and sculptors is found in delighting the eye; when this is fulfilled their task is done. Eloquence which does nothing but delight is not really eloquence, for it was intended to gain a different end; and if it does not succeed, it ill

becomes a good man. Even granting that the eloquence of
Cicero was useful once, what is its use today? In the courts,
you say? There the case is presented in legal provisions and
formulas by attorneys and lawyers who are anything but Ciceronians before judges in whose eyes Cicero would be a barbarian. Nor is there much more use for him in councils
where individual men state their views to a small group in French
or German. And business of especial importance is done today
in a secret committee composed of scarcely three men and these
almost illiterate whom the rest may consult. Furthermore, even
if today the cases were tried in Latin, who would endure such
a peroration as Cicero made in the cases against Verres, Cata-
line, Clodius, and the testimony of Vatinius? What senate so
amply supplied with time and patience that it would abide the
orations he delivered against Antony, though in these the eloquence is that of an older man, is less redundant and less
boastful?

Therefore for what useful end, pray, are we securing this
laboriously won eloquence of Cicero? For popular assemblies?
The common people do not understand the language of Cicero;
and in popular assembly no state business is transacted. In
church councils certainly this style of oratory does not belong
at all. What use then is it, unless perchance in embassies, which
at Rome especially are carried on in Latin by force of tradition
rather than from choice and for the sake of display rather than
utility; for in them practically no serious business is transacted,
all speech being spent in words of praise of him to whom you
are sent, in testimony of the goodwill of him by whom you are
sent, and in set common-places. In a word, all this is of such
a nature that you have accomplished a great thing if you have
avoided the appearance of adulation, even though perhaps you
have been really guilty. The response is customarily rather
dull, distressingly prolix, embarrassing to him who is praised
immoderately, mortifying to the speaker and also risky, for he
sweats while reciting what he has learned, is perplexed and sometimes does not know how to proceed either because of forgetfulness or confusion. What admiration, moreover, could such
speeches elicit, when they have been learned from some rhetorician so that no reputation comes to our orator except the courage of recitation? Thus at Rome nothing is done except the

exchange of courteous greetings. The serious business is transacted privately by letter and by conferences at which French is spoken. Then what theater of action will our Ciceronian seek? He will write Ciceronian epistles? To whom? To the learned; but they are very few and care nothing about the language's being Ciceronian provided it is sane, prudent, elegant, and learned. To whom then? To the four [1]Italians who recently have begun to boast themselves Ciceronians, though, as it has been shown, there is nothing more unlike Cicero than they, who have scarcely the faintest trace of him.

Perhaps nothing ought to be despised, however trivial, if it comes without effort, if it hinders not greater and more important things. But ask yourself whether this reputation ought to be bought at the expense of sleep, of great toil, perhaps of health itself, in order to be taken into the list of Ciceronians by four silly Italian youths.

No.—You do not approve of the study of eloquence then?

Bu.—Cicero does not require eloquence from a philosopher. Do you think any one among the heathen philosophers weightier than any Christian?

Hyp.—No, indeed. All the philosophy of the Greeks compared to the philosophy of Christ is a dream and bauble.

Bu.—Then how brazen are we to exact of a Christian Ciceronian eloquence, which is both inimitable and even in a Pagan's opinion ill becoming a serious man? And it does not follow that a style is bad because it differs from Cicero's. Nor can it be too oft repeated that fitness is absolutely essential to good style. Add to this that any armor which is only for show and not at hand when the occasion demands is useless. Business sometimes urges us to write twenty letters in one day. What will my Ciceronian do in such a case? And again how few there are now who care for Ciceronian style? What about the fact too that Cicero has many styles? He has one when, in relaxed and quiet conversation, he teaches philosophy; another in the pleading of cases; another in letters where the language is not studied but even almost careless,—very appropriate for a letter which follows the turn of familiar conversation. Would it not be absurd for one to write a letter on a matter of business as carefully as Cicero wrote the oration *Pro Milone?* And shall

---

[1]Aonio Palerio, Jacob Sadolet, Peter Bembo, etc.

we put a month's work on a brief note about matters of little importance? Not even Cicero would have bought that eloquence which he displays in court if it had cost him as many vigils as a letter costs us; though in his day the exercise of eloquence in the Republic was great, its study both in private and official life flourishing, and that facility was far more easily gained. Rightly was the man ridiculed who tormented himself for days and still was not able to compose the exordium of his oration because he was striving to speak better than he could. There is in Cicero a certain happy, natural ease, and a native clearness. If nature has denied us this, why do we vainly torture ourselves? Why do others, madder far than we, torment themselves in these times, when all the conditions are changed and when there is hardly any practice of Ciceronian speech, with this one desire of being Ciceronians and nothing but Ciceronians?

No.—Your rhetoric is beautiful, but I cannot rid myself of this longing, it has taken such hold of me.

Bu.—From a moderate desire of imitation I do not call you, but imitate only his best; emulate rather than follow; desire more truly to rival than to be exactly alike; work along the line of your natural ability; do not endeavor to make your speech harmonize so with Cicero's that it does not fit your subject. Above all, show no anxiety; for anxiety is always unfortunate and never anywhere more than in speaking. Finally, do not take the matter so seriously that, if you do not succeed, you will count life bitter and not worth living, although you know that many thousands of learned men without this title have attained great reputations in life, and immortality after death.

No.—That is indeed the way I feel now.

Bu.—I too felt that way once but I have recovered from the disease.

No.—How pray?

Bu.—I called a doctor.

No.—Whom, pray?

Bu.—An eloquent, an efficacious one.

No.—Whom, I say?

Bu.—In comparison to whom Aesculapius and Hippocrates are as nothing.

No.—You are playing with me.

Bu.—Than whom no one is more ready, more friendly, more faithful; than whom no one cures more perfectly; he heals one all over.

No.—If you will not give his name, at least give his remedy.

Bu.—Both his name and his remedy you shall know   ὁ λόγος Τῷ λόγῳ[1] has cured me.

Hyp.—You speak most truly.   ψυχῆς νοσούσης ἐσὶν ἰατρὸς λόγος[2]

Bu.—So I have recovered from that disease, Nosoponus. And now, if you wish to take my character for a time, I will play the physician.

No.—I'll play the part.

Bu.—When the paroxysm of the disease was upon me, the doctor spoke to me just as I am now speaking to you. "A false shame," he said, "is overwhelming you" because you cannot endure a taunt common to so many thousands of men.

No.—What taunt?

Bu.—Because you are denied the title of Ciceronian.

No.—This hurts me, I acknowledge.

Bu.—But answer me in the name of the Muses, what Ciceronians can you mention to me, save only Cicero himself? Let us begin with the ancients. In the very long list of orators which Cicero has compiled in the *Brutus* there are scarcely two whom he deems worthy of the title of orator at all, to say nothing of being Ciceronians. Caius Caesar cannot be called a Ciceronian, in the first place because he was contemporary, and in the second place because he aimed at a very different style of oratory, content to speak gracefully and in his own distinctive way. How little there is of Cicero in this! For it is not so commendable for an orator to speak elegant Latin, as it is disgraceful for him to be ignorant of elegant Latin. Then too, Caesar's works are not extant except some letters and the *Commentaries* about the authorship of which there is much dispute among scholars. There is certainly no oration extant, while in this Cicero especially excelled. I may say the same of Marcus Caelius, Plancus, and Decius Brutus, whose letters we have in abundance, thanks to the zeal of Tiro. I may say the same also of Cneius Pompeius, L. Cornelius Balbus, Lentulus, Cassius, Dolabella, Trebonius, Publius Vatinius, Servius Sulpicius, Aulus

---

[1]Reason with reason.
[2]Reason is the physician of a diseased mind.

Caecina, Bithynius, Marcus Brutus, Asinius Pollio, Caius Caesar, and others, fewer of whose letters we have but who were contemporaries of Cicero, so that it is not more fitting for Marcus Caelius to be called a Ciceronian than for Cicero to be called a Caelian. Nor is there any resemblance to Cicero's letters except the clear and natural elegance of the Roman language. You object on the ground that in his letters you have not that complete Cicero whom you set before yourself as model! At this point I would say something of Crispus Sallust, a contemporary of Cicero, but very unlike him in style.

No.—Do not mention those rough, uncombed ancients in whose time eloquence as well as manners had not yet become polished, nor the contemporaries of Cicero, but those who lived after him.

Bu.—Well, does Seneca seem to you a Ciceronian?

No.—By no means, particularly in prose. And the *Tragoediae*, which are esteemed by scholars, could hardly have been written by Seneca.

Bu.—Valerius Maximus?

No.—He is as much like Cicero as a mule is like a man. So different indeed is he that you would scarcely believe he was an Italian or that he lived in that age which he describes. So different is his whole style that you might say he was an African. Never was poetry more labored.

Bu.—What about Seutonius?

No.—Just as different from Cicero as Seneca was, reproducing him neither in words, nor structure, nor clearness, nor ornamentation, nor elegance.

Bu.—Do you consider Livy worthy the honor?

No.—In the first place he is a historian, in the second place he is careless in style, and has been criticised for his Patavinity.

Bu.—I do not dare now to suggest Cornelius Tacitus.

No.—It isn't worth while.

Bu.—Perhaps you will allow Quintilian in your list.

No.—He really strove to be unlike Cicero; but I wish his *Declamationes* were extant, for the writings which we possess have the faintest suggestion of Cicero.

Bu.—But I have one you would not scorn, Quintus Curtius.

No.—He is a historian.

Bu.—Yes, but in his histories there are some orations.

No.—He is a more promising candidate than the others, but nothing, they say, to the swine of Parmeno. He has many tricks of style different from Cicero.

Bu.—If you reject him, you will not accept, I presume, Aelius Spartianus, Julius Capitolinus, Aelius Lampridius, Vulcacius Gallicanus, Trebellius Pollio, Flavius Vopiscus, or Aurelius Victor.

No.—In these there is scarcely anything which you would commend, except historical fidelity. They are so far from deserving the name of Ciceronians that they ill preserve the purity of the Latin tongue.

Bu.— Well, here is [1]Probus Aemelius!

No.—He praises fair-mindedly all whose biographies he writes so that you might call him eulogist more fittingly than historian.

Bu.—Perhaps you will accept Ammianus Marcellinus?

No.—Slow of speech, but with style approaching the poetic, when he urges us to give up our captives. I should accept more quickly Velleius Paterculus, and yet I do not deem even him worthy this honor.

Bu.—You will not grant the honor, I suppose, to the compilers of epitomes,—Florus, Eutropius, and Solinus?

No.—I will if any scholar recognizes them as such, but on this ground, because they reflect what they imitate.

Bu.—But I must go back. We have omitted the two Scipios. I know you will not allow the elder to be mentioned here. Perhaps you will the younger?

No.—No, indeed, the censors of this case especially forbid his letters to be read by youths, lest they become Plinians, instead of Ciceronians.

Bu.—But he wrote a pretty clever speech in praise of Trajan.

No.—Very clever, but not Ciceronian.

Bu.—I purposely omit the poets, easily divining your answer, if I should bring forward the most illustrious and charming of all,—Vergil, Horace, Ovid, Lucan, and Martial.

No.—In Horace there is not a trace of Cicero; in Vergil some, though faint. Ovid might be the Cicero of the poets. Lucan is more orator than poet though very different from Cicero. Martial comes very close to the charm of Ovid and something of Ciceronian praise he could have won, if he had not prefaced sev-

[1]Cornelius Nepos.

eral of his books with letters—Goodness knows how different
from Cicero's!

Bu.—What if I should suggest Lucretius?

No.—At the same time bring forth Ennius and Lucilius.

Bu.—Scholars admire the fair phrases of Aulus Gellius.

No.—Neither his themes nor his language pleases. His speech
is affected and verbose, his range of subjects is meagre.

Bu.—Consider Macrobius.

No.—He's exactly the poor little crow of Aesop. From the
patches of others he has woven his patchwork, so his own tongue
does not speak; and if ever it should, you would think a Greekling
were stammering Latin. An example of this you will find in the
Second Commentary on the Dream of Scipio. All his wisdom
is borrowed and as old as Homer.

Bu.—Well, some admire Symmachus who is clever in his letters.

No.—Let them admire him who prefer a labored style.

Bu.—But hold, we have passed Apuleius by!

No.—I shall compare him with Cicero when I may compare
a jackdaw with a nightingale.

Bu.—That may be true in reference to his *Golden Ass* and
Florida, but he approaches Cicero at least in his *Apology.*

No.—Yes, he approaches but still is far behind. But you
have forgotten Martianus Capella also, if you care to include
such as he.

Bu.—Suppose we take up those who are half Christians. What
do you think of Boethius?

No.—A worthy philosopher, not a mean poet, but far removed
from Ciceronian.

Bu.—What about Ausonius?

No.—I grant him talent and training, but his style smacks of
the pleasure and licentiousness of the court just as does his life:
instead of being a Ciceronian, he seems to have designedly spoken
in different fashion. If one, therefore, should call him a Ciceronian one would disgrace instead of honor him, just as you would
if you should call him a German who wished to be counted a
Frenchman even if he were a German.

Bu.—To make a long journey short, let us come, if you please,
to the Christians and see if we may find perchance some one who
deserves to be called a Ciceronian. I suppose you will approve

of Lactantius who is reputed to send forth a *lactean* stream of Ciceronian eloquence.

No.—Reputed yes, but by one who was not a Ciceronian.

Bu.—But this you cannot deny that Lactantius strove for the eloquence of Cicero. The preface of the third book of the *Institutiones* declares this, where intent upon the truth of the Christian philosophy he longs for eloquence, if not Ciceronian, at least approximately Ciceronian.

No.—And certainly he did not try without some success, though he did not attain his desire.

Bu.—How so?

No.—For he said in the very first of the preface of that work: [1]*Alioqui nihil inter Deum hominemque distaret, si consilia et dispositiones illius majestatis aeternae cogitatio assequeretur humana.* When did Cicero ever use *dispositiones* for *decreta?*

Bu.—By no means has he become unlike Cicero in his desire to be a Ciceronian. For it is a characteristic of Cicero to emphasize a thing by two words meaning the same, or almost the same. This is the reason for the words, *consilia et dispositiones.* Who knows but that he seized upon the hiatus in *consilia atque* and again in *cogitatio assequeretur* in order to be Ciceronian? Perhaps he had in mind the rhythm too, finishing the clause with the close of a scazon, as in *balneatore* and *archipirata.* Endings of this kind he frequently uses in the same preface, as in the very first sentence, *inhaerere,* and again *instruere possimus,* and soon *apud Graecos, luce orationis ornata,* and *honesta suscepta,* and immediately after *honorasti,* then soon after *nominis tradas,* and *ut sequerentur hortarer,* likewise a little after, *reliquerunt.* That certainly is Ciceronian which frequently ends in a double trochee, as *contulerunt, convocamus, sopiamus, inchoamus;* and once in the close of a period he puts *quaesisse videatur.* This shows that he tried very hard to imitate Cicero. But, with some justice you refuse Luctantius the title of Ciceronian on the ground that he did not bring to the defense of the Christian philosophy the erudition, vigor, and feeling that Cicero brought to the pleading of civil cases.

Bu.—In what order shall I present the rest? Shall Cyprian be first?

---

[1]"Otherwise there would be no difference between God and man, if human thought could attain to the plans and disposition of that divine power."

No.—He wrote as a Christian rather than as a Ciceronian.

Bu.—Hilary?

No.—Soho! Nothing like. He is tedious and obscure and raises himself on his Gallic buskin, as they say, dragging with him many words that are not of Ciceronian purity.

Bu.—Sulpicius, I presume, will seem worthy of this honor?

No.—He is indeed more delicate, more pleasing, clearer, and more spontaneous than Hilary, but his language declares him to be a Frenchman. Piety is not lacking but force and dignity are. He has a florid rather than a vigorous style.

Bu.—You will admit Tertullian?

No.—You are jesting. He purposely and consciously hid good thoughts under mean words and was even more rugged than Apuleius himself.

Bu.—Certainly you will not reject that most eloquent and learned St. Jerome?

No.—I recognize in him a man distinguished for learning and eloquence. I do not recognize a Ciceronian who has to be driven from the imitation of Cicero by a scourge.

Bu.—St. Augustine then?

No.—He is like Cicero in that he makes his periods very long and involved. But he is not so clever in breaking up the extended structure of his oration into divisions nor has he Cicero's ready speech and felicity in handling subjects.

Bu.—Paulinus?

No.—He shows hardly a vestige of Cicero—commonplace in thoughts and words.

Bu.—St. Ambrose then.

No.—You cite a Roman orator, not a Ciceronian. He delights in clever allusions and general reflections, expresses himself only in aphorisms, abounds in rhythmical divisions and clauses and nicely balanced periods, has his own inimitable style but it is very different from Cicero's.

Bu.—At least acknowledge Pope Gregory I.

No.—I recognize in him a pious and sincere man. He is more like Cicero than St. Ambrose but his speech flows sluggishly and shows the influence of Isocrates, which is foreign to Cicero, for in his boyhood he had been so trained in the schools.

Bu.—Every one marvels at the eloquence of Pope Leo.

No.—His language is, I admit, rhythmical, clear and sensible, but not Ciceronian.

Bu.—What if I should suggest St. Bernard of Burgundy.

No.—I recognize in him a good man, which is a requisite for an orator, naturally disposed to refined and pleasing speech but so far from being a Ciceronian that you would scarcely gather from his writings that he had ever even read Cicero.

Bu.—Since you have rejected St. Bernard, I should not dare to propose to you Bede, Remi, Claudius, Hesychius, Anselm, Isidore.

No.—Do not mention those κολοζώτας[1] for their translations are miserable and their native speech worse. In them eloquence languished.

Bu.—I fear you will say *died* if I mention those who lived later. I shall omit therefore Alexander of Hales, Peter of Ghent, and innumerable writers of this calibre. I will suggest two κορυφαίους,[2] Bonaventure and Thomas.

No.—Bonaventure is fluent enough in his way; while Thomas is a true Aristotelian ἀπαθὴς,[3] aiming only to instruct the reader.

Bu.—That is true in investigations; but when he becomes rhetorician or poet you see the spirit of Cicero distinctly enough.

No.—Poet you say? Nowhere does he seem less eloquent than when he aims at oratorical fluency in the handling of the Eucharist. But come, to dismiss those scholastic theologians in whom you will seek in vain for any, much less Ciceronian, eloquence. Present others if you have them.

Bu.—Well, we will come back to another class of writers nearer to our own time. For several generations eloquence seems to have died out entirely, but not so long ago it began to come to life among the Italians, then later among our own people. And thus, the chief of the reflowering eloquence seems to have been the Italian, Francesco Petrarch, celebrated and great in his time, but now scarcely read—a man of burning genius, wide knowledge, and extraordinary eloquence.

No.—I admit it. And yet there are times when he halts in the use of Latin and his whole diction smacks of the rudeness of the preceding age. Moreover, who would call one a Ciceronian who did not even strive for the distinction?

[1] Mutilators.
[2] Eminent men.
[3] Without passion.

Bu.—There's no use then in suggesting Biondo and Boccaccio, who were inferior to Petrarch, both in eloquence and in the understanding of Latin. Nor even Giovanni Tortelli.

No.—No, indeed!

Bu.—He had a host of learned followers who eagerly set themselves to the imitation of Cicero. Do you consider any of them worthy of the name? Francesco Filelfo?

No.—Evidently he would be if he had pleased all as well as he pleased himself. He tried industriously to imitate Cicero but not very successfully. When he tried hardest, he failed most completely; for example, in his orations. Now in his letters there is some suggestion of Cicero. I would not have you think that I have meant to disparage these men. I recognize them as worthy of immortality and as having done great service to literature, but it is something divine to be a Ciceronian.

Bu.—[1]Leonardo Aretino seems to me a second Cicero.

No.—In ready speech and clearness he is much like Cicero, but he lacks Cicero's strength and some of his other virtues. He rarely gets a glimpse of pure Latinity. Aside from this, he is as learned as he is good.

Bu.—Guarino, I know well enough you would not allow, or Lapo, or Acciaiolo, or Antonio Beccaria, or Francesco Barbatius, or Antonio Tudertino, or Leonardus Justinianus, or Achille Bocchi, or others whose names do not occur to me, especially since most of them we know only through their translating from the Greek where originality, the chief part of eloquence, has no place.

No.—I scorn none of them yet I deem none worthy of the honor.

Bu.—I will present the Florentine, Poggio, a man of rather spirited style.

No.—He had natural ability enough but little training and sometimes his speech lacked purity, if we are to believe Lorenzo Valla.

Bu.—Then let us substitute Valla.

No.—He uses the purest idiom of all and is the most polished but he approaches nearer to the carefulness and subtlety of Quintilian than to the careless ease of Cicero.

---

[1]Leonordo Bruni.

Bu.—I consciously am passing over many whom I know you will not listen to and am proposing only the exceptional. If you confer the honor of this name upon any one at all, you will certainly grant it to Ermolao Barbaro the Great.

No.—You have introduced a truly great and divine man, but very unlike Cicero in style and more labored almost than Quintilian himself and Pliny whose eloquence the study of philosophy injured somewhat.

Bu.—What about Giovanni Pico della Mirandola?

No.—You mention an almost divine talent, an unbounded genius, but one whose zeal for language, philosophy and even theology has marred his eloquence.

Bu.—You know his namesake, Francesco?

No.—'Οὐδ' ἐγγὺς,[1] as the saying is, too much a philosopher and theologian, otherwise a great man. But how does it happen that you count him among the Ciceronians, when in his dispute with Pietro Bembo, he denounced the devotees of Cicero?

Bu.—Granting that one can be too much of a theologian, you have praised him most highly.

No.—One can be for the gaining of this palm.

Bu.—The chances are that there is one, unless I am mistaken, to be found whom you will not reject—Angelo Politian. For Marsilio Ficino I do not dare to introduce.

No.—I confess that Angelo was of perfectly *angelic* mind, a rare miracle of nature in any field he has tried; but when compared to Cicero's style he is as nothing. His virtues are of a very different kind.

Bu.—Suppose I put into the list Codrus Urceo, George of Trebizonde, Theodore Gaza, John Lascaris, George Merula, Marcus Musurus, Marullo. I can almost guess your answer. You would bar from this contest the whole race of Greeks because you would say they hated your beloved Cicero. But no sentiment of anger, hate, or love should influence this election.

No.—Nor shall it. We must speak rather guardedly of John Lascaris, since he is still alive. He is a man of courteous manner, good breeding, and keen judgment. His epigrams are very clever. He might have been a promising candidate for Ciceronianism, if business of the state had not diverted his mind. Codrus Urelo had no skill in Latin nor culture. A man of the Epicurean

---

[1] Not near.

type, he troubled not himself about a prize which is as difficult to obtain as it is uncommon. George of Trebizonde, I acknowledge, is a remarkably learned man who has done noble service to letters, and yet Theodore Gaza is more finished. The one has devoted himself to Cicero, the other to Aristotle; and no one has made more elegant translations, whether from Greek into Latin or Latin into Greek, than George of Trebizonde. When he speaks his own tongue, however, two definite things annoy the fastidious reader: his zeal for philosophy, in which he was absorbed; and that γνήσιον[1] of the Greek which is hard to unlearn.

Bu.—What hinders a Greek from mastering Latin, if a Briton or a Frisian can? Especially when the Greek language, not only in words but also in figures, has most affinity to the Latin?

No.—What the Britons and the Frisians have done I leave to others. Affinity seems to me to stand in the way of purity. More quickly will an Irishman speak pure Latin than a Frenchman or a Spaniard. More quickly will a Frenchman learn to speak pure German than he will learn to speak Italian or Spanish. However, I shall proceed. George Merula is an Alexandrine. I do not know whether he is a Greek or not but his Greek translations are so fine that he can be compared favorably with many of the classical scholars. I have read a few things by Marullo which would be tolerable if they contained less paganism. Marcus Musurus I know better. He is a remarkably well informed man, somewhat obscure and affected in his poetry, and leaving nothing, so far as I know, in prose, except one or two prefaces. I used to wonder how a Greek knew so much Latin. He did little writing, because he was summoned to Rome by Pope Leo to the office of archbishop and soon after died.

Bu.—You will accept Pomponio Leto then?

No.—Content with the elegance of Latin conversation he learned nothing else.

Bu.—Well, Platina?

No.—He would have been a worthy historian if he had lighted upon a happier theme. In his *optimus civis* and *Panegyricus* he resembled Cicero but not enough to earn the name of Ciceronian. In general, he was a learned man, versatile, and, I think, good.

Bu.—What of Filippo Beroaldo, the Elder? I see you shake your head. I knew it.

---

[1] Accent.

7

No.—I will assent if you recommend him to me as a man of unusual merit in the realm of literature but if you demand that he be enrolled in the list of Ciceronians I must say no. Filippo Beroaldo, the Younger, stands a better chance, although he has made but small contribution to letters.

Bu.—In vain do I enumerate Giorgio Valla, Christophoro Landino, Mancinelli, Peter Marsus, Baptista Pius, Cornelio Vitelli, Nicolo Leoniceno and Leonico, Bartolommeo Scala, Paolo Cortesi, Pietro Crinito, Jacopo Antiquario.

No.—What a hodgepodge! Do not mention Mancinelli, Vitelli, and Marsi, when style is the subject for discussion. Baptista Pius tried for a style of his own. Scala in his own estimation was a Ciceronian but in that of Politian he had not even common sense, much less Latin scholarship. Paolo Cortesi I will discuss later. Pietro Crinito is a scholar yet he falls far short of being a Ciceronian. Leoniceno is a physician, not a rhetorician. Leonico ever busied in the sanctuaries of philosophy, especially in those of Plato, set himself to imitating the dialogues of Plato and Cicero and gained as much eloquence as we could expect from a philosopher; but he would not desire to be called a Ciceronian, I'm sure, for he is a man of rectitude as well as of profound learning.

Bu.—What of Domizio Calderino?

No.—He had a good start and would have stood a fair chance if dissipation at Rome and death had not cut him off in his youth.

Bu.—Next Scipio Carteromacho.

No.—I recognize in him a man without ostentacion, and versed in both Latin and Greek, but from his writings it does not appear that he aimed at Ciceronian eloquence.

Bu.—You will not reject, I suppose, Girolamo Donato, the noble Venetian?

No.—His letters—about the only thing of his we have—show that he could have accomplished anything he turned his mind to but politics distracted him from literary work.

Bu.—Antonio Sabellicus?

No.—I acknowledge he has natural ability and some skill in speaking. And he uses his rhetoric not unsuccessfully at times. He has done brilliant work in that kind of history which calls for his particular style.

Bu.—Thus far the host of dead. Now we ought, as they say, to remember the living, of whom perhaps you will hesitate to say what you think.

No.—Not at all, since I admit that this measure of praise has been the good fortune of practically no one up to the present time

Bu.—You know Paolo Aemilio?

No.—The man's profound learning, painstaking care, purity of life, and entire trustworthiness in history, I greatly admire. Ciceronian style he neither aimed at nor has.

Bu.—I bring Battista Egnazio.

No.—You have mentioned a man as honest and blameless as he is learned and eloquent but to whom the votes of the doctors deny the honor of the Ciceronian name. He preferred to speak learnedly rather than in Ciceronian style and he gained what he wished.

Bu.—See, I bring to you Paolo Bombasio.

No.—Indeed I admire Paolo Bombasio, a man of absolutely golden heart, the best friend in the world; but, on account of his health, he did not indulge much in writing. Of sensitive nature, he was soon offended at the wicked contentions of mean rivals. He taught Greek at Bologna for a salary; devoted himself to the business of the state; and, when at length summoned to Rome, he preferred to increase his estate rather than to grow old in letters.

Bu.—Perhaps you will be more favorable to younger men. What do you think of Andria Alciati?

No.—I will give you the opinion of scholars who knew the man better than I. The virtues which Cicero divided between Quintus Scaevola and Marcus Crassus, the one of whom he called the most legal minded of orators and the other the most eloquent of lawyers, both in this one man are said to meet. His power of eloquence we have seen in the preface of Cornelius Tacitus. For in the *Annotations* he meant to teach, not to speak as an orator.

Bu.—We have omitted few Italians, I suppose, worthy of mentioning. But Jerome Aleander, who was recently a favorite of Clement VII and Archbishop of Brundusium, ought not to be overlooked.

No.—His ability is not sufficiently clear from what he has written; for few of his things have been published and in these particular ones he does not seem to have striven for Ciceronianism. For a long time business of state turned him in a different direction and, though he was skilled in both Latin and Greek, he was absolutely unworthy the honor because a slave to business.

Bu.—Indeed I think Albert, Prince of Carpi, approached nearer to Ciceronian phrase than Aleander. He has written nothing, so far as I know, except a single book, or, if you prefer, a lengthy letter in answer to Erasmus, and even of this some declare positively that he is not the author.

No.—Whatever his merits, he approaches Cicero just so far as one may who has been trained from his youth in theology and philosophy.

Bu.—You see how many writers of most celebrated name I have called to mind, Nosoponus, no one of whom you admit to have attained the dignity of a Ciceronian. Perchance some escape me. Suggest if you know any, Hypologus.

Hyp.—The two Cælii, Rhodiginus and Calcagini you have intentionally omitted?

Bu.—Certainly not intentionally.

No.—Rhodiginus was a good man and widely read but not to be entered in the contest of eloquence at all; Calcagini was not only superior in eloquence but also in learning, of elegant and ornate style, but smacking somewhat of scholastic philosophy which does not hinder him from being numbered among the eloquent but bars him from the Ciceronians.

Bu.—A very few I pass by consciously, to the mention of whom our discussion will naturally bring us around at a more fitting time. Meantime, if you please, let us go across for a little while into France, always most flourishing in letters, to bring up for consideration at least the principal ones who have recently won a reputation for eloquence through their writings. Robert Gaguin not so very long ago was very popular, more however, on account of his speeches than his writings.

No.—Yes, but in his own age. Now he would hardly be counted a Latin scholar.

Bu.—What if I should introduce the two brothers Ferdinand?

No.—I would not allow it.

Bu.—Jouvenneaux Gui?

No.—Much less.

Bu.—Jodocus Badius?

No.—More quickly I should admit him into the contest than Apuleius, for his attempts have not been fruitless; he has ability and skill and would have attained greater success if domestic cares and avarice had not interrupted the leisure conducive to the Muses and necessary for an aspirant to this honor.

Bu.—Perhaps the honor of this title you will grant to Guillaume Budé, the glory of France.

No.—Why should I grant what he does not strive for and would not recognize if I should? Still, he deserves admiration in other respects for his great and varying gifts.

Bu.—Jacob Faber is very highly esteemed.

No.—A good man and a scholar but one who preferred to speak in the language of theology rather than in that of Cicero.

Bu.—Jean Pins perchance you will take.

No.—He might have been numbered among the competitors if the stress of business and ecclesiastical office had not turned him away from his studies. Once indeed at Bologna he demonstrated his power when he made offerings to the Muses. Now, I hear, he has been made a bishop and what increase of eloquence has come to him I do not know. Perchance he has gained more learning than honorable employment.

Bu.—Do you recognize Nicolas Bérauld?

No.—I recognize that he is not unlike Pins in spontaneity but he has never directed his strength to Ciceronian style. He is more successful in speaking than in writing. I divine perfectly well his abilities but he is rather inclined to be lazy.

Bu.—Franciscus Deloinus I should not hesitate to suggest, if he could have shown himself as great in oration or essay as in letters written extemporaneously to friends. It would surely have seemed strange if he had wasted almost his whole life *in Accursiis, Bartholis, ac Baldis,* and if in his old age he had fortunately grown young again in more polite letters. Death recently has called him away; timely for himself because he was an old man, but prematurely for letters because he seemed destined to their elevation and adornment. If Lazare de Baif, who by a single little essay on clothes won great renown and raised the highest hopes, only had gone on as he began! Although fitted for teaching, he preferred to be witty as it seems, and a representative of the Attic school rather than a Ciceronian.

Bu.—There occurs to me at this moment a pair, by no means, I fancy, to be scorned. You know Claude Chansonnette of Metz, and Cornelius Scepper?

No.—Both, intimately. Chansonnette is of a playful turn of mind, sings most sweetly any theme whatever, especially in prose; in poetry I do not know his ability. Not unsuccessfully does he imitate Cicero. The fluency, perspicuity, wealth of language, and wit of Cicero he has almost attained, and though for a long time he has been playing a vivacious role in the legations of princes, in spite of the fact that this task requires the deepest quiet, he has conquered himself, just as if he took all the Muses as his companions with him when flitting over land and sea. He has this remarkable distinction, viz., that he has combined eloquence with knowledge of law and philosophy. Scepperus in addition to skill in every department of learning weaves with equal facility poetry and prose even though he now for a long time has been taking active part in politics.

Bu.—What do you think of Ruel?

No.—That which is worthy of a man most skilled in medical lore and most religiously faithful in translating Greek authors. This kind of a reputation he preferred to being called a Ciceronian.

Bu.—But where must I place Peter Mosellanus of Treves, among the Germans or the French?

No.—That has nothing to do, surely, with our present discussion.

Bu.—Among the Ciceronians?

No.—I admire his scholarship, equal in Latin and Greek, his practical knowledge, his pure and unalloyed genius, his untiring care, his lively, figurative, and clear diction. Much would have been expected of him if he had not died in his youth, when just entering the contest for this honor, causing sorrow to all scholars and a great loss to letters.

Bu.—From France then, if you please, let us turn to England, the fortunate nurse of geniuses. But hold, I had almost forgotten German Brixius. You would not ignore a man equally skilled in Latin and Greek, in poetry and prose, and successful in Latin translations of Greek. Will you then class Brixius among Ciceronians?

No.—Although he is still in the heat of the race and has attained fluency and clearness, yet he is unlike Cicero in some things, but in such things that he may have hope, if, as at present, he goes on devoting himself wholly to this study. Meantime, I like to applaud him because he is running zealously.

Bu.—Now then into England; and, since she has so many candidates, I will name only those who have sought fame through their writings. If I cite William Grocyn, you will say that there is nothing extant of his except a single letter, very carefully elaborated, clever, and in good Latin. Fitted for epistolary cleverness, he loved brevity and propriety; you would call him a representative of the Attic School in this surely, for he aimed at nothing else and could not endure Cicero's fulness of expression. He was laconic not only in writing but also in speaking. Therefore I shall not urge his claims. But I do not hesitate to propose Thomas Linacre.

No.—I know him as a man of excellent training but so disposed toward Cicero that, if he could have been like either he pleased, he would have preferred Quintilian to Cicero. Thus, you see, he was not much more kindly disposed toward Cicero than the common run of Greeks are. Urbanity he never strives for; he surpasses an Attic in the repression of his feelings; brevity and elegance he loves, and he is extremely didactic. He studiously copies Aristotle and Quintilian. You may attribute him as much praise as you wish but he cannot be called a Ciceronian for he has studied to be unlike Cicero.

Bu.—There is Richard Pace.

No.—He indeed could have been counted among the candidates for Ciceronian eloquence, if the speed of extemporaneous writing had not been too alluring and if the business of popes and kings had not distracted him in his youth and almost buried him in worldly cares.

Bu.—I will leave England when I have mentioned Thomas More.

No.—A most fortunate genius. I confess there is nothing he could not have accomplished if he had devoted himself wholly to letters. But in his boyhood scarcely a trace of the better literature had crossed into England. Then the authority of his parents compelled him to learn English Law, the farthest possible from literature; next he was exercised in pleading cases, then called to the duties of the state. With difficulty he could at odd hours turn his attention to the study of oratory. Finally he was dragged into Court and immersed in the business of the King and the Kingdom where he could love study but not cultivate it. Though the style he gained tended rather to Isocratic rhythm and logical subtlety than to the outpouring river of Ciceronian eloquence, yet he is not inferior at all in culture to Cicero. Furthermore, you recognize a poet even in his prose for in his youth he spent much time in writing poetry.

Bu.—Then let us leave England for I will not mention William Latimer or Reginald Pole—one of whom, a pious man, preferred to be proficient in theology rather than in the eloquence of Cicero, and the other, though a very great admirer and not a bad imitator of Cicero, has not cared to publish anything over his own name but has shown his ability in private letters. In other lines, England has innumerable youths of the highest hopes. We are, however, playing the part of the censor, not the soothsayer. Yet what wonder that youth flowers there where the King himself not only encourages talent by prizes but also spurs it on by his example, already having testified in two pamphlets his love of piety and shown his genius and his eloquence.

No.—I have admired those essays very much and they are not so different from Cicero except that the theme and royal dignity seem to require their own peculiar style.

Bu.—What then remains except to sail over to Holland?

No.—First to Scotland, I vote.

Bu.—I should not care, if I thought there was any one there whom you would consider. I'd rather go to Denmark for she has given to us Saxo Grammaticus who wrote a splendid history of that people.

No.—I admire so much his lively and burning genius, his rapid, flowing speech, his wonderful wealth of words, his numerous aphorisms, his wonderful variety of figures that I cannot wonder enough where a Dane of that age got so great power of eloquence; yet you will find scarcely a trace of Cicero in him.

Bu.—Now to Holland.

No.—No, to Zeland first, lest you slight some one.

Bu.—That land too has produced skillful minds but most of them are buried in luxury. Thence if you will I shall bring Adrian van Barland, in whose writings you can recognize the purity and ease of Cicero.

No.—He approximates Cicero, to be sure, in those qualities, but not in all.

Bu.—From Zeland it is an easy journey to Holland, prolific parent of native genius; but no honor is paid there to eloquence and pleasures do not easily allow talent to mature. From there I will bring Erasmus of Rotterdam, if you will allow.

No.—You profess to speak of writers. I do not call him a writer, much less a Ciceronian.

Bu.—What do I hear? Anyway he was counted among the πολυγράφοι.[1]

No.—Yes, if a πολυγράφος is one who smears a great quantity of paper with ink. It is a different thing to write in the sense in which we are using the term, and writers make up a different class. Otherwise those who make money by transcribing books with the hand might be called writers, though scholars prefer to call them scribes. But that is writing in my mind which brings fruit from the field. Reading corresponds to the fertilizing; digesting and correcting corresponds to the harrowing, digging, trenching, pruning, pulling out of tares, and the rest of the work without which neither the seed will sprout nor, after sprouting, grow.

Bu.—What then is your opinion of Erasmus?

No.—He degrades and hurries everything; he does not give natural birth to his creations; sometimes he writes a whole volume at one sitting; nor can he ever have patience to read over even once what he has written; and he does nothing but write, notwithstanding the fact that not till after long reading should one come to writing and then but seldom. What of the fact too that he not even tries for Ciceronian style but uses theological words and sometimes even vulgarisms?

Bu.—William Gaudanus was terser.

No.—Brief as an Attic in his letters, good in poetry, but— O accursed ease! how much of fine natural ability do you either spoil or utterly destroy!

Bu.—You know Gilles de Delft?

No.—A man of wide learning, not a bad versifier, if he had added strength to facility.

Bu.—Martin Dorpius died but recently.

---

[1] Writers of many books.

No.—Fruitful, versatile, and inclined to elegance, but preferring to be led by others' counsels. Finally, theology separated him from the Muses.

Bu.—What do you think of Jacob Ceratinus?

No.—He gave promise but is far from a Ciceronian.

Bu.—Thence then, if you please, let us journey together into Friesland. For that country produces minds absolutely white, as the saying goes. But Como is ill suited to the Muses. Therefore I shall omit the Langes, and the Canters; Rodolph Agricola alone is a sufficient representative.

No.—I recognize in him a man of divine heart, of profound learning, of no common style, genuine, strong, painstaking, orderly, but smacking somewhat of Quintilian in style and of Isocrates in structure, yet more sublime than either, also more fluent and clearer than Quintilian. He accomplished his aim and I do not doubt that he could have portrayed Cicero if he had wished. And yet there were certain other things that stood in the way of his attaining this highest reputation—the misfortune of place and time, for in his day and country practically no honor at all was paid to polite letters and the national life was extravagant. In Italy he could have excelled but he preferred Germany.

Bu.—Hayo Hermanus is of the same race.

No.—A young man of divine talent; yet there is extant no specimen of his power except some letters, unrivalled in purity, healthy tone, and sweetness. He perchance would have gained the palm if he had been as industrious as he was gifted.

Bu.—I vote that we cross to Westphalia, which has given us Alexander von Heck.

No.—Yes, you mention one who is learned, pure, and eloquent but who has accomplished nothing great because of his contempt for fame.

Bu.—Westphalia has given us Hermann von dem Busche also.

No.—In poetry successful, in prose showing great strength of mind, wide reading, keen judgment, plenty of force; but his style is more like Quintilian than Cicero.

Bu.—Conrad Goclenius, I presume, you do not know.

No.—Do you mean him who in Brabant has for so long adorned not only the college *Busleidianus*—called by some *Trilingue*—but also that whole Academy, and who was otherwise most distinguished?

Bu.—That very one.

No.—I know him Καὶ οἴκοθεν.[1]

Bu.—Do you find any deficiency in him whereby he may not be counted among the Ciceronians?

No.—I think that that mind could accomplish whatever it seriously wished but he prefers to take life easy rather than to be voluminous.

Hyp.—I know one point in which he is very unlike Cicero.

Bu.—What is that?

Hyp.—We picture Cicero with a long and slender neck. Goclenius had a beautifully plump one, and so short that the chin almost touched his breast.

Bu.—We are not discussing his neck but his pen. Suppose, however, we leave Westphalia. Saxony has young men of hope and extraordinary promise among whom Christophorus Carlebitzius is very distinguished on account of the services of his ancestors to the state, and even more on account of his own exemplary character and literary work; but I will not weary you with the enumeration of men whose genius is still growing, who, so to speak, are still in the blade. I will proceed to the other Germans, chief among whom was Reuchlin.

No.—A great man, but his speech is redolent of his age which was still somewhat rough and unpolished. In the same class are Jacob Wimpheling and others whose works contributed not a little to the literature of Germany. And yet he, in a certain way, had his second youth in his grandson, Jacob Spiegel.

Bu.—Then you recognize Philip Melancthon as a pupil of Reuchlin?

No.—Most successful would he have been if he had devoted himself wholly to the Muses. As it was he exerted himself but little and, content with the gifts of nature, he showed little practice or care in his writing and it may be his health would have failed him if he had tried. He seems naturally fitted for extemporaneous speaking but absorbed in other things he seems to have largely given up the study of oratory.

Bu.—Then let me bring to you Ulrich von Hutten.

No.—Splendor and wealth enough he shows in prose, more in verse; but he was far from being the image of Cicero.

---

[1] Intimately.

Bu.—Bilibaldus I ought to have mentioned before, for under his leadership eloquence first began to flourish in Germany, which he illuminated by the purity of his character and the splendor of his fortune.

No.—I do not know whether he aspires, surely he has not attained and his native ability is not so much in the way as business of state and poor health, though no one is more worthy of the best. Yet writing so happily without preparation shows how much he might do if he could put his strength to it.

Bu.—All Germany gives the highest praise to Ulric Zazius.

No.—Yet less than he merited, for besides an exact knowledge of the law, which is his profession, he has a certain very happy faculty of speaking and writing even extemporaneously so that you might say his speech flows out from some rich spring in good, well-chosen words and sentences unceasingly; and there is in his writings a youthful alacrity, and if I may use the term, vivacity which would make you say that it is not the work of an old man you are reading. Yet, withal, he imitates Politian more nearly than Cicero.

Bu.—Well, from a spot near by I will bring Bruno Amerbach, of Augst than whom nature has never fashioned any more promising.

No.—As far as one may know from a taste, he would have been great if death had not snatched him away prematurely from his studies.

Bu.—Henricus Glareanus, the Swiss, you know?

No.—He preferred to spend his time on philosophy and mathematics rather than to imitate Ciceronian phrase, which hardly fits the subtleties of mathematicians.

Bu.—There is one left whom if you do not accept we shall go across into Pannonia.

No.—Who?

Bu.—Ursinus Velius.

No.—Successful in poetry but not in prose. He has plenty of feeling and culture; but when the history which he is said to be writing on the exploits of King Ferdinand of Pannonia and Bohemia is published we can decide more definitely.

Bu.—I am certain he will respond with vigor and eloquence to the renown of his chief and his great deeds. Mention of him has brought us into Pannonia, where I know no one except Jacob

Piso, a zealous candidate for Ciceronian eloquence, who was first snatched away from us by the Court, then by misfortune, and recently by death itself.

No.—I heard and was much grieved.

Bu.—And Sarmatia has men whom you could not despise, but I shall mention none except those who by publishing have given proof of themselves. Chief among these is Bishop Andreas Critius, who surely has wit at command, as the saying goes, who composes verses happily, even more happily prose, who writes extemporaneously with ease and makes conversation pleasing by his perpetual humor.

No.—I have tasted some little bits of his which surely raise in me high hopes, if he is not compelled to give up the leisure needed for the pursuit of the Muses because of embassies of State and Church.

Bu.—Spain who has begun to flower again and to vie with her early glory has very many learned and eloquent men and a few who have become famous through their writings, among whom is Antonio de Lebrixa, a man of wide knowledge. But the mention of him you would not allow in the catalogue of Ciceronians.

No.—You have guessed rightly.

Bu.—Not even Lopes, I think, or Sanchez.

No.—One is a theologian and did not strive for this reputation, the other is much less successful in eulogy than in panegyric, neither the one nor the other is a Ciceronian.

Bu.—I wonder if you will reject John Louis Vives.

No.—Indeed I find lacking in him neither talent, learning, nor memory; he has a ready store of thoughts and words; he was a little too stilted in the beginning, but he grows more eloquent daily; and if neither life nor zeal fail there is hope that he will be numbered among the Ciceronians. There are those however whose attempts at writing come out as the gifts of Mandrabulus. He excels himself daily. He has a versatile mind and thus is fitted especially for public speaking. Yet some of the virtues of Cicero he has not attained, particularly that of pleasing speech and flexibility.

Bu.—Also I know some learned Portuguese who have given public proof of their genius. But I have direct knowledge of none of them except a certain Hermicus, who is successful at epigram, quick and facile in prose, and of very skillful wit in prattling; and Genesius, who recently showed great hope of himself through his pamphlet published at Rome.

See how many lands we have traversed seeking a single Ciceronian, Nosoponus; and not one has been found whom you deem worthy of the honor of the name of your lover! How many ancients we have called to mind, how many of later ages, how many of the age preceding our own, how many of our own contemporaries! Some of them, I grant, a fastidious censor would not accept; but many of them have ornamented, illuminated, and ennobled their age, country, church, and literature by their learning and eloquence; and, up to the present point, we have found no Ciceronian. What remains for us but to go to the Islands of the Blessed for the purpose of seeking there one to whom we may give this name?

With more content we suffer a misfortune common to all. A Spaniard does not grieve if he has not yellow hair, nor an Indian because he is of sallow complexion, nor an Ethiopian because he is black and his nose is flat. Then why do you torture your mind and chafe because you are not a Ciceronian? This may be an ill; but, if it is, can you not bear an ill common to you and such men as we have mentioned?

No.—But Christophe de Longueil, a native of Brabant and educated among the French, attained the reputation. To him alone on this side the Alps the Italians granted this palm; all others they cast aside as barbarians.

Bu.—To be sure De Longueil won highest praise but he won it at too great a price. Long he tortured himself and finally died in the midst of his struggle, causing no small loss to letters to which he would have been in his lifetime of greater use if he had not turned his mind and all his strength of genius to the desire of an empty name. And yet he did not devote himself entirely to Cicero but read every kind of author, studied carefully all the liberal arts, and had a practical knowledge of law besides. Nor was he content to follow in the footsteps of Cicero, but was seemingly very clever in invention, and fertile, skillful, and happy in argument, never failing to show proof of a genius worthy of admiration. It amounts to nothing that these apes of Cicero throw De Longueil in our teeth; he would have been great for his other gifts, even if he had not been a Ciceronian; and this very ambition for an empty title almost destroyed the fruit of his studies and finally cost him his life. Still he was very different from Cicero for he lacked the opportunity of exercising that wonderful eloquence which Cicero exhibited in grave and serious cases in court.

De Longueil published letters, which, though elegant and cleverly wrought, were, I confess, many of them on very trivial subjects and many more were as far-fetched as those of Pliny the Younger. Such products I think ought not to be ranked as letters. Tell me what characteristics of a letter have the *Epistolae* of Seneca except the name? But you say that in Cicero's letters nothing is far-fetched. Either he writes on weighty and serious business as he would speak in public, or he talks with absent friends on familiar themes or about literary pursuits as friends do in ordinary conversation. What of the fact that he did not publish his letters and that he seems to have written some more carelessly than he was accustomed to talk? Why did a great part of those which Tiro, the freedman, collected perish? I think they would not have perished if scholars had judged them worthy of immortality. In the first place then, Cicero's simplicity and charm of unaffected speech; in the second place, his truthfulness is lacking in most of the letters of De Longueil. And inasmuch as neither the fortune nor the business of De Longueil was the same as Cicero's, his imitation lacks fitness and life. To illustrate—Cicero, when a senator and of consular rank, writes to his peers what the generals are doing in the provinces, how the legions are drawn up, points out the dangers, and prophesies the outcome; De Longueil, in imitation of Cicero, writes similar things to learned friends in times of peace and shows anxiety about the outcome of affairs. Do not his efforts fail? Consider that in the privacy of his library he committed to writing most idle rumors such as commonly float about, unworthy to be mentioned even in the conversation of sensible men.

But you say that in the two orations which he left, as if delivered in the Capitol, he has given us Cicero. These, I confess, I have read not only with great admiration but also with great delight; for they caused me to feel far more than ever before the genius of the man. So much so that, though I had formed a fine opinion of him, he far surpassed my expectation; for he seems to have brought forth in these orations whatever power he had of his own and what he had drunk from the orations of Cicero. Yet these speeches which were worked on for so many years, revised so many times, so many times subjected to the censorship of critics,—how little have they of Cicero! No fault indeed of De Longueil, but of the times. Cicero spoke in perfect keeping with his times, not so De Longueil; for at Rome today there are neither the Conscript Fathers, nor the Senate, nor the authority of the people, nor the votes of the tribes, nor the regular magistrates, nor the laws, nor the comitia, nor legal procedure, nor provinces, nor towns, nor allies, nor citizens,—and Rome, there is no Rome, for there is nothing but ruin and rubbish, scars and tracks of old-time calamity. Take away the pope, the cardinals, the bishops, the curia and its officials, the embassadors, the churches, colleges and abbeys, and the rabble—a part of whom live on trafficking and the other part are such as have drifted thither seeking liberty or fortune—and what will Rome be? You answer that the authority of the Popes handed down by Christ is grander than was formerly the rule of the Senate and the Roman People, or even, if you please, of Octavius Caesar. Suppose it is, only acknowledge that the kind of rule is different. Then you see that the same language will not fit, if we decide that it is Ciceronian to fit the language to the present theme. But that celebrated youth fitted his speech to the emotions of men who dream of ancient Rome, *rerum dominam gentemque togatam,* just as the Jews dream of their Moses and the temple at Jerusalem. Young Christophe was great, I say, not on account of office, or exploits, or for any other reason except for his own ability, which I think is much finer than if he had ruled a kingdom.

This however, has nothing to do with Cicero. Back to the case. A dispute arose between him and a certain Italian youth, who I suppose, was primed to protect Ciceronian eloquence against the barbarians. And there is, I hear, now a sort of society at Rome of such men who have more learning than piety, who are called scholars and are held in high esteem by many. Through the influence of these idlers the dispute kindled into fires of partisanship on both sides, for Rome seeks material for pleasure from every source. As time went on the actions of Luther injured De Longueil; for, on account of Luther, whatever had to do with Germany, in fact any one on this side the Alps, was in bad repute at Rome. Some few, more fair-minded than the others, thought it proper to bestow upon De Longueil the title of Roman citizen, as a mark of honor, notwithstanding the fact that he was a barbarian by birth—they still use words of this kind as if the whole face of the world had not changed—because of the admirable elegance of his language. In ancient days this was done and it was a gift as useful as it was honorable. But now, what is it to be Roman citizen? Indeed something less than to be a citizen of Basle. Out of this grew the rivalry of the youth and his coterie against the barbarian De Longueil. The society of idlers sought satisfaction by having De Longueil plead his case in the Capitol (for so they called the hall in which plays are accustomed to be performed by the boys for the sake of practice). An upstart of a youth was suborned to present the indictment, which had been drawn up by some one else and had been memorized. The headings of the indictment were:—first, Christophe de Longueil, once in his boyhood, when, for the sake of testing his strength, he was praising the country where he was then living, had dared to compare France favorably with Italy; second, he had praised the barbarians, Erasmus and Budé; third, incited and delegated by them he had come into Italy to carry back to the barbarians all the best books so that thus they might vie with the Italians for the chief place of learning; and finally, on the ground that he was an uncivilized man and of obscure family he did not seem worthy of so great an honor as to be called a Roman. Here is a theme on which you may test the powers of Ciceronian eloquence. De Longueil treated with utmost seriousness this plainly ridiculous charge, manifesting a truly wonderful pomp of words, a great show of talent, the greatest vehemence, at times much urbanity, using the age of Cicero just as the author of "The Battle of Frogs and Mice" made use, in sport, of the Homeric Iliad, fitting to frogs and mice and equally ridiculous things the splendid words and deeds of gods, goddesses, and heroes. He exaggerated the danger of his position, picturing armed cohorts and bands of gladiators by whom the authority of the Senate and the free action of the law had been hindered. He set before them in fancy early Rome, the Queen of the World, and Romulus with his *Quirites* as her guard and protector; then the Common People and the ruling Senate, the people divided into classes and tribes, the Praetorian

8

right, the veto of the Tribunes; he pictured provinces, colonies, towns, allies of the Seven-hilled City; he quoted a decree of the Senate; he cited laws:—I marvel that he did not remember the water-clocks, nine of which I think are allowed to the defendant. Next the emotions were called into play; the old statesmen of the Roman Republic were appealed to and summoned forth from their tombs. What was not done? The proceeding was exceedingly humorous.

I, for my part, confess it would be a good thing if our young men were trained thus in the schools of declamation, in spite of the fact that Quintilian teaches that the practice of declamation should approach as nearly as possible to the real pleading—no doubt because some like to seek themes from the stories of poets which are neither real nor probable; and because, though the preparatory exercises bear valuable fruit even when the subject is taken from history and the words and thoughts are made to suit the conditions of other times, yet the youth will be better instructed to plead a real case if he handles an investigation involved in the circumstances of the present day. For example, these would be more useful subjects: whether it would profit the state for princes to give their daughters and sisters in marriage to distant regions; whether it would be to the advantage of Christian piety for the leading churchmen to be burdened with secular rule; whether a young man can gain a better education by wide reading than by traveling through distant lands; or whether it is profitable for a boy, elected to rule by choice of the people or by birth, to spend much time on letters and the liberal arts.

Since De Longueil's theme was not taken from history, how could it be made consistent with its time by fictitious assumption? and since, on the other hand, it was not of such a kind that it could be consistent with its own time and characters, how could he imitate Cicero exactly, who, when the arms of Antony had been defeated, laying aside the fear of death, spoke freely before the Senate and the Roman People? The distinguished youth, in spite of these difficulties, conducted the case with so much zeal and skill that I know of no one today even among the Italians, with due respect to all I say it, who could do as well. Thus you see I have no desire to detract from the glory of De Longueil, for such genius I should have to admire even if found in an enemy.   What I have said has only this in view that I may keep youthful students from superstitiously torturing themselves by striving after the likeness of Cicero to such an extent that they are turned away from more useful and necessary studies by the effort.   You have the case before you, Nosoponus, the orations are extant to refute me if I have misrepresented anything.   Now I should like to have you explain to me whether it is worth while for brilliant minds to spend so much time and trouble on these displays, to say nothing of killing themselves by such anxieties.   How much more use De Longueil would have been to the Christian religion, to letters, and to his fatherland, if the nights he spent on these ridiculous indictments he had spent on serious subjects!

No.—Indeed, I am sorry for De Longueil and I have practically nothing to answer.

Bu.—Besides, he bears witness that he has written five orations in praise of Rome.   O labor beautifully spent!   How much better if he had sought to kindle that state and those men who professed belles-lettres there to the adoration of Christ and the love of piety by a few carefully wrought orations!   You understand, Nosoponus, what I mean.   And, pray tell me for whom so much labor was spent.   For the Senate?   The Senate, if there is any at Rome, does not know Latin.   For the people?   So far are they from being captivated by Ciceronian language that they speak a barbarian tongue.   So farewell to these ostentatious displays!

He enters into a serious and weighty case against Martin Luther.   In this can he be a Ciceronian when he is discussing things of which Cicero knew absolutely nothing!   He cannot, for the oration cannot be perfectly Ciceronian which does not accord with the age, the characters, and the circumstances.   He could assail in a fashion truly Ciceronian, but when it comes to the enumeration of the charges Cicero's phraseology would be rather obscure and hardly understood by those who held the tenets of Luther.   Here the case requires the utmost clearness of expression, if he wishes to be a Ciceronian.   Furthermore, from the way he sets forth the facts, it would not be difficult to guess what he would have been in refuting the doctrines of his adversary and in establishing his own.   He carefully avoids the words of our religion, never using the word, *fides* (faith), but substituting in its place, *persuasio* (conviction), and many others which we have spoken of before. Yet time and again he uses the name of Christian, inadvertently, I presume, for this word never occurred in the books of Cicero. Withal, there was much in the speech very praiseworthy; and the greatest fault was that he was so anxious to be a Ciceronian that he preferred to fit his language to Cicero rather than to the case.

No.—And yet it is wonderful how much at the present time some Italians praise these orations.

Bu.—I confess that they praise them, but they read others. How many more thumb the pages of the popular trifles of the [1]Dutch orator which are called the *Colloquia* than the writings of De Longueil however carefully wrought, however finished, however Ciceronian, or to put it in Greek better, κεκροτημένα![2] What is the reason? Why, I say, unless because in the latter the subject itself holds and attracts the reader, no matter in what style it is handled; while over the former the reader sleeps and snores because they are lifeless and artificial? Usefulness recommends even mediocre eloquence. That which merely furnishes amusement cannot continue to please, especially if those who are reading have the end in view not only to speak with greater polish but to live better. In fine, those who inflamed this youth to the striving after Ciceronianism did not deserve the highest reward either from him or from the literary world. But of De Longueil perchance too much.

No.—You have hurried past Jacob Sadolet and Pietro Bembo with reason, I suppose.

Bu.—Yes, for I was not willing to mix excellent men and rare examples of their time with the mob. None of Pietro Bembo's work is extant that I know of except some letters in which I admire the very clear, sane, and I may say Attic style of speaking, as well as the honesty, gentleness, and singular purity of genius, reflected in the language as in a mirror. In nothing do I think De Longueil more fortunate or more adorned than in the friendship of such men. Jacob Sadolet in almost all respects equals Bembo; but he does not strive so much, in that most elegant commentary which he published on the fiftieth psalm, to be considered a Ciceronian that he fails to preserve the charm of his

---

[1] Erasmus himself
[2] Applauded.

character, for he was Bishop of Carpentras and had full regard for his theme. And he used some ecclesiastical words in his letters too. What then? Did he not speak in Ciceronian style? No, or rather yes; for he spoke as Cicero would probably have spoken of the same things if he had lived at that time,—that is, of Christian themes in Christian language. Ciceronians of this kind I can endure, who, gifted with the highest genius, finished with every kind of training, of singular judgment and wisdom, cannot but use the best language whether they have as examples Cicero alone, or a few superior men, or all the scholars.

No.—The scholars think very well of Battista Casellius.

Bu.—The oration *De Lege Agraria* which was published a little while before his death shows that he strove for the formal part of the Ciceronian style with all his might, and that in this he succeeded very well for there was a very high degree of illustration, brilliance of language, and persuasion. For the rest, his deficiency is great if you compare him with Cicero.

No.—Surely all unanimously praise Pontano. The votes of scholars grant to him the palm of Ciceronian style.

Bu.—I am not so stupid nor so envious as not to confess that Pontano was of the first rank in many excellent gifts of genius. And he captivates me too with the quiet flow of his style; he charms my ear by a lovely tinkling of sweet sounding words; and he overpowers me with a kind of splendor and majestic dignity of style.

No.—What hinders then your acknowledging him to be a Ciceronian?

Bu.—What I have said does not make him a Ciceronian. I have read a few of his works. He handles secular subjects and what may be called commonplaces, such as fortitude, obedience, excellence, which shine most easily and of themselves furnish an abundance of maxims, in a way that you could scarcely tell whether he were a Christian or not. Thus he manages his pen in the pamphlet *De Principe*. I cannot remember what else I have read of his except some dialogues modelled after Lucian. But I do not recognize in him a Ciceronian unless he is a Ciceronian who handles modern life with Ciceronian felicity. In epigrams he would have won more praise if he had shunned obscenity, which is not entirely lacking in his *Dialogi* either. In *Meteora* and *Urania* he found material that easily became brilliant, and handled a happy theme in a happy way, using at times the vocabulary of the Christians. In his other works I find at times propriety and fitness and that pungency which lingers in the mind after one of Cicero's works is laid aside. Certainly, according to that law which you have laid down to us, he will not be a Ciceronian in whose writings I could show six hundred words not in Cicero. Finally, think how little Pontano is read, though he is one of the most prominent writers.

No.—Accius Syncerus, who succeeded Pontano, described the birth of the Virgin Mother in a wonderfully clever poem which was applauded beyond measure in the theater at Rome.

Bu.—The breviaries (for so they call them today) of Leo and Clement testify abundantly to this. Then a preface was added of Cardinal Aegedius, not to mention others, and it had reason to be pleasing. Indeed I read both books with delight. He wrote eclogues on fishing too. Who would not admire such talent in a noble youth? He must be placed before Pontano because he was not ashamed to write on a sacred theme and because he treated it neither in a sleepy nor in a disagreeable fashion, but he would have deserved more praise if he had treated his sacred subject somewhat more reverently. Indeed Battista Mantuano could excel him. What was the use of his invoking so many times in a sacred poem the Muses and Phoebus? of his painting the Virgin intent upon the verses of the Muses? of introducing Proteus foretelling Christ? and peopling the whole world with nymphs, hamadryads, and neriads? How harsh this verse sounds to Christian ears which, if I mistake not, is spoken to the Virgin Mary: *Tuque adeo spes fida hominum, spes fida Deorum!*[1] Of course *Deorum* for the sake of the meter was put in place of *Divorum*. Among so many virtues his frequent elisions count for little, but they mar the smoothness. To be brief: if you should cite this poem as a typical work of a youth studying to write poetry, I should think it good; but if as a poem written by a serious man on the subject of piety, I should far prefer the single hymn of Prudentius, *De Natali Jesu,* to the three little volumes of Accius Syncerus,—so far does this poem fail to suffice for the overthrowing of Goliath as he threatens the church with a sling, or for soothing Saul in his madness with the harp as the preface declares him to do. And I do not know which is more blame-

[1] And you therefore the sure hope of gods and men.

worthy for a Christian to handle secular themes in secular language, pretending that he is not a Christian, or in pagan tongue; for the mysteries of Christ ought to be treated in both a scholarly way and reverently. It is not enough to arouse in the reader little temporary feelings of delight; emotions worthy of the Lord must be aroused. And you cannot do this unless you have the subject you are handling thoroughly mastered: for you will not inflame if you yourself are cold; you will not set the reader's mind on fire with the love of celestial things, if you yourself are but lukewarm. If you have at hand either spontaneously or at the cost of no great labor fine phrases and figures to attract the fastidious reader and cause him to linger, I think they ought not to be despised, provided those things which are of chief importance have the first place. Would it be possible for a religious theme to be distasteful to us because it has been clothed in religious language? How can you use religious language if you never take your eyes from Vergil, Horace, and Ovid?—unless, perchance, you approve of those who have described the life of Christ by gathering fragments of Homeric and Vergilian verses from everywhere and sewing them into a patchwork. Surely a painstaking kind of writing,—but have they ever brought tears to the eyes of any? Whom have they moved to pious living? Whom have they recalled from an impure life? And yet not so different is the attempt of those who clothe Christian argument in words, phrases, figures, and rhythms gathered from Cicero. To return, what reward of praise does this rhapsodist gain? This, to be sure, that he has busied himself carefully with Homer and Vergil. What reward of Ciceronianism? That he is applauded only by those who are busied in the same and recognize what has been gathered and whence. This sort of thing certainly furnishes a kind of pleasure, I confess, but to very few and of such a kind that it is easily turned into satiety, and in the end it is nothing more than pleasure. That power of arousing the emotions, without which, in the estimation of Quintilian, there can be no eloquence worthy of admiration, is absolutely lacking. Notwithstanding, we think we are Vergils and Ciceros. Tell me, Nosoponus, if one should break into parts the story of Ganymede elegantly constructed in mosaic and with these same little blocks, by arranging them differently, should attempt to represent Gabriel bearing the divine message to the

Nazarene virgin, would he not produce a rude and disappointing work, out of excellent blocks to be sure, but not fitted to the subject?

No.—Licence granted by the ancients makes excuse for poets.

Bu.—Listen to what Horace says about this:

> [1]*Sed non ut placidis coeant inmitia, non ut*
> *Serpentes avibus geminentur, tigribus agni.*

It is more inappropriate, I think, to join the Muses and Apollo and the rest of the gods of poetry with the mysteries of the Christian religion than to unite snakes with birds and lambs with tigers, especially if in a serious piece of work. And I think that if any thing is sprinkled in by way of a joke from the stories of the ancients, it ought to be endured rather than approved of; for it behooves every speech of Christians to be centered in Christ whereby it will become persuasive, eloquent, and learned. Even boys may practice on serious themes. Who would allow those pagan exercises when practicing for real, serious, and what is still more important, religious subjects?

No.—What then is your advice? That I reject Cicero?

Bu.—No. He should always be in the bosom of the youth who is a candidate for eloquence, but that over-nicety and fastidiousness which causes one to reject a learned and elegant piece of work and to consider it not worth reading simply because it has not been wrought in imitation of Cicero must be absolutely rejected. In the first place, Ciceronian style does not always accord with one's bent of mind, in which case the effort will turn out badly; in the second place, if one has not the natural ability to attain an inimitable felicity of speaking, what is more stupid than to agonize oneself over the impossible? Add to this that the Ciceronian style does not fit all subjects nor all characters, and, if it did, it is better sometimes to underdo than to overdo. If his eloquence had cost Cicero as much as it costs the Ciceronians he would have left off some of the ornaments from his orations, I venture to say. That is overdone which is bought at so great a sacrifice of time, health, and even at the price of life itself. That is overdone for the sake of which we neglect the branches

---

[1] But 'twill not screen the unnatural and absurd,
Union of lamb with tiger, snake with bird. Ars Poetica 12, 13.—Conington.

of knowledge more necessary to know. And lastly, that is overdone which is bought at the expense of piety. If eloquence is
learned to delight the idle, what profits it to learn by heart the
lines of our role by so many vigils? On the contrary, if it
is learned that we may persuade people of those things that are
honorable, Phocion, the Athenian, spoke more effectively than
Demosthenes, Cato of Utica than Cicero. Again, if eloquence is
acquired that our books may wear out with much reading, and if
we could attain without effort the likeness of Ciceronian style,
yet we ought to strive for variety because it would be healing to
the sick stomach of the reader. Variety has such efficacy in human affairs that it is not always expedient to follow even the
best. Ever true is the Grecian proverb, μεταβολὴ πάντων γλυκύ·[1]
Homer and Horace are to be praised for nothing more than
for the fact that their wonderful variety of subject and figure
never allows the reader to grow weary. Besides, nature has
fashioned us in such way, by granting us each his own genius,
that you will scarcely find two who can do the same thing
or who love the same. And again, since nothing is more
delicate and fastidious than the human stomach and since
there is such a volume to be devoured by us in order to
gain learning, who could hold out in the continual reading if
all had the same style and diction? Therefore, it is better in
books as it is in banquets that some parts be inferior than that
all be alike. Another illustration: what kind of a host would he be
who would serve many guests of varying taste with the same food
seasoned all alike, even if he were serving Apician delicacies?
The result is now, since one is captivated by one kind of speaking and another by another, that everything is read. Nature too
who intended speech to be a mirror of the mind rebels against
that effort. To carry the figure further, there are as many kinds
of minds as there are forms of voices and the mirror will be
straightway deceptive unless it give back the real image of
the mind, which is the very thing that delights the reader especially—to discover from the language the feelings, the characteristics, the judgment, and the ability of the writer as well as
if one had known him for years. Out of this has grown the
great variety of preference for books, according as the writer's
genius is kindred or alien, as it wins or repels the reader; just

---

[1] Change in all things is sweet.   Aristotle, Rhet. 1. 11, 20.

as in form and feature different types delight different men. Let me tell what happened to me. As a youth I was madly in love with all the poets. But as soon as I became more familiar with Horace, all others, in comparison to him, began to offend. What do you think was the reason for this, if not that a kind of secret affinity of minds was recognized in those mute letters? This genuine, native quality does not breathe out in the language of those who express nothing but Cicero. What about the fact that honorable men though born with only ordinary beauty are never willing for a portrait to misrepresent them by flattery, and insist upon being painted in exactly the form that nature has given them, declaring that it is disgraceful to put a false face upon any one and that a deceptive mirror or a flattering picture is a ridiculous thing? The deception would be more disgraceful if I, Bulephorus, should wish to be thought Nosoponus or any one else. Are there not some dishonest men who are rightly ridiculed by the scholars because they reject, as it were, and throw out of their libraries learned and eloquent authors worthy of immortality, simply because they preferred to express themselves rather than Cicero, feeling that it would be a kind of imposture to cast before the eyes of men an illusion of another's beauty instead of their true selves? I doubt whether, if our Divine Maker were willing, we could find many who would wish to exchange the whole type of their bodies with others, and still fewer I suppose there would be who would be inclined to exchange their minds; because, in the first place, no one would be willing to be different from what he is and, in the second place, each one by Providence has been attuned by his own gifts in such a way that even if he should have some faults he can counterbalance them by virtues. Each mind has an individuality of its own reflecting in speech as in a mirror and to fashion it in a different shape is nothing else than going out in masquerade.

No.—Be careful, lest, as the saying is, your language overleap the bounds, for it seems to me that you have reached the point where you condemn all imitation, overlooking the fact that the rhetorical schools depend very largely upon rules, imitation, and practice, unless perchance you believe that those who imitate Cicero take upon themselves the shape of another while those who imitate others keep their own.

Bu.—I favor imitation but imitation that aids rather than hinders nature; that corrects rather than destroys nature's gifts. I approve of the imitation of a model agreeing with your genius or at least not antagonistic, for otherwise you would be fighting the battle of the gods and giants. Further, I do not approve of the imitation of one copy from whose lines you would not dare to depart, but that which culls from all authors, and especially the most famous, what in each excels and accords with your own genius,—not just adding to your speech all the beautiful things that you find, but digesting them and making them your own, so that they may seem to have been born from your mind and not borrowed from others, and may breathe forth the vigor and strength of your nature, causing those who read to recognize, instead of a mosaic drawn from Cicero, an offspring of your own brain as they say Minerva was of the brain of Jupiter, reflecting the living image of the parent, so that your speech may not seem a patchwork, but a river flowing forth from the fount of your heart.

But let your first and chief care be to know the subject which you undertake to present. This will furnish you wealth of speech and true, natural emotions. Your language will live, breathe, persuade, convince, and fully express your self.

Nor do I maintain that every thing gained from imitation is spurious. There is some care of the person which is not unbecoming to a man and which sets off native beauty to advantage, —bathing, for example, an office which is of prime importance to good health but which at the same time contributes to beauty of face. Now if you should wish to shape your face after the type of one who is very unlike you, you would accomplish nothing; but if you see that the beauty of some one not so very unlike yourself is lessened by grinning, frowning, wrinkling the forehead, sneering, pouting, winking, and by other like actions, you can, by avoiding these things, make your beauty greater and yet not take on the face of another but mould your own. Likewise if you see that long and shaggy hair is not becoming to another, you may correct yours; if you see that a merry face, a truthful eye, and a countenance so ordered to uprightness that it shows nothing grim or insolent, trivial or unseemly add very much to another's charm, you will be justified in fashioning your face in imitation, since it is natural for the mind to respond to the

face.   Moreover inasmuch as the charm of beauty varies, do
not make up your mind that that beauty is inferior which is
different from the beauty which you admire, for, as we have
said, those who are most unlike may yet be equal.   And there
is no reason why one very unlike Cicero may not be even
greater than one copying his form more perfectly.   Come then,
let us lay aside our preferences and vote from judgment rather
than feeling.   If your Goddess of Persuasion should give you
the choice of being Quintilian or Cornificius instead of Nosoponus
which would you choose?

No.—For my part, I should prefer to be Quintilian.

Bu.—But yet the other is much more like Cicero.   Which
would you prefer to be, Sallust or Quintus Curtius?

No.—I should prefer Sallust.

Bu.—But Quintus Curtius is more like Cicero.   Would you
prefer to be Leonardo Aretino or Lorenzo Valla?

No.—I should prefer Valla.

Bu.—Yet Leonardo is more like Cicero.   Would you prefer
to be Hermolao Barbaro or Christoforo Landino?

No.—Barbaro.

Bu.—The other is more like Cicero.   Would you prefer to be
Politian or Paolo Cortesi?

No.—Politian.

Bu.—But the other demands that he be called Ciceronian.
Well, would you prefer to be Tertullian, leaving out of consideration his heresy, or Bede?

No.—Tertullian.

Bu.—But Bede has more the phraseology of Cicero.   Would
you prefer to be St. Jerome or Lactantius?

No.—St. Jerome.

Bu.—Yes, but the other, how great an ape of Cicero is he!
You see now that he who is more like Cicero does not necessarily
speak better, and that he who is more unlike does not necessarily
speak worse.   In fine, just as it is possible for many people to
be Atticists and yet be very different, so there is no reason why
many may not be called Ciceronians who are equal though unlike
in power of speaking.   Who can abide those sciolists who reject
with a scowl whatever does not show the lineaments of Ciceronian style which they estimate only by petty words, figures, and
rhythms!   He makes but a feeble effort toward Ciceronian style

who approaches the task without being previously trained by the reading of many authors, by the knowledge of many branches of study, and by acquaintance with a wide range of subjects, not to repeat what has been said about natural ability and practical judgment. I might overlook this foolish little conceit in youth, I might stand it in scholars who counterbalance the fault by many great virtues; but who could endure old men whose only ambition is to be like Cicero, who erase from their list of authors men more learned and more eloquent than themselves because these men dare to vary a little from the lines of Cicero, though they themselves as a rule are so far from being Ciceronians that their speech is even ungrammatical at times? I will not give the names of some I am acquainted with who may perchance hope to become famous thus.

I will speak next of Bartolommeo Scala who thinks Hermolao Barbaro and Politian but indifferent Ciceronians, yet deems himself a true one, however much he tries to conceal it. I, for my part, prefer the dreams of Politian to sober Scala's laborious writings.

Paolo Cortesi acknowledges this ambition but—good heavens! how much farther is his letter from the image of Cicero than the one of Politian which it answers! And in nothing else does Cortesi seem more unlike Cicero than in missing the point in almost the whole argument. He argues the case just as if Politian were keeping him from imitating Cicero and as if he were unwilling that a writer should set before himself a model of any kind; for he reproaches those who, trained by no reading of good authors, no learning, no practice, strive only to gain the form of Cicero and calls them for this reason the apes of Cicero. He reproaches those who borrow words in little bits from Cicero, who walk in others' tracks and create nothing, who do nothing but imitate and imitate only the mere words. He says that he cannot bear those who, though they are anything but Ciceronians, nevertheless laud themselves under the title and do not hesitate to express their opinion of the best writers. Then he advises his friend, after he has by long continued reading dissected, learned by heart, and digested Cicero first and many great writers afterward, to prepare as at any time to write, putting aside that peevish and anxious care to imitate only Cicero, because that anxiety would cause him to attain less perfectly the very thing he is striving for. Is this keeping one from imitating Cicero? Does it teach that no one at all is to be imitated? Does he who is so crammed with reading that the best from all comes to him for use when writing imitate no one, even though granting that he is not a slave to any, that he consults his own feelings and takes into consideration the nature of his subject? Cortesi declares that the apes of Cicero do not please him, saying: "I wish, my dear Politian, to resemble Cicero not as an ape resembles a man but as a son resembles his parent," making the same remark that Politian had made. Continuing this speech at length he finally admits, as if forgetting himself, that he would rather be an ape of Cicero than a son of others. If this word, *others,* includes Sallust, Livy, Quintilian, Seneca, who would not prefer to be like them as a son is like a parent rather than to be like Cicero in the way that an ape is like a man? Next he makes many charges against those who gorge themselves with wide reading and do not digest what they read. Their speech comes out rough, uncouth, and harsh, he says. But what has this to do with Politian's letter? If he agrees with him why does he answer as if he disagrees? If he disagrees, why does he not disprove what Politian says? For it is particularly Ciceronian to discern the subject of dispute, the points of vantage for the adversary and the main point at issue, and to say nothing outside the limits of the question. You see then that Cortesi with much pains worked out an epistle which was more lengthy than Ciceronian, which elicited no answer from Politian because of its irrelevancy.

But Politian, who was not styled a Ciceronian, how much better, albeit in a shorter letter, he expressed Cicero, not only by the charm of his aphorisms but also by apt, elegant, and telling language!—though I remember there is a story among the scholars of Italy that he answered for some reason or other more curtly than the man deserved. And believe me these things are not said in disparagement of Cortesi, for it is not a mark of disrespect for any one to be rated lower than the inimitable Politian; but they are said to make clear to young men what it is to be a true Ciceronian.

Hyp.—You lead us by such a round-about way, Bulephorus, that I am almost Hyponosus instead of Hypologus. Now tell us simply what you think of Cicero and of imitating him.

No.—This very thing I too should like very much; for your talk has brought me to the point where I have decided to take your advice.

Bu.—I think nothing remains but to summarize what in a scattered fashion has thus far been discussed.

No.—What kind of a man does Cicero seem to you to be?

Bu.—A most excellent orator, and, even though a pagan, a good man, who I think if he had known the Christian religion would have been reckoned among those who now are honored as saints on account of their innocent and pious living. Skill and practice, I confess, aided him very much; but he owed far the greatest part of his eloquence to natural ability, which no one can gain for himself. Nor do I think that any of the other Latin writers ought to be more cherished by boys and young men who are being trained to win praise in the field of eloquence.

Yet I would that the reading of the Latin poets at least came before the study of oratory, for poetry is more in harmony with early youth. Nor would I have any one called to the careful imitation of Cicero until the precepts of the art of rhetoric had been learned. After this I would have a teacher of the art of oratory at hand, just as painters are wont to point out to their pupils when looking at some great picture what has been done in accordance with the principles of art and what in violation of these principles.

I would have Cicero form the first and foremost part of the curriculum but not the only part, and not simply for the purpose of being followed but for being imitated rather and emulated; for he who follows walks in the steps of another and becomes a slave to rules. True indeed is the saying that he cannot walk well who always puts his foot in the track of another, nor swim well who does not dare to throw away the cork. To amplify—an imitator does not desire to say the same things so much as he does to say similar things, nay sometimes not even similar but even equal; an emulator strives even to speak better if he can, and no one was ever so finished an artist that you could not find in his work something which could be done better. But I should not want this imitation to be sought too anxiously and too religiously; for this very thing hinders us from accomplishing our desire.

Nor do I think that Cicero should be adored to the ex-
clusion of all others. You should first read the most noted
authors and cull from them what is best; for it is not necessary that you should imitate any one entirely. Nor do I think
that those ought to be scorned who do not take great delight
in nicety of language but furnish abundance of material for
thought, such as Aristotle, Theophrastus, Pliny. Further I
should not like any one to be so devoted to the imitation of Cicero
that he would depart from the bent of his own genius and follow
at the cost of his health and life what he could never attain because of the limitations of his natural ability; or what, if he
could attain, would be at so great a cost. I should not wish one
to occupy his time exclusively with Cicero, nor do I think that
Ciceronian diction should be aimed at to such a degree that the
liberal arts and especially the necessary ones are neglected. You
must avoid those as you would a pest who cry out that it is
wrong to use any word that is not found in the books of Cicero.
For now that the Latin speech has ceased to be in control, whatever words are discovered in reputable writers, let us use on our
own authority whenever there is need, and if they seem rather
harsh and obsolete, because they are rarely used, let us bring
them forth and by frequent and timely use let us soften them;
for what ground of criticism, pray, can there be if we, aware
that the ancients borrowed words of the Greeks whenever Latin
words were lacking or were considered inadequate, modify what
we find in approved authors when the occasion demands? Not
less zealously ought you to avoid those who declare that whatever
has not been fashioned in imitation of Cicero's words, phrases,
and rhythms must be rejected as entirely unworthy of reading,
notwithstanding it may have other virtues if not similar at least
equal to Cicero's. Let us not have that over fastidious nicety,
or rather let us show seriously in the reading of authors what
Ovid jestingly relates as happening to him in his love affairs:—A
tall girl pleased him because she seemed half divine, a short one
because of her active motion; youth recommended itself to him
through its inherent charm, maturity by its experience of the
world; an ignorant girl delighted him with her simplicity, an
educated one with her intellect; a blond with her wealth of color,
a brunette with some hidden charm or other. If we gather as
freely from the individual writers what they have which is

worthy of approval, we shall spurn none but shall gain something from all to give spice to our speech.

But provision must be made, first of all, that youth, in the simple and untutored time of life, be not deceived by the illusion of a Ciceronian name and become pagan instead of Ciceronian. For we see pests of this kind, not yet absolutely uprooted, from time to time sprouting up again under the guise of old heresies, of Judaism, of paganism. Many years ago, factions of Platonists and Peripatetics began to arise thus among the Italians. Let these names, as sources of discord, be abandoned; let us rather inculcate doctrines which in the pursuit of learning, in religion, and in every phase of life will win and increase our mutual good-will. That belief in sacred things which is truly worthy of a Christian must first be gained. When this is accomplished, nothing will seem more ornamental than the Christian religion, nothing more persuasive than the name of Jesus Christ, nothing more charming than the words by means of which the great men of the Church show forth her mysteries. Nor will the speech of any one seem charming which is not in accord with his character and not accommodated to the subject in hand; that will seem unnatural too which treats of a sacred theme in secular language and which contaminates a Christian theme with pagan baubles. But if some indulgence here is granted to youth, let not more advanced age assume for itself the same right. He who is so much of a Ciceronian that he is not quite a Christian is not even a Ciceronian because he does not speak fittingly, does not know his subject thoroughly, does not feel deeply those things of which he speaks; lastly he does not present his religious beliefs with the same adornment with which Cicero presented the philosophy of his times. The liberal arts, philosophy, and oratory are learned to the end that we may know Christ, that we may celebrate the glory of Christ.

This is the whole scope of learning and eloquence. And we must learn this, viz., that we may imitate what is the essential in Cicero which does not lie in words or in the surface of speech but in facts and ideas, in power of mind and judgment. For what advantage is it if the son reproduce the parent in lines of face when he is unlike him in mind and character? To conclude, if it is not our good fortune to be called Ciceronians by the vote of the ultra Ciceronians we must bear it patiently for the great men whom we have enumerated above suffered the same fate. It is foolish to strive after that which we cannot attain. It is effeminate to torture ourselves pitiably for what so many illustrious writers have borne tranquilly; it is stupid to wish to speak otherwise than the subject demands; it is mad to buy at the price of such vigils what will probably never be of any use. A physician with some such remedy as this cured me, and if you are not too loth to take it, I hope it will cause this fever to leave you, Nosoponus, and you, Hypologus.

Hyp.—I surely have long since been cured of the disease.

No.—And I too, except that I still feel some remnants of that long familiar illness.

Bu.—They will gradually vanish, but if there be any need we will summon again the physician, Reason.

NOTES OF CORRECTION ON PART II

Read the following instead of the forms found:

p. 21   καλά
p. 28   συμμύσαις
p. 30   Ennius, . . . *prosiluit*
p. 41   *Orator* and not *De Oratore*
p. 45   *consule Romam*
p. 46   *orationis* and not *oratis*
p. 49   *salutem*
p. 62   Camillo
p. 71   Pacuvius
p. 74   Theocritus
p. 85   Catiline
p. 92   Lactantius
p. 96   Angelo Poliziano, Codrus Urceus
p. 98   Giorgio da Trebisonda, Cartermachus, Antonius Sabellicus
p. 99   Andrea Alciati
p. 100   Calcagninus
p. 101   Francis Deloin
p. 102   Germain de Brie
p. 106   Busleiden College
p. 109   Juan Luis Vives
p. 116   Giacomo Sadoleto

BIBLIOGRAPHY

ABELSON, PAUL. The seven liberal arts, a study in mediaeval culture. New York 1906.

ASCHAM, ROGER. Letters to Sturm. In Ascham's Works. London 1864. The Schoolmaster. London 1570. In iii, 88–276 of Ascham's Works. 3 voll. London 1864.

AENEAS SYLVIUS, POPE PIUS II. De liberorum educatione. In opera. f°. Basil. 1551. Translation in Woodward's Vittorino da Feltre. p 134.

BALZAC, J. L. GUEZ DE. Vivi magni judicium de imitatione Lipsianae latinitatis. In Socrate Chrestien, etc. p. 228. Paris 1652.

BAILLET, ADRIEN. Jugemens des Savans. 8 voll. in 4. Amsterdam 1725.

BAYLE. Dictionaire historique et critique. f°. 2 voll. in 4. Rotterdam 1697.

BEMBO, PIETRO. De imitatione libellus. In Opera iii, 17–41. 3 voll. ed. Basil. 1556.

BORRICH, OLAF. Cogitationes de variis Latinae linguae aetatibus. An appendix on Latin lexicons. Hafriae 1675.

BRUNI, ARETINO LIONARDO. De studiis et literis. Liptzick 1496. First edition probably 1472.

BUDÉ, GUILLAUME. Commentarii linguae graecae. f°. Paris 1548. First edition, Paris 1529.

BUISSON, FERDINAND ÉDOUARD. Répertoire des ouvrages pedagogiques du XVIᵉ siècle. In memoires et documents scolaires publiés par le musee pedagogique. Fascicule No. 3. Paris 1886.

BURCKHARDT, JACOB. The civilization of the Renaissance in Italy, translated by S. G. C. MIDDLEMORE. 4th Ed. London 1898.

BURIGNY, JEAN LÉVESQUE DE. Sur la querelle qui s'eleve dans le XVIᵉ siècle au sujet d'estime qui était due á Cicéron. In Histoire de l'Académie Royale des inscriptions et belle-lettres. xxvii, 195–205. Paris 1756.

CAMILLO, GUILIO. Trattato della imitatione. In Opera pp. 197–232. Vinegia 1560.

CHRISTIE, RICHARD COPLEY. Etienne Dolet. London 1880.

CHUTRAEUS, DAVID. De ratione discendi et ordine studiorum in singulis artibus recte instituendo. Witebergae 1564.

CORTESI, PAOLO. De hominibus doctis dialogus. c. 1490. ed. Florentiae 1734.

DOLET, ETIENNE. Responsio ad convitia Floridi Sabini. Lyons 1540. In liber de imitatione Ciceroniana adversus Floridum Sabinum. pp. 23–48.
De imitatione Ciceroniana adversus Floridum Sabinum. 56 pp. Lyons 1540.

DOLET, ETIENNE. Dialogus de imitatione Ciceroniana adversus Erasmum Rot. pro C. Longolio. 200 pp. Lyons 1535.

DURAND DE LAUR, H. Erasme précurseur et imitateur de l'esprit moderne. 2 voll. Paris 1872.

ENGEL, CHARLES. L'ecole Latine et l'ancienne académie de Strasbourg, 1538–1621. Paris 1900.

ERASMUS, DESIDERIUS. Opera omnia, emendatiora et auctiora: cura F. Clerici. 10 voll. f°. Lugd. Bat. 1703–6.

ESTIENNE, HENRI. Nizoliodidascalus sive Monitor Ciceronianorum Nizolianorum Dialogus. 200 pp. Geneva 1578.

Pseudo-Cicero. Geneva 1577.

FITCH, Joshua. Educational aims and methods. New York 1900.

FLORIDO (SABINO), Francesco. Liber adversus Stephani Doleti Aurelii calumnias. 40 pp. Romae 1541. Rare: Copy in Bodleian Library at Oxford, bound with Caroli Signonii Disputationum Patovinarum ad F. Robortellum. 1542.

Lectiones Succisivae, Libri Tres. Basil. 1539. In vol. I of Grüter's Lampas sive fax partium liberalium, etc. 7 voll. Francof. 1602.

GAULLIEUR, ERNEST. Histoire du Collége dé Guyenne. Paris 1874.

GRESWELL, W. PARR. Memoirs of Angelus Politianus, Joannes Picus of Mirandula et al. Manchester 1805.

GUARINO, BATTISTA. De ordine docendi et studendi. Verona 1459. Translation in Woodward's Vittorino da Feltre, pp. 159–178.

HALLAM, HENRY. Introduction to the literature of Europe in the fifteenth, sixteenth and seventeenth centuries. 5th ed. 3 voll. London 1873.

HENDRICKSON, G. L. The de analogia of Julius Caesar. *Classical Philology*, April, 1906.

JORTIN, JOHN. The life of Erasmus. 3 voll. London 1808.

LANDI, ORTENSIO. Cicero relegatus et Cicero revocatus. Lipsiae 1534. In De latinitate of J. Vorstius, pp. 85–168. Leipsic 1722. Christie says this was published at Lyons in 1534.

LENIENT, C. De Ciceroniano bello apud recentiores. 74 pp. Paris 1855.

LONGUEIL, CHRISTOPHE DE. Epistolae. In epistolae Ciceroniano stylo scriptae Petri Bunelli et Pauli Manutii et al. Paris ed. 1581.

MAITTAIRE, MICHEL. Annales typographici ab artis inventae origine ad annum 1664. 3 voll. in 6. Hagae-Comitunn 1722–33.

MORHOF, DANIEL G. Polyhistor, literarius, philosophicus, et practicus. 2nd ed. Lubecae 1714.

MURETUS, M. ANTONIUS. Opera. Ed. Ruhnken. 4 voll. Leyden 1789.

In Ciceronis Catilinarias commentarius, Praefatio 1556. In Opera ii, 523–528.

Sermo habitus cum Dario Bernardo de stultitia quorumdam qui se Ciceronianos vocant. 1580. In Opera, ii, 340–347.

Oratio xxi—De via et ratione ad eloquentiae laudem perveniendi. Delivered at Rome, 1572. In Opera, i, 167–179.

NETTLESHIP, HENRY. Lectures and essays. Oxford 1895.

NISARD, CHARLES. Les gladiateurs de la république des lettres aux XVᵉ, XVIᵉ, et XVIIᵉ siècles. Vol. I. Paris 1860.

PERION, JACOBO. Pro Ciceronis oratore contra Petrum Ramum oratio. 52 pp. Paris 1547.

PICO, GIANFRANCESCO. Ad Petrum Bembum de imitatione libellus. In Bembi Opera, iii. 1–17. ed. Basil. 1556.

POGGIO BRACCIOLINI. Opera. f°. ed. Basil. 1538.

POLIZIANO, ANGELO. Opera. f°. Basil. 1533.

PONTANO, GIOVANNI. Antonius. In Opera, ii, 72–101. 3 voll. Venice 1519.

QUINTILIAN. Institutes of Oratory. J. S. Watson, translator. 2 voll. London 1882.

RAMUS, PETER. Rhetoricae distinctiones in Quintilian. Paris 1549.

Brutinae quaestiones in Oratorem Ciceronis. 44 pp. Paris 1547.

Ciceronianus. Paris 1557.

Oratio de studiis philosophiae et eloquentiae conjugendis. In Brutinae questiones, pp. 44–50. Paris 1547.

RICCI, BARTOLOMMEO. De imitatione tres libri. 88 pp. Venice 1545.

RICHARD, JAMES WILLIAM, Melancthon, the protestant praeceptor of Germany. In Heroes of the Reformation. New York 1898.

ROCCHUS, PILORCIUS. De scribendi rescribendique epistolas ratione opusculum. 31 pp. Perusiae 1563.

SABBADINI, REMIGIO. Storia del Ciceronianismo e di altre questioni letterarie nell età della Rinasceuza. 74 pp. Torino 1885.

SADOLETO, GIACOMO. De liberis recte instituendis. 172 pp. Basil. 1538. First edition c. 1530.

SANDYS, JOHN EDWIN. A history of classical scholarship, vol. ii, from the Revival of Learning to the end of the eighteenth century. Cambridge 1908.

Harvard lectures on the Revival of Learning. Cambridge 1905.

A history of classical scholarship from the sixth century B. C. to the end of the Middle Ages. Cambridge 1903.

SANTI, P. Rabelais et J. C. Scaliger. In revue des Études Rabelaisienses, iii, 12–44. Paris 1905.

SCALIGER, J. C. Oratio pro M. T. Cicerone contra Desiderium Erasmum Rot.Oratio ii. Toulouse 1621. First edition, Paris 1537.

Oratio pro M. T. Cicerone contra Desiderium Erasmum Rot. Oratio i. Toulouse 1621. First edition, Paris 1531.

Epistolae. In J. G. Schelhorn's Amoenitates literariae vi, 512 ff., and viii, 551 ff. 14 voll. in 7. Frankfurt 1725–31.

Epistolae et orationes. Hanoviae 1612.

SCALIGER, J. J. Scaligerana, Editio Altera. Coloniae Agrippinae. 1667.

SCHOPPE, GASPAR. Consultationes de scholarum et studiorum ratione. Amst. 1660. Prefatory letter 1636. First consultation, 1629; second, 1616.

SHEPHERD, WILLIAM. The life of Poggio Bracciolini. Liverpool 1837.

SMILEY, CHARLES NEWTON. Latinitas and Hellenismos. Dissertation. Madison, Wisconsin 1906.

STURM, JOHANN. De imitatione oratoria libri tres. Argentorati 1574.

Classicae epistolae, sive scholae Argentinenses restitutae. Argentorati 1565.

Ad Werteros fratres, nobilitas litterata. Argentorati 1549. In Crenius' Consilia studiorum. pp. 235–277. Rotterdami 1692.

De literarum ludis recte aperiendis liber. pp. 45. Argentorati 1543. First published in 1538.

TACITUS, CORNELIUS. De oratoribus claris.

TAUBMANN, FRID. Dissertatio de linguae Latinae. 119 pp. Witebergae 1602.

VINET, ÉLIE. Schola Aquitanica. Docendi ratio. Bordeaux 1583. In memoires et documents scolaires publiés par le musée pedagogique. pp. 4–36. Fascicule No. 7. Paris 1886·

VALLA, LORENZO. Opera. f°. ed. Basil. 1543.

VILLANI, FILLIPPO. Liber de civitatis Florentiae famosis civibus. Florentiae 1847.

VIVES, JUAN LUIS. De tradendis disciplinis. Colon. Agr. 1536.

De studii puerilis ratione. London 1521.

VOIGT, GEORG. Die Wiederbelebung des Classischen Alterthums: oder des erste Jahrhundert des Humanismus. 3ᵗᵉ Aufl., besorgt von Max Lehnerdt. 2 voll. Berlin 1893.

VORST, JOHANN. De latinitate et cetera. Leipsic 1722.

VOSSIUS, GERARDUS JOANNES. De imitatione, cum oratoria, tum praecipue poetica liber. In Crenius' Consilia studiorum. pp. 743–820. Rot. 1692.

Oratoriarum institutionum libri sex. 4th ed. Lugduni Bat. 1643. Prefatory letter dated 1633.

WALCH, J. C. Historia critica Latinae linguae. Lipsiae 1729.

WADDINGTON, CHARLES. Ramus (Pierre de la Ramée), sa via, ses ecrits et ses opinions. Paris 1855.

WATSON, FOSTER. Mathurin Corderius: Schoolmaster at Paris, Bordeaux, and Geneva, in the sixteenth century. *School Review*, xii, 284–298, April, 1904.

The English grammar schools to 1660. Cambridge 1908.

WOODWARD, WILLIAM H. Erasmus concerning education. Cambridge 1904.

Studies in education during the age of the Renaissance 1400–1600. Cambridge 1906.

Vittorino da Feltre and other humanistic educators. Cambridge 1897.

CRITICAL BIBLIOGRAPHY OF SCHOOL TEXTS AND BOOKS
ON THE THEORY OF TEACHING, PUBLISHED BY MEN
INTERESTED IN THE CICERONIAN CONTROVERSIES

DICTIONARIES

CALEPINO, AMBROSIO. Dictionarum latinarum e greco pariter dirivantium.
f°. Basil. 1512. First edition f° 1502.
Said to be a transcript of Perotti's Cornu Copiae.
"The Aldine press alone issued between 1542–92 eighteen editions
of this work. Little by little Greek, Hebraic, French, Italian, German, Spanish and English meanings were added to the Latin words
and it was published in a great many editions before the end of the
seventeenth century."—*Graesse.*

CELLARIUS, CHRISTOPH. Thesaurus Ciceronianus with added index.
Prefaces of previous editions by Squarcialupus (1576), Curio
(1548), and Nizzoli (no date). f°. Basil. 1583. Nizzoli's lexicon.

CURIO, CAELIUS SECUNDUS. Nizolius, sive Thesaurus Ciceronianus, omnia
Ciceronis verba, omnemque loquendi atque eloquendi varietatem
complexus. f°. Basil. 1548.

In M. T. Ciceronem observationes secundo atque iterum locuple-
tatae perpolitatae. f°. Lyons 1552. Nizzoli's lexicon.

Thesaurus linguae latinae s. forum Romanum. Basil. 1561. 3 voll.
f°. (Ed. Alb. Burer.) ib. 1576. 3 voll. f°. (Anonyme.)—*Graesse.*
Morhof says this was the Thesaurus of Robert Estienne.

DOLET, ETIENNE. Commentariorum linguae Latinae tomi duo. f°.
Lugd. 1536–38.

Phrases et formulae Latinae lingae elegantiores. Preface by Sturm
1576. No place 1585. First edition Lyons 1539.

ERASMUS, DESIDERIUS. De copia rerum et verborum. Paris 1512.
It was first published 1509 to be used by Colet in St. Paul's and
was widely used as a text-book.

ESTIENNE, ROBERT. Dictionarium seu thesaurus linguae Latinae. f°.
Paris 1531.
Said to be at first a transcript of Calepino. Enlarged to a 3 voll.
edition, 1536. Best edition, 3 voll. f°. 1543. Morhof says that this
was published later under many titles and authors. Under its own
author and title it was frequently reprinted and widely circulated.
Chutraeus (1564) ranks it with the lexicons of Dolet and Ricci and
says they were all celebrated.

FACCIOLATI, JACOPO. Lexicon Ciceronianum ex recensione Alex. Scoti
nunc crebis locis refectum et inculcatum. Accedunt phrases et
formulae linguae Latinae Étienne Doleti. f°. Padua 1734.
In the preface to the 1820 edition of the same work it is stated
that this lexicon is the most eminent of all and has been much criticised.. London 1820. The lexicon was that of Nizzoli.

GODSCALCUS, JOANNES. Latini sermonis observationes. Coloniae Agrippinae 1561.
Preface dated 1536 in which are mentioned Ricci's Apparatus, Valla's Elegantiae, and a great volume called Linguae Latinae Thesaurus.

HELLIUX, SEVERINUS. Ciceronianae phraseos seu dictionis varietas, et copia ex Mario Nizolio, Aldo Manutio et aliis. Latin-German. 12°. Coloniae 1595.

MANUTIUS, ALDUS, Pauli filius. Elegantes et copiosae Latinae linguae phrases. Venice 1558.

NIZZOLI, MARIO. In M. T. Ciceronis Observationes. f°. Brescia 1535.
No other lexicon between 1535 and 1820 had so many editions. It was by far the most influential lexicon of that period.

PEROTTI, NICCOLO. Cornu Copiae linguae Latinae. f°. Venice 1480.
It was the source of Calepino's dictionary which in turn was the basis for that of Robert Estienne. Perotti was educated by Vittorino da Feltre.

RICCI, BARTOLOMMEO. Apparatus Latinae locutionis ex M. T. Cicerone, Caesare, Sallustio. Coloniae 1535.
Borrich (1675) says this was based on the Roman forum.

SCOT, ALEX. Apparatus Latinae locutionis, inusum studiosae juventutis olim per M. Nizolium ex M. T. Ciceronis libris collectus. Lugduni 1588.

SANCTIUS, FRANCISCUS. Minerva seu de causis linguae Latinae commentarius. Amst. 1714. First edition, Salmant. 1587.

SCHORUS, ANTONIUS. Thesaurus verb. linguae Latinae Ciceronianus. Argentorati 1570. Additions by Sturm and Lambini. Argentorati 1597.

SQUARCIALUPUS, PLUMBIENSUS. Nizolius sive Thesaurus Ciceronianus post Mar. Nizolii, Basilii Zanchi, et Caelii Secundi Curionis, numquam satis laudatas operas, cum insigni accessione quam te sequens docebit pagina digestus et illustratus. f°. Basil. 1576.

SUSSANNAEUS, HUBERT. Dictionarium Ciceronianum. 8°. Paris 1536.

ZANCHIUS, BASILIUS. Verborum latinorum epitome, ejusdem verborum quae in Nizolii observationibus in Ciceronem desiderautur appendix. Romae 1541. Basil. 1543.

GRAMMARS

ALVEREZ, EMMANUEL. De institutione grammatica. Ulyssip. 1572.
First edition of a Latin grammar composed by a Jesuit, and introduced into almost all the schools directed by this order where it was used to the end of the seventeenth century.—*Graesse.*

CORDIER, MATHURIN. Exempla de Latino declinatu partium orationes. Paris 1540.
Mentioned as a text-book in the program of the Collége de Guyenne.

DESPAUTERE, JEAN. Orthographiae Isagoge (Paris 1510), Rudimenta (1512) and Syntaxis (1515), were combined in the Commentarii Grammatici. Lyons 1536; Paris 1537.

ERASMUS, DESIDERIUS. De octo partium orationis constructione libellus. Paris 1511.

Printed in Florence, Venice, London, Mayence, Lyons, before 1550.

GUARINO, DE VERONESE. Regulae grammaticae. s. l. c. 1480.

Of no wide influence. Used in Guarino's school at Ferrara.

LEONICENUS (OGNIBENE DA LONIGO). Grammaticae libellus sive de octo partibus orationis liber. Venice 1473.

LILLY, WILLIAM. De octo orationis partium constructione libellus. London 1513.

This book was widely used with various editions abridged or modified. Authorized in England by the King.

LINACRE, THOMAS. De amendata structura Latina sermonis. 1524.

This book was used generally as a text-book and was recommended by Melancthon for the German schools. Chutraeus (1564) says that it was the best book on rules of syntax.

MANUTIUS, ALDUS. Institutionum grammaticarum libri quatour. Venice 1501.

Many times reprinted during the sixteenth century.

MELANCTHON, PHILIP. Grammatica Latina. Paris 1527.

Various editions and revisions of this were in general use for several centuries. Authorized text for Germany.

PEROTTI, NICCOLO. Rudimenta grammatices. s. l, s.n. 1471.

This went through a very great many editions before 1500 and was most popular in Italy during that period.

RAMUS, PETER. Rudimenta grammaticae. Paris 1559.

Published under several titles with modifications. Perhaps not extensively used.

RHETORICS AND GUIDES IN WRITING AND SPELLING

ADRIAN, CARDINAL. De sermone Latino et modis Latine loquendi. Coloniae 1543. First edition Venice 1505.

A phrase book widely used throughout all Europe.

BRITANNUS, ROBERTUS. De ratione consequendae eloquentiae liber. Paris 1544.

Ratio conscribendum epistolarum. Paris 1545.

Text-book used in colleges of the University of Paris. The author was an ultra Ciceronian.

CAMERARIUS, JOACH. Elementa rhetoricae, sive capita exercitionum studii puerilis et stili, ad comparandam utriusque linguae facultatem collecta. Basil. 1541.

CAPELLA, MARTIANUS. De nuptiis Philologiae et Mercurii et de septem artibus liberalibus novem libri optime castigati. ed. Lyons 1539.

CORDIER, MATHURIN. De corrupti sermonis apud Gallos emendatione et loquendi Latine ratione libellus. Paris 1530.

A manual of conversation containing phrases to be used in church, class, disputes, public exercises, and recreation. The content is given in an analysis by Foster Watson, *School Review*, xii, 284–298, April, 1904.

Colloquiorum scholasticorum libri iv, ad pueros in sermone latino paulatim exercendos recogniti. Gen. 1563.

DRESCHER, MATTH. Rhetoricae inventionis, dispositionis et elocutionis libri iv, exemplis illustrati et emendati. Lipsiae 1588.

ERASMUS, DESIDERIUS. Colloquia. Basil. 1516.

There were many editions and translations. It was extensively used in Europe and England as a school text-book in the sixteenth and seventeenth centuries.

De ratione conscribendi epistolas. Coloniae 1522.

Very widely used.

GASPARINO DA BARZIZZA. Epistolae ad exercitationem accommodatae. Paris 1470.

This was used as a text-book in Italy and France. It is mentioned in the program of the Collége de Guyenne.

GIORGIO DA TREBISONDA. Rhetoricorum libri v. f°. s.l. 1493.

A number of editions published during the sixteenth century at Basle, Paris and Lyons.

MACROPEDIUS, GEORGIUS. Epistolica studiosis trajectinae scholae tyrunculis nuncupata, quae nihilominus quicquid ad prima rhetorices elementa attinet, brevibus praeceptis plane complectitur. Antverpiae 1543.

MELANCTHON, PHILIP. Institutiones rhetoricae. Paris 1522.

Widely used under various titles and revisions.

SCALIGER, J. C. De causis linguae Latinae libri xiii. Prefatory letter. 1540. No place 1609.

There were several editions but the book had no extended influence.

SANCTIUS, FRANCISCUS. De arte dicendi liber unus. Salmanticae 1558.

Libellus de auctoribus interpretandis, sive de exercitatione. Antverpiae 1581.

SCHORUS, ANTONIUS. Phrases linguae Latinae ratioque observandorum eorum in auctoribus legendis quae praecipuam ac singularem vim aut usum habent. Coloniae 1573. First edition Basil. 1557.

STURM, JOHANN. De exercitationibus rhetoricis liber academicus. Argentorati 1575.

Seems to have had but one edition.

VALLA, LORENZO. De elegantia Latinae linguae. Romae 1471. Written c. 1450.

The most widely influential book of rhetoric and textual criticism during the Renaissance.

VIVES, JUAN LUIS. Rhetorica, sive de recte dicendi ratione libri iii. Lovanii 1533.

De conscribendis epistolis. Antverpiae 1534.

Colloquia, sive linguae Latinae exercitatio. Basil. 1538.

All of Vives' books were very popular.

INDEX